The Drunken Journalist

The Biography of a Film Stereotype

Howard Good

The Scarecrow Press, Inc.
Lanham, Maryland, and London
2000

SCARECROW PRESS, INC.

Published in the United States of America
by Scarecrow Press, Inc.
4720 Boston Way, Lanham, Maryland 20706
http://www.scarecrowpress.com

4 Pleydell Gardens, Folkstone
Kent CT20 2DN, England

British Library Cataloguing in Publication Information Available

Library of Congress Cataloging-in-Publication Data

Good, Howard, 1951–
    The drunken journalist : the biography of a film stereotype / Howard Good.
        p.   cm.
    Includes bibliographical references and filmography.
    ISBN 0-8108-3717-X (cloth : alk. paper)
    1. Journalists in motion pictures. 2. Alcoholism in motion pictures. I. Title.

    PN1995.9.J6 .G57 2000
    791.43'652097—dc21

                                                        99-057930

♾ ™ The paper used in this publication meets the minimum requirements of American National Standard for Information Sciences—Permanence of Paper for Printed Library Materials, ANSI/NISO Z39.48–1992.
Manufactured in the United States of America.

To my brothers,

Larry Good, M.D.
Eliott Good, Esq.
Arnold Good, M.D.

L'Chayim!

Contents

Acknowledgments

I wish to thank the following people and institutions, all of whom contributed in some way to the completion of this book: Professor Matthew C. Ehrlich of the University of Illinois at Urbana-Champaign for taking time from his own research to guide me to appropriate films and make helpful comments on them; Madeline F. Matz, reference librarian in the Motion Picture, Broadcasting and Recorded Sound Division of the Library of Congress, for sharing her lunch hour as well as her film expertise with me; the State University of New York at New Paltz for awarding me a grant for archival research; my children, Gabriel, Graham, Brittany, and Darla, for giving me something else to think about besides the next chapter; and my wife, Barbara, for being sweet vermouth.

1

A Hundred Bottles of Beer

That the greatest writing is made out of loneliness and despair magnified by booze is an idea for arrested adolescents.

—Donald Newlove

I don't drink . . . much. The one time in my life I got really drunk, I threw up my guts. I was fourteen and in ninth grade. Neil's parents were away for the weekend. A bunch of us guys sat around the kitchen table on Saturday night, playing poker and polishing off a quart of his father's Chivas Regal. It seemed at the time a cool thing to do. Later, when I had my head in the toilet, it didn't seem so cool.

My friends and I weren't bad kids, just kids who somewhere had gotten the notion that drinking was manly. Probably we had gotten it from observing our fathers and older brothers and from partaking of popular culture, particularly the movies. Men drank a lot in the movies we grew up watching. They drank with their buddies and they drank alone. They drank hurriedly, tossing back shot after shot. They drank glumly, staring for long moments into their whiskey glass with hard, flat eyes. They drank before work, during work, after work. They drank when something was weighing on their minds, and they drank when their minds were untroubled. They drank in cowboy saloons, at elegant nightclubs, straight from the bottle. They drank with a tough expression on their faces. They drank, but never got sick or fall-down drunk. They drank and only got tougher.

Looking back, I can see that we were being indoctrinated in a brutish, militaristic conception of manhood. Men were supposed to

1

be courageous, laconic, self-contained; we weren't any of those things. We hoped that alcohol might supply us with the manly qualities that as confused, pimple-faced adolescent boys we lacked.

I'm not the first to suggest that drunkenness entails more than the impairment of sensorimotor capabilities.[1] Others have noted that drinking is deeply connected in American life with gender roles and social status. It isn't necessary to drink large amounts to feel the effects of alcohol. We live surrounded by its symbolic uses.[2]

"Any important disease whose causality is murky, and for which treatment is ineffectual," Susan Sontag wrote in her short but brilliant book *Illness As Metaphor,* "tends to be awash in significance."[3] Alcoholism seems just such a disease—or, as some prefer to call it, addiction. Herbert Fingarette reported in the late 1980s that "the current dominant consensus among researchers is that no single explanation, however complex, has ever been established as the cause of alcoholism."[4] Alcohol abuse has been variously ascribed to genetic inheritance, moral weakness, social conditioning, and psychiatric problems.

No agreement prevails either as to the best treatment for alcoholism. Many different types of treatment exist, including the twelve-step program of Alcoholics Anonymous, which preaches total abstinence; cognitive-behavorial therapy, which provides ways to manage the desire for alcohol and avoid situations leading to drinking; and motivational enhancement therapy, which promotes the alcoholic's responsibility for helping himself.[5] Despite the multitude of approaches, at least half of the alcoholics who get treatment will relapse in two to four years.[6]

Sontag devoted most of her brief book to analyzing the use of tuberculosis as a metaphor in the nineteenth century. When she pointed out a twentieth-century equivalent, it was insanity, not alcoholism. As tuberculosis once did, insanity now serves as "the index of a superior sensitivity, the vehicle of 'spiritual' feelings and 'critical discontent.' "[7] *One Flew over the Cuckoo's Nest* by Ken Kesey and *The Bell Jar* by Sylvia Plath are examples of novels (and films) in which insanity becomes a kind of moral statement.

Alcoholism has, as a metaphor, parallels to both insanity and tuberculosis, the incandescent "white death." In the nineteenth century tuberculosis was closely linked with creativity. The link was so well established, in fact, that one critic at the end of the century blamed the progressive disappearance of tuberculosis for the decline of literature.[8] Alcoholism has since become the writer's disease.[9] "Of course, you're a rummy," Ernest Hemingway told F. Scott Fitzgerald, "but no more than most good writers are."[10]

The journalist is popularly presumed to be a cut-rate version of legendary writer rummies like Hemingway and Fitzgerald. Alex Barris, in his *Stop the Presses! The Newspaperman in American Films*, cited as "one of the indestructible cliches of American belief" that "all newspapermen keep a bottle of booze in the bottom drawer of their desks, that the corner saloon claims more of their time than the newsroom, that tippling among reporters is as inevitable as gambling among Las Vegas tourists." Films have done a good deal to spread this stereotype. "No other human problem," Barris remarked, "seems to have afflicted movie newspapermen more often than drinking."[11]

He was only half right. While journalists do drink heavily in films, their drinking isn't always problematic. Sometimes it is presented in neutral or even positive terms. Sontag observed that "all really successful metaphors" are "rich enough to provide for two contradictory applications."[12] Drinking is rich enough to provide for at least eight.

What are these applications? The answer, based on my own and others' findings, is that drinking has functioned in films as: (1) a natural accompaniment of the creative occupations of writer, artist, actor, or musician; (2) a sign of moral corruption and mental instability; (3) a stimulus to memory, truth-telling, and poetic speech; (4) a "gateway to comic disinhibition";[13] (5) a symbol of "cosmopolitan affluence and the insouciant good life";[14] (6) a source of solidarity among men; (7) a visual code for sexual license in women; and (8) a form of protest against the modern bureaucratic order.

Which applications predominate in any given era depends on a complex set of factors, including the relative status of various film genres, the prevailing conception of alcoholism, and the current historical circumstances. I should add that the relationship between films and social history isn't necessarily one of direct correspondence. During the long, supposedly dry years of Prohibition, for example, films were never wetter.

Here is a song we used to sing coming home from class trips to the Museum of Natural History or the Brooklyn Botanical Gardens, our

thin, quavery 9- and 10-year-old voices straining to outshout the boom-
ing engine of the school bus: "A hundred bottles of beer on the wall, a
hundred bottles of beer, if one of those bottles should happen to fall,
ninety-nine bottles of beer on the wall. . . ." And here is a version of
"Marjory Daw" I learned so long ago that I don't remember having ever
learned it, that I seem to have been born knowing how to sing: "See-
saw, Marjory Daw. Who's there? Grandpa. Whaddya want? A bottle of
beer. What for? Because. Get outta here, ya drunken bum." It is this version I taught my own children when they were small, joggling them on
my knee. And now I wonder why I did and what it means that I did.

Maybe it doesn't mean anything. Maybe it is just one of those
meaningless vestigial customs. But anyone who has read my previous books—has *anyone* read my previous books?—knows that I'm
not likely to leave it at that. If my books have a common thread, it is
their underlying assumption that popular culture is invasive, duplic-
itous, ideologically charged. I agree with something Pulitzer Prize-
winning philosopher Ernest Becker once said: "It is fateful and ironic
how the lie we need in order to live dooms us to a life that is never
really ours." Popular culture is the lie we need in order to live. We
need it, Becker would say, because we are human and because we
live in an overwhelmingly tragic and demonic world.

This book is in part about drinking, another way in which people
try to forget themselves and their fears. It analyzes the stereotype of
the hard-drinking journalist, with the goal of discovering why the
stereotype exists and how it operates not only in films, but also in real
life. That journalists, to a certain extent, imitate the alcohol use of
their glamorous film counterparts is probably to be expected; it is just
the sort of behavior that sociologist Norman K. Denzin predicted
when he wrote that "cultural texts, like alcoholism movies, create
possibilities of experience that are then lived out in the lives of ordinary interacting individuals in the contemporary postmodern
period."[15] Less expected is the fact that there are several distinct
styles of drinking portrayed on the screen and that these tend to reinforce gender, ethnic, and class divisions. "If we look back at the cinema . . . ," Richard Dyer noted in his essay "The Role of Stereotypes,"
"it is fairly clear that the alcoholic did serve *to distinguish clearly* alcohol use from abuse, as if a definite line could be drawn, in order to
legitimate the 'social' use of alcohol. . . . The question that such an

analysis poses is, in whose interest was this distinction maintained?"[16] It is a good question, one that moves film study beyond plot summaries and the mere description of images, and I try to address it in the following pages.

Unlike this chapter, the rest of the book is organized quite straightforwardly. Chapter 2, "The Pictures in Our Heads," defines what a stereotype is and considers whether there is a historical basis for the stereotype of the hard-drinking journalist. Chapter 3, "Drink, Drank, Drunk," reviews the shifting conceptions of alcoholism from colonial days to the present. Chapter 4, "The Ghosts of Printing House Square," explains how the authors of turn-of-the-century newspaper novels translated the temperance movement's model of alcoholism as a degenerative, disease-like addiction into a pessimistic vision of the stages of a typical newspaper career.

In chapters 5–10, I deal with films from across the decades. Chapter 5, "Hello Darkness," identifies the fate of the romantic couple as a major—if not *the* major—concern of silent films featuring drunken journalists. Chapter 6, "Bottoms Up," explores the many and often conflicting meanings associated with drinking in the 1930s, the so-called "golden age of newspaper films." Chapter 7, "The Dog That Bit You," discusses, among other things, the influence of Alcoholics Anonymous on newspaper films of the 1940s and 1950s. Chapter 8, "Happy Hour," examines the portrayal of the hard-drinking journalist in films of the 1960s and 1970s, while Chapter 9, "Mixed Drinks," examines it in films of the 1980s, and Chapter 10, "Last Call," in films of the 1990s. There is also an epilogue in which I point out that down through history, American culture has marginalized troublesome subgroups—for example, Indians, blacks, and Irish immigrants—by stereotyping them as drunks or at least as peculiarly susceptible to drink. I suggest that the stereotype of the hard-drinking journalist may have a similar aspect.

Many years ago, when I wrote my first book, I included in the preface a quotation from George Orwell that compared writing a book to "a long bout of some painful illness." I was young and, as only the young can be, infatuated with the idea that suffering was an essential ingredient of good writing. Suffering now seems to me to be nothing but suffering and worth avoiding if at all possible. I have come in middle age to believe that Laurence Sterne, the sharp-nosed eighteenth-century English clergyman and author, was closer to the truth. "To write a book," he said, "is for all the world like humming a song." Even—or maybe especially—a drinking song.[17]

2

The Pictures in Our Heads

I believe that those who speculate that a full apprehension of man's condition would drive him insane are right, quite literally right.

—Ernest Becker

Jewish mothers. Drug addicts. Thirty-something stockbrokers. Korean grocers. Homosexuals. Members of Congress. These are just a few examples of people who have stereotyped public images.

Stereotypes are "simple mental models" that lead us to have certain fixed expectations about the world and the things in it.[1] "For the most part," as Walter Lippmann said decades ago, "we do not first see, and then define, we define first and then see. In the great blooming, buzzing confusion of the outer world we pick out what our culture has already defined for us, and we tend to perceive that which we have picked out in the form stereotyped for us by our culture."[2]

This has its advantages. "Stereotypes," Professor D. B. Bromley of the University of Liverpool noted, "provide us with simple cognitive frameworks that are fast and require little mental effort. We rely on these conceptual routines in organizing our behavior when dealing with objects, people, and events."[3] To try to see all things freshly and in detail, rather than as stereotyped shapes, would be exhausting and, amid a busy life, impractical.[4]

On the other hand, there is the danger that stereotypes overgeneralize and prevent us from recognizing reality. It was with this in mind that Lippmann warned not about stereotypes per se, but about the gullibility with which most of us employ them.[5] "Uncritically held," he wrote, "the stereotype not only censors out much that needs to be taken into account, but when the day of reckoning comes, and the stereotype is shattered, likely as not that which it did take wisely into account is ship-wrecked with it."[6]

Today's social scientists believe that stereotypes are resistant to change.[7] "There is nothing so obdurate to education or to criticism," Lippmann himself said in the twenties, "as the stereotype."[8] A stereotype is often shared by the people with whom we associate, which gives us extra confidence that it is valid.[9] If experience happens to contradict the stereotype, we just discount the contradiction as the exception that proves the rule.[10]

Stereotypes may be irrational, may have blind spots, may oversimplify. We cling to them, anyway. They constitute a world with which we have grown familiar and in which we have invested our emotions. It isn't necessarily an ideal world. In fact, it is typically a world that seems overrun with conspiracies and mongrel races and sleazy, self-serving professions. But at least we feel at home there.

The stereotype of the drunken journalist has had a long and complicated history. We might begin exploring this history by noting that the term "stereotype" itself is of journalistic origins. Before Lippmann coined its modern meaning in his 1922 book, *Public Opinion,* stereotype referred to the oldest and cheapest kind of duplicate plate used in printing newspapers. The plate was cast by making a mold, or "matrix," from composed type in papier-mâché and then pouring hot lead into it. Once the matrix was made, duplicate plates could be produced in less than a minute.[11] It was a relatively plausible leap from this process to the definition of stereotype as a widespread, standardized image of a race, religion, nationality, or occupation.

Many occupations suffer from negative stereotyping. For example, politicians are often represented as crooks; the clergy as hypocrites; scientists as madmen; and teachers as tyrants and sadists. Journalists usually don't fare much better. The stereotype of the hard-drinking, sarcastic journalist prevails throughout American popular culture. It has appeared in fiction about journalists, as well as in memoirs by journalists, including H. L. Mencken's *Newspaper Days* (1941) and Pete Hamill's *A Drinking Life* (1994). "Between 1899 and 1904 there was only one reporter south of the Mason & Dixon Line who did not drink at all," Mencken remembered, "and he was considered insane. In New York, so far as I could make out, there was not even one."[12] The biggest contributor to this stereotype, though, has been mainstream Hollywood films, and at least part of the reason may lie in the nature of the film-viewing experience.

About seventy-five years ago, when feature films were still in their infancy, Lippmann sensed, perhaps in a way we no longer can, what a revolution in image-making film had wrought. He noted that moving pictures now had the kind of authority over the imagination that the printed word once had. "Any description in words, or even any inert picture," he said, "requires an effort of memory before a picture exists in the mind. But on the screen the whole process of observing, describing, reporting, and then imagining has been accomplished for you. Without any more trouble than is needed to stay awake the result which your imagination is always aiming at is reeled off on the screen." As evidence, he cited how one's shadowy idea of the Ku Klux Klan took vivid shape when watching D. W. Griffith's *The Birth of a Nation* (1915). "Historically it may be the wrong shape," he pointed out, "morally it may be a pernicious shape, but it is a shape, and I doubt whether anyone who has seen the film and does not know more about the Ku Klux Klan than Mr. Griffith will ever hear the name again without seeing those white horsemen."[13]

The truth or falseness of a stereotype apparently has very little to do with its public acceptance. Art codifies reality, not the other way around. "What with our insensitiveness and inattention," distinguished critic Bernard Berenson once said, "things scarcely would have for us features and outlines so determined and clear that we could recall them at will, but for the stereotyped shapes art has lent them."[14] Having borrowed our standard of reality from the art with which we are acquainted—best-sellers, mall movies, video rentals, television—we tend to label as unreal or insincere anything that doesn't conform to this standard. Although the historical basis for the belief that all newspapermen keep a bottle of booze in their desks has withered away, the belief itself survives, preserved and sanctified by popular art.[15]

The reputation of journalists for hard drinking dates back to at least the last quarter of the nineteenth century.[16] No less a judge of men than Harvard University President Charles W. Eliot called reporters "drunkards, deadbeats, and bummers." Frank Luther

Mott, after quoting Eliot in his history of American journalism, added, "Certainly there was too much drinking by reporters."[17]

Some nineteenth-century commentators attributed this "bohemianism"—the then-popular term for a lifestyle of dissipation and artistic pretension—to the rush and strain of a reporter's life.[18] "One could hardly lead a more unsettled existence," an observer wrote in 1871. "His hours of sleep and meals vary almost daily, and unless a man has strong self-command, these irregular habits . . . will have a bad effect on him."[19] In 1888 the *Journalist*, a trade magazine, blamed bohemianism specifically on the space system, which paid reporters a low rate per column inch of story rather than a fixed salary. "It is not from choice that there are so many Bohemians in journalism," the magazine stated. "They are forced into Bohemia by the men who buy their work."[20]

Others thought that journalism held a natural appeal for vagabonds and wastrels. Charles J. Rosebault, a reporter at the *New York Sun* in the 1880s, claimed that his colleagues were often "strays in the social sense, for whom the irregular habits imposed by their calling were not its least attraction. Not a few had drifted into journalism from other vocations for the very reason that they could not tolerate the conventional life."[21]

But by the turn of the century, drunkards and misfits were said to be going, or even already gone, from the newsroom. The *Journalist* celebrated its 17th year of publication in 1900 by remarking that "the old, picturesque, Bohemian element is dying out. Nowhere is this more noticeable than on the staffs of the great dailies where the well dressed, well mannered alert young news-gatherers have taken the places of the impudent, unshorn, rum-soaked old vagabonds who used to disgrace the profession."[22]

Memoirists also testified to the increasing professionalism of the press. In *The Making of a Journalist* (1903), Julian Ralph wrote that journalism had once been "a haphazard, unmethodical business managed by printers and led by geniuses, ne'er-do-wells, Bohemians—often men of disorderly lives or irresponsible natures." Now, however, "all newspaper men must be ready to work at every moment of every day; they must be sober; they must appear well, and they must be able at least to present the external signs of refinement."[23] Samuel Blythe agreed, claiming in his memoir, *The Making of a Newspaper Man* (1912), that the "days of the frowsy, alleged-bohemian, drunken reporter and editor have passed."[24]

We don't have to entirely believe this. In fact, some evidence suggests that the tradition of hard drinking and unconventional living survived on newspaper staffs even through the depths of the Depression. Alfred McClung Lee, a journalism historian working in the late 1930s, observed that a reputation for bohemianism "continues to characterize" reporters.[25] These were also the years when there were fifteen "healthy newspapers in New York," each with a saloon next door.[26] It may be no coincidence that many alcoholic writers of the first half of the twentieth century—among them Ring Lardner, Sherwood Anderson, and Ernest Hemingway—began their careers at newspapers.

At a National Council on Alcoholism forum on alcoholic writers in 1979, the legendary drinking capacity of journalists came up for discussion. Ring Lardner Jr. noted that heavy drinking was common among New York newspapermen in the thirties when he became a reporter and that it was probably even greater in his father's time.[27] Another discussant, sportswriter Roger Kahn, confirmed that heavy drinking was socially acceptable in journalism. "It was a way of being macho," he said.[28]

Every decade from the 1920s through the 1950s produced at least one film about a newspaperman with a drinking problem. In the 1920s, it was *Big News;* in the 1930s, *The Sisters;* in the 1940s, *Welcome Stranger;* and in the 1950s, *Come Fill the Cup.* The stereotype of the hard-drinking newspaperman, however, grew mostly out of other films—scores of them—that showed reporters and editors boozing it up, but socially, casually, without complications. Through these films, heavy drinking came to seem part of the job description of a newspaperman, like typing with two fingers or wearing a hat indoors.

When I first began this book, Professor Matthew C. Ehrlich of the University of Illinois at Urbana–Champaign compiled as a favor to me a list of films in which there are scenes of drinking newspapermen. The list, with his annotations, included:

Platinum Blonde (1931): Part of the action takes place in a speakeasy as the reporter hero is torn romantically between an heiress and a fellow reporter.

Nothing Sacred (1937): Movie starts in a banquet hall in which reporter Frederic March is clearly soused.

The Philadelphia Story (1940): Reporter James Stewart gets drunk while pursuing Katharine Hepburn.

Citizen Kane (1941): The Jed Leland character is a drunk who tells hard truths about Kane and his opera singer wife.

Meet John Doe (1941): Editor James Gleason has a long drunk scene with Gary Cooper in which Gleason affirms his belief in democracy and reveals to Cooper that he (the John Doe character) is being duped.

Roxie Hart (1942): The movie begins and ends in a bar; near the beginning, a veteran reporter tells a cub that the public expects all reporters to drink and that it's always important to do what the public expects.

Deadline U.S.A. (1952): Editor Humphrey Bogart is trying to win back his reporter ex-wife; he gets drunk and wakes up hung over in her apartment. There's also a wake in a bar for the dying paper.

Park Row (1952): Editor Gene Evans gets drunk near the end of the film when he thinks he's lost his paper.

While the City Sleeps (1956): The characters hang out in a bar; reporter Dana Andrews gets drunk and cheats on his girlfriend.

Teacher's Pet (1958): Editor Clark Gable gets drunk while trying to get a romantic rival intoxicated; later, he goes to the rival's apartment and tends to the man's hangover with still more alcohol.

Lonelyhearts (1959): Editor Robert Ryan is a cynical boozer; idealistic columnist Montgomery Clift gets disillusioned and goes on a bender.[29]

There are still more scenes of this sort in later films. In *Absence of Malice* (1981), editor Josef Sommers shares his office bottle with reporter Sally Field; in *Under Fire* (1984), photojournalist Nick Nolte, arriving in war-torn Nicaragua, is immediately apprised by a colleague of the different kinds of beer available in the country; in *The Paper* (1994), editor Robert Duvall spends almost the entire second half of the film sulking in a bar. From the 1920s through the 1990s, the journalist has been identifiable in Hollywood films as much by the drink in his hand as by the cynical gleam in his eye.

That has never sat too well with the journalistic establishment, and editorials attacking the "false portrayals" of newspapermen on the screen have let Hollywood know it.[30] The trade magazine *Editor & Publisher* reported in 1947 that "recurring criticisms that movie journalists are characterized as inebriated or unscrupulous have recently led the Motion Picture Association to make a breakdown of pictures intended to prove that Hollywood is not doing newspapermen wrong."[31] Naturally, the breakdown—a survey of 378 films from 1946 and 398 from 1945—proved nothing less.

Hollywood's defenders also pointed out to *E&P* that "many newspaper movies are written by former newspapermen and the direction of the film versions is often in the hands of the newspapermen," which was quite true.[32] In the words of one historian of the genre, "Many of the best newspaper films were created as fondly bitter reminiscences of lost youth by men graduated from the world of newswriting to screenwriting."[33] And here we come to a paradox: that while the heavy drinking of reporters and editors in films was seen by some in journalism as offensive, it was generally meant to be seen as romantic, though in a dangerous and decadent way. To the extent that it was seen so, the films may have contributed to the heavy drinking among actual journalists.

This isn't as far-fetched as it probably sounds. "People," psychiatrist Donald W. Goodwin noted, "*do* what is expected of them," even if it is to drink themselves to death.[34] American writers are a good example.[35] Because of the literary success in the 1920s of alcoholics like Hemingway and F. Scott Fitzgerald, the gifted alcoholic writer became "a cult figure, a model for less gifted writers to follow into the later part of the century."[36] And follow they did. Dan Wakefield, a novelist, screenwriter, and recovered alcoholic, told a 1989 conference on "Alcohol and Other Drugs in Literature":

> I grew up with the glamor of alcohol. The first time I went to the White Horse Tavern in Greenwich Village, someone showed me the table where Dylan Thomas had his last drink before he died—and pointed to St. Vincent's Hospital across the street, where he was taken. I thought, Wow! That'll be me.[37]

The hard-drinking, wisecracking, crime-busting reporters of old newspaper films apparently attracted a similar cult following. Tom Wolfe recalled that when he entered journalism in 1957, he wanted the "whole movie, nothing left out": "Drunken reporters out on the

ALL THE PRESIDENT'S MEN *(1976), starring Robert Redford (left) and Dustin Hoffman (right) as* Washington Post *reporters Bob Woodward and Carl Bernstein, respectively, has been called "the most popular and honored picture about journalism of modern times." Significantly, it presents its reporter heroes and their editors and colleagues as hard-working rather than hard-drinking, as workaholics rather than alcoholics.*

ledge of the *News* peeing into the Chicago River at dawn . . . Nights down at the saloon listening to 'Back of the Yards' by a baritone who was only a lonely bull dyke with lumps of milk glass for eyes . . . Nights down at the detective bureau."[38] The influence of the made-in-Hollywood reporters was great enough for Goodwin to use the term "the Front Page tradition"—after the classic 1931 film—to designate the heavy drinking that was still occurring on newspapers not so very long ago.[39]

As late as 1977, Knight Ridder was combating in its corporate advertising the stereotype of the hard-bitten, boozy reporter. Under the headline "Scoop McClain? He doesn't work here anymore," and alongside a photograph of Scoop relaxing with his feet up on his desk and a bottle by his typewriter, the ad copy said:

Scoop graduated from the school of hard knocks. . . . Murder was his speciality, but he fought City Hall, too, and saved widows from eviction. He never forgot a friend and he never told a lie—except to get a story. So here's to Scoop McClain; they don't make 'em like that anymore.

You remember Scoop McClain—sarcastic and swaggering, a tough guy with a press card in his hat who liked pretty girls and whiskey and telling the world to go to hell. He was something else. Scoop was a star reporter, streetwise and cynical, but with a heart of gold. He never let the facts get in the way of a good story.

And, of course, they never did. The movie stereotype of American newspaper reporters is part of our folklore; it never had much to do with reality. But there's no question that journalism and the people who practice it have changed over the years.

I got my first job in journalism in 1977 and later worked on two Knight Ridder papers, the *Charlotte Observer* and the *Grand Forks (N.D.) Herald*. There wasn't a reporter nicknamed "Scoop" on the staff of either. Most of us were upward-striving young professionals, and if we drank, it was a couple of beers at a phony English pub after we put the paper to bed. Journalism and the people who practiced it had indeed changed. We were living a new film, the sanctimonious *All the President's Men* (1976) rather than the down-and-dirty *Front Page*.

3

Drink, Drank, Drunk

I never drink 'cept when alone or with somebody.

—Frontier saying

Why do people drink? "People drink," Alfred Kazin said, "for hereditary reasons, nutritional reasons, social reasons. They drink because they are bored, or tired, or restless. People drink for as many reasons as they have for wanting to 'feel better.' "[1]

The vast majority of Americans who drink are social drinkers—that is, they take a drink to relax, to be convivial, to enjoy themselves—but problem drinkers are still numerous.[2] About 9 percent of adults in the United States, almost 14 million people, suffer from alcoholism or a less severe form of alcohol abuse. All forms of alcohol abuse cost the nation an estimated $100 billion a year in lost productivity and direct health spending. Moreover, alcohol abuse is a major factor in traffic accidents, suicides, and violent crime.[3] One survey found that Americans drove while intoxicated an average of 14,000 times an hour in 1993, and that almost one in every 12 instances involved a driver under age 21—too young to drink legally in any state.[4]

Kazin noted that "America has always been a hard-drinking country despite the many places and times in which alcohol has been forbidden by law."[5] Even in the colonial era, Americans "drank often and abundantly."[6] They drank on rising, during work breaks, with meals, and in the evening before the tavern fireside. They drank when the night was cold or when the day was hot. They drank at har-

17

vests, elections, weddings, baptisms, holiday celebrations, ordinations, militia musters, and funerals. They drank to keep off chills and fevers, and as an aid to digestion.[7] "All this drinking," alcohol historians Mark Edward Lender and James Kirby Martin said, "added up. Under most modern definitions, the majority of [colonists] easily would qualify as moderate or heavy drinkers."[8]

But though they drank a lot, their drinking wasn't considered problematic. Lender and Martin cited three related reasons for this lack of anxiety over alcohol: 1) popular wisdom held that alcohol was essential to good health; 2) the social norms of the day kept public drunkenness in check; and 3) people generally drank fermented beverages—beer, wine, and cider—rather than more potent distilled liquors.[9] John Adams downed a tankard of cider every morning with breakfast.[10]

Not until the late eighteenth and early nineteenth centuries, when Americans moved away from fermented beverages to distilled liquors, did concern erupt over the ill effects of alcohol. The availability of cheap whiskey after Independence led to "unprecedented lusty drinking" among all social groups and occupations.[11] W. R. Rorabaugh, in an analysis of American drinking patterns in the post-Revolutionary period, described a nation of drunkards:

> When southerners served barbecue, they roasted hogs and provided "plenty of whiskey." Guests at urban dances and balls were often intoxicated; so were spectators at frontier horse races. Western newlyweds were customarily presented with a bottle of whiskey to be drunk before bedding down for the night. Liquor also entered into moneymaking and business affairs. When a bargain was negotiated or a contract signed, it was sealed with a drink; auctioneers passed the bottle to those who made bids. . . . Whiskey accompanied traditional communal activities such as house-raisings, huskings, land clearings, and reaping. It was even served when women gathered to sew, quilt, or pick the seeds out of cotton.[12]

Foreign travelers were amazed at the great quantities of alcohol Americans drank. A Swedish visitor reported "a general addiction to hard drinking," while a visitor from England noted that intoxication pervaded all segments of society. The nation's foremost statesmen voiced similar views. George Washington, who brewed a molasses-based beer at Mount Vernon, thought that distilled liquors were "the ruin of half the workmen in this Country." And Thomas Jefferson worried that the use of redeye was "spreading through the mass of our citizens."[13]

The temperance movement that arose in the 1820s and culminated 100 years later in national Prohibition was a response to America's post-Revolutionary spree. It was also a response to the kind of society in which sprees were permissible, or at least possible. "Drinking customs and habits," Rorabaugh pointed out, "are not random but reflective of a society's fabric, tensions, and inner dynamics, of the psychological sets of its people."[14] Between the Revolution and the Civil War, the Industrial Age dawned, loosening traditional communal bonds, destroying familiar moral standards, creating new economic dependencies—and inducing middle-class anxiety. Attempts to prohibit alcohol were, in a sense, attempts to prohibit a future flaming with nightmare cities and pockmarked by social decay.

Except for abolition, the temperance movement became the most powerful reform effort in antebellum America. By the end of the 1830s, the traditional notion of alcohol as "a positive good" and drinking as "a normal and necessary part of life" was collapsing under the pressure from drys. Few employers, for example, still provided their workers with mid-morning and mid-afternoon breaks for a pick-me-up (the forerunner of today's coffee breaks). Some employers had even begun to fire anyone found drinking on the job.[15] Increasingly, too, there were objections that drinking was something immigrants, rather than "true" Americans, did.[16]

The temperance movement emerged from the Civil War stronger and more popular than ever. Many Americans feared in the postwar period that the onrush of industrialization would topple the nation into anarchy unless precautions were taken. Since drinking was seen as being at the root of other social evils—crime, poverty, political corruption—the attack on it appeared particularly important.[17]

Important enough, in fact, to win the support of business leaders. To men like John D. Rockefeller and Henry Ford, who believed a steady, sober workforce was essential in industrializing America, drinking symbolized wastefulness and sloth, the breakdown of Victorian standards of propriety. Lender and Martin noted that the first item in "Andrew Carnegie's Advice to Young Men," even before "Never speculate" and "Save a little always," was "Never enter a bar-room, nor let the contents of a bar-room enter you."[18]

After the repeal of Prohibition—"that flawed battle against grief and plague," as Donald Newlove called it, which lasted from 1920 to 1933—business leaders were offering very different advice.[19] By then, the basis of the American economy had shifted from production to consumption, with a corresponding shift in moral and social values.[20] No longer were the middle and upper classes encouraged to set an example of abstinence for the lower classes. Instead, all classes were urged to spend, spend, spend. Alcohol fit easily into this glossy new world of consumption and enjoyment. In a nation where fanatics once smashed saloons with axes and churches once rang with denunciations of "demon rum," drinking had become stylish.

We can't understand what the hard-drinking journalist of American popular film represents unless we also understand popular attitudes toward drinking and drunkenness. Whether the journalist is a saint or sinner or a combination of both depends on whether drinking is defined as a normal social activity, an insidious addiction, or a moral evil. And if there is no single agreed-upon definition, as some scholars have claimed, then that ambiguity has an effect, too.[21]

Colonial Americans didn't regard alcohol as addicting. They believed that there was nothing inherent in the individual or alcohol that prevented someone from drinking moderately. A drunkard was someone who wanted to drink and get drunk, not someone who "had" to.[22] Or, as alcoholism expert H. G. Levine put it, "Drunkenness was a choice, albeit a sinful one, which some individuals made."[23]

In 1784 Dr. Benjamin Rush of Philadelphia published a pamphlet, *An Inquiry into the Effects of Ardent Spirits upon the Human Body and Mind,* that introduced the modern concept of alcoholism. Probably the foremost physician in the nation, Rush argued that alcohol was inherently addicting and that drunkards became addicted gradually and progressively. The old colonial idea that drunkenness was the fault of the drinker, he said, was true only in the early stages, when the drinker might still pull back. Once addicted, the drinker no longer controlled his drinking; his drinking controlled him.[24] Rush described this loss of control as a "disease of the will" and gave a vivid example: "When strongly urged by one of his friends, to leave off drinking [a habitual drunkard] said, 'Were a keg of rum in one corner of the room, and were a cannon constantly discharging balls between me and it, I could not refrain from passing before that cannon, in order to get at the rum.' "[25]

Rush would become known as the "Father of Temperance."[26] His notion that alcoholism was a progressive disease, as well as his recommendation that total abstinence was the only way to cure it, were at the core of temperance ideology during the nineteenth century. But though Rush's ideas circulated widely after the Civil War, the colonial view of drunkenness hadn't died out.[27] An 1882 pamphlet by a Rev. John E. Todd echoed the seventeenth-and eighteenth-century belief that drunkards chose to drink to excess:

> I consider it certain that the great multitude of drunkards could stop drinking today and for ever, if they would; but they don't want to. . . . I observe that there is no apparent difference between drunkenness in its first and drunkenness in its last stages. In both cases there is an appetite, and a will to gratify it. The man drinks simply because he likes to drink, or likes to be drunk.[28]

Around the turn of the twentieth century, the temperance movement lost interest in promoting the concept of alcoholism as a disease-like addiction. Instead, the movement committed its resources to the drive for national Prohibition in hopes of preventing, in historian Andrew Sinclair's phrase, "the wet cities from swamping the dry country."[29] After repeal, Alcoholics Anonymous and the Yale Center of Alcohol Studies revived the disease concept, but with a significant change.[30] The idea that alcohol was inherently addicting was abandoned in favor of the more congenial (for the mass of drinkers) idea that alcohol was addicting to only some people—those from alcoholic families, for example, or from heavy-drinking cultures.[31]

It isn't always clear today just what the prevailing American attitude toward drinking is.[32] "The many political battles over the regulation of sales [of alcohol]; the special restrictions on time of sale, especially to adolescents; the numerous legal measures enacted to limit its availability and use all attest to public ambivalence," sociologist Joseph R. Gusfield said.[33] While Americans annually drink an enormous amount of alcohol—they consumed 135 million cases of whiskey, vodka, and other distilled liquors in 1996—and generally believe that alcoholism is a disease, they still regard the alcoholic with disapproval."There is a stigma to alcoholism not seen with any other disease," Newlove, a novelist and member of AA, lamented. "It says, if you're a victim, you have poor moral fibre, a weakness that makes you a victim by choice."[34]

Until Prohibition imbued drinking with the romance of outlawry, the alcoholic was most commonly portrayed in fiction and graphics as a skid row derelict. This stereotype originated in so-called "Temperance Tales"—short stories, novels, and plays that showed the progressive ravages of drink and that propagandized for total abstinence. Although the popularity of temperance fiction peaked just before the Civil War, the genre remained vital throughout the nineteenth century. Books by such dry authors as Timothy Shay Arthur and Lucius Manlius Sargent reached hundreds of thousands of readers. Indeed, Sargent's works were translated into several languages, and Arthur's classic *Ten Nights in a Bar-Room* was still in print as a play and novel in the late 1970s.[35]

The typical temperance tale traced the career of an alcoholic from his first drink through years of physical, social, and economic decay to his final arrival at the grave or skid row. Temperance illustrations similarly emphasized the "gradual and cumulative destruction wrought by alcohol."[36] Illustrators often presented the alcohol addiction process in a series of prints, each print depicting yet another stage in the descent of a middle- or upper-class man to derelict status.[37]

Almost by definition, temperance tales were overly dramatic and entirely predictable, but while they made bad literature, they made good propaganda.[38] The temperance-tale image of the alcoholic as a skid row derelict dominated popular thinking until at least the 1930s. And thanks to mandatory temperance education in every state and classroom materials supplied by dry groups, even public-school students absorbed it.[39] "The drunkard, with his foul breath, his noisy tongue, his foolish and dangerous acts, his bloated face, and reeling gait," a typical text read, "is in many communities an everyday warning to young and old of the sad effect of drink."[40]

A study of turn-of-the-century "best-sellers" found that the skid row stereotype reeled through nontemperance fiction, too. Even though most of the authors viewed alcohol itself as acceptable, they portrayed alcoholics as social outcasts and physical wrecks.[41] An early work of newspaper fiction from 1899, "The Old Reporter" by Jesse Lynch Williams, took just this slant. Excessive drinking inevitably destroys its well-born protagonist, a reporter named Billy Woods, who ends up in the gutter with DTs.[42]

There have been other stereotypes of the alcoholic, including some related to or derived from the skid row stereotype. Perhaps the most enduring has been the "comic drunk," a species of which was the tramp comic. In the first decade of the 1900s, tramp comics swarmed through American vaudeville. One of the best was Lew Bloom, who wore a simple, shabby suit on stage and used virtually no makeup. He delivered his monologue in a serious, almost lugubrious tone.[43] "But I don't spend all my time in saloons," he would say. "I can't do it. They have to close up some time."[44]

The comic drunk has since migrated to films, television, and even greeting cards.[45] Norman K. Denzin, who wrote a book on alcoholism in Hollywood films, noted that the tradition of the comic drunk extends from the drunken millionaire in Chaplin's *City Lights* (1931) to the drunken millionaire played by Dudley Moore in *Arthur* (1981) and *Arthur 2 on the Rocks* (1988). In between there have been so many comic drunks that Denzin was able to divide them into several distinct types: the rich, pampered playboy drunk; the quiet, mellow tippler; the crude, boisterous W. C. Fields-type drunk; the witty, urbane drunk (William Powell in *The Thin Man* series, Cary Grant in *Topper*); and the eccentric, gentle-humored drunk (James Stewart in *Harvey*).[46]

While filmgoers like to laugh at these characters, the idea that drunkenness is comic doesn't strike alcoholism experts as particularly funny. They have claimed that the humorous portrayal of drunkenness promotes heavy drinking and deflects attention from the problems that may underlie and result from repeated drunken episodes.[47] Donald Newlove's boyhood experiences in Jamestown, New York, seem to support this. "When I was five," he recalled, "I began going to the movies alone and later acting out everything about alcohol I saw on the screen. . . . I knew about redeye before I could spell my name."[48]

But the comic drunk isn't the only cultural stereotype to leave the impression that drinking is an approved activity. So does the stereotype of the heavy-drinking artist or writer. American literature is crowded with writers who are nearly as famous for their drinking as for their poems, plays, or novels: Edgar Allan Poe, Jack London, Ring Lardner, Dorothy Parker, e. e. cummings, Dashiell Hammett, Ben Hecht, James Thurber, Raymond Chandler, Robert Benchley, Sinclair Lewis, F. Scott Fitzgerald, Thornton Wilder, Hart Crane, Ernest Hemingway, Thomas Wolfe, William Faulkner, John Steinbeck, Eugene O'Neill. "All these boozers on their mountaintops," Newlove said, "wrestling with their geniuses—what better life can there be?"[49] Until he went into an alcoholism recovery program, he thought none.

It is often assumed that writers hit the bottle in order to achieve disinhibition; that is, in order to stimulate or free up their creativity. But for at least some writers, the exact opposite has been the case. "One rule I observed," London said in his memoir of his drinking life, *John Barleycorn* (1913). "I never took a drink until my day's work of writing a thousand words was done. And, when done, the cocktails reared a wall of inhibition between the day's work done and the rest of the day of fun to come. My work ceased from my consciousness. No thought of it flickered in my brain till next morning when I sat at my desk and began my next thousand words. This was a desirable condition to achieve. I conserved my energy by means of alcoholic inhibition."[50] Hemingway apparently also used alcohol to regulate his creative rhythms. Drinking for him was "an anodyne, a reward, a soporific—a way to cut the overheated engine of imagination and cool it down restoratively at the end of a good day's work."[51]

The problem is that alcohol, consumed in large enough quantity and over sufficient time, causes physical and mental deterioration. It rusted out even the iron constitutions of London and Hemingway, both of whom ended as suicides. London's craving for alcohol grew so incessant that he found himself breaking his one rule. He started taking a drink halfway through his daily stint and, eventually, before he sat down to write.[52]

Despite the potential health hazards, heavy drinking has been accepted as "a natural accompaniment of literary life," and perhaps never more so than in the 1920s.[53] John W. Crowley, who has astutely analyzed the motif of alcoholism in modernist American fiction, attributed the Lost Generation's "reverence for strong drink" to the fact that its members grew up in the heyday of Prohibition, as well as lived through World War I. "Both experiences," he said, "bred deep skepticism about the wisdom and integrity of the elders and provoked rebellion against authority that exceeded the ordinary friction between generations."[54] Drinking in defiance of the Eighteenth

Amendment became fashionable, glamorous, a sign of emancipation. "It was the only period," *New Yorker* writer (and chronic alcoholic) A. J. Liebling reminisced, "during which a fellow could be smug and slopped concurrently."[55]

One indication of the rising interest in drinking was the proliferation of terms for drunkenness. H. L. Mencken, a devoted student of both the American language and alcoholic beverages, traced some of the terms for drunkenness used during Prohibition—"boiled," "canned," "cock-eyed," "fried," "oiled," "ossified," "pifflicated," "stewed," "stuccoed," "tanked," "woozy"—to frontier days.[56] But other old terms fell out of use as new synonyms came into vogue. By 1927 literary critic Edmund Wilson had collected more than a hundred words for drunkenness, including such neologisms as "lit," "crocked," "soused," "polluted," and "embalmed." He thought it significant that one heard less often of people going on "*sprees, toots, tears, jags, bats, brannigans,* or *benders*," all terms suggesting "an exceptional occurrence, a breaking away by the drinker from the conditions of his normal life." Fierce protracted drinking, he speculated, had now become "universal, an accepted feature of social life instead of a disreputable escapade."[57]

Although Wilson overestimated the amount of alcohol people were actually consuming in the twenties—annual alcohol consumption rates were between 55 and 33 percent *less* than those of pre-Prohibition years—he was right that they were consuming it with a new eagerness, even seriousness.[58] Fitzgerald said he and his generation "drank cocktails before meals like Americans, wines and brandies like Frenchmen, scotch-and-soda like the English. This preposterous melange . . . was like a gigantic cocktail in a nightmare."[59] But it wasn't only their excessive boozing at parties in Greenwich Village or their relentless bar-hopping through Paris nights that created the stereotype of the drunken literary genius. The books that made them famous were also saturated with alcohol. For example, drinking occurs on nearly every page of *The Sun Also Rises* (1926), which Hemingway later described as "one book about a few drunks."[60]

Something similar might be said of other well-known modernist texts, from London's *John Barleycorn* through Fitzgerald's *Tender Is the Night* (1934) and John O'Hara's *Appointment in Samarra* (1934) to Malcolm Lowry's *Under the Volcano* (1947). "The avant garde," Crowley noted, "reacted against the Victorian ideal of inebriation by pro-

ducing a literature that idealized intoxication as iconoclasm and lion-
ized the drunk as an anti-Puritan rebel."[61]

This romantic vision of alcohol, alcoholism, and the alcoholic influ-
enced the screen portrayal of the hard-drinking journalist, particularly in the 1930s, the so-called "golden age of newspaper films."[62]
While the old concept of the alcoholic as morally defective still sur-
faced on occasion—*The Famous Ferguson Case,* a "B" film from 1932,
would be an example—most newspaper films of the era took a more
liberal view. And this despite the Motion Picture Production Code,
which went into effect in 1934 and closely governed conduct on the
screen. The code was quite explicit about drinking: "The use of liquor
in American life, when not required by the plot, or for purpose of
characterization, will not be shown."[63]

Liquor must have been required by reporters, for they are certainly
shown drinking a lot of it. When I asked a film archivist if she knew
of any films from the thirties with drunken reporters, she replied,
"Gosh, there must be a drunken reporter in most thirties films, don't
you think?"[64]

Drunks can be entertaining, sociable, pleasant. The social drinker
is bound to end up a skid row bum with swollen eyes, broken nose,
shabby clothes, and ruined family. "All good writers are drunkards,"
Hemingway said.[65] "No one," Ring Lardner insisted, "ever wrote
anything as well after even one drink as he would have done without it."[66] Alcoholism is a vice and a sin. Alcoholism is a disease-like
addiction.

Obviously, there is no culturally agreed-upon definition of alcoholism or the alcoholic. Americans have long felt ambivalent about
alcohol, and as Norman Denzin pointed out, this has been reflected
on the screen.[67] It is my theory that because attitudes about alcohol
are so conflicted, the symbolic significance of the hard-drinking journalist in Hollywood films is curiously unfixed, varying according to
the context in which he (or, on rare occasion, she) appears.

Anthropologists Craig MacAndrew and Robert B. Edgerton found
that "what people do when they are drunk is almost everywhere sit-
uationally variable."[68] I'm suggesting that something of the same
principle applies to the film journalist who hits the bottle. Depend-
ing on the situation, his drinking has different implications. Some of

the implications are positive, and some are negative, but all comment on his moral, social, and professional status. Now drinking implies that the journalist is tough and manly, a throwback to an earlier and more virile age; now that he is suave and stylishly cynical, an example of the modern cosmopolitan. Now drinking implies that the journalist is an easygoing, humorous, irresponsible loafer; now that he is a corrupt, scoop-crazy bastard. Now drinking implies that the journalist lives more fully and sensitively than the average person; now that he must anesthetize himself against the pain of being alive.

4

The Ghosts of Printing House Square

There are two kinds of newspapermen—those who try to write poetry and those who try to drink themselves to death. Fortunately for the world, only one of them succeeds.

—Ben Hecht

Jesse Lynch Williams is remembered today, when he is remembered at all, for receiving in 1917 the first Pulitzer Prize ever awarded for drama. Yet Williams was a prolific and versatile author who wrote short stories and novels as well as plays.[1] In 1899 he published *The Stolen Story and Other Newspaper Stories*, which joined Richard Harding Davis's "Gallegher, A Newspaper Story" (1890) and Elizabeth G. Jordan's *Tales of the City Room* (1898) as an early entry in the fledging genre of newspaper fiction.[2]

Williams had been a reporter for the *New York Sun*, and so knew whereof he wrote. "Few people," an anonymous reviewer said in the *New York Times*, "know very much about how their favorite paper is made up. It is generally enough for them that the paper is. Mr. Williams not only knows how it is done, but . . . he also knows how to present the facts in story form. . . ."[3] In the days before there were college courses or textbooks in journalism, Williams's collection somewhat filled their role. As an aspiring young journalist in turn-of-the-century Baltimore, H. L. Mencken eagerly read it.[4]

One of the stories Mencken devoured was "The Old Reporter," the

29

last and by far the longest in the book. The story is historically significant because it served as a kind of crossover between dry literature and newspaper fiction. It grafted the temperance-tale concept of
alcoholism as a gradual and progressive disease and the temperance-
tale stereotype of the alcoholic as a skid row bum onto the characterization of the reporter.[5]

The story opens with the recommendation that we take a walk
along Park Row, the street of newspapers in late nineteenth-century
New York, with a veteran newspaperman and make him talk about
the fellow craftsmen he meets. "If it were the right time of day, and
he were the right kind of newspaper-man [sic]," Williams notes,

> you might pass a score of them between Broadway and the Bridge. Per-
> haps a half-dozen would have left a hard-luck story trailing behind
> them. There would be one main cause assigned for it by your experi-
> enced companion. In your walk you would have passed just about that
> number of places where the staple article of merchandise was dis-
> pensed in glasses. And yet these places alone are not to blame.[6]

After this general introduction, Williams turns to a detailed exam-
ination of the newspaper career of Billy Woods, following him from
his first fumbling efforts as a cub through his triumphs as a star
reporter to his descent into unemployment and poverty. Williams is
ambiguous about the ultimate cause of Billy's downfall. Alcohol
plays a part, but so does the strenuous nature of newspaper work. In
fact, alcohol and newspaper work seem to have the same long-term
effects on a body. Both are addicting and debilitating, and both inflict
their misery by slow degrees.

Williams implies that Billy would have escaped ruin if he had quit
newspaper work in time, a notion that parallels the addiction model
of alcoholism publicized by the temperance movement in the nineteenth century.[7] Friends urge him to try some other line of work after
he has won fame as a reporter, something less difficult and draining,
but he refuses. "I could no more settle down to a roll-top-desk life,"
he says, "than Cherokee Indians can run farms."[8]

Unfortunately, the excitement of newspaper work comes with a
heavy price: cynicism and a distorted sense of reality. Billy, Williams
points out, "had little to do with anything normal, because his job
was to hunt and handle The News, which means the interesting, the
unusual, surprising, shocking, remarkable, wonderful, wicked, hor-

rible. . . ." To make matters worse, his work hours were abnormal, too, "extending far into the night intended for rest." He had no chance to recuperate physically or mentally from digging up scandal and the like. Although Williams doesn't use the term "burnout," Billy eventually exhibits many of its symptoms, including "in-growing thoughts," "disquieting sensations," and taut nerves.[9]

And so he begins not only to drink, but to get drunk. "He got drunk," Williams adds, "because he liked it. It was glorious. . . . everything swung around, soothingly straightened out, and became sunny and warm."[10] At this point, the story reflects the seventeenth- and eighteenth-century assumption that "people drank and got drunk because they wanted to, and not because they 'had' to."[11] Later, though, Billy's drinking becomes compulsive, which conforms more closely to the modern understanding of alcoholism as a disease—or two diseases.

Berton Roueché, longtime science writer for the *New Yorker*, once explained that "Beneath the blunted mind, the ravaged body, and the compelling, insatiable thirst of the familiar alcoholic syndrome sits some far more savage disorder, whose torments . . . can be wonderfully assuaged by alcohol. The seeds of alcoholism are thus implanted in its victims before they ever take a drink."[12] In Billy's case, the underlying or primary disorder is the loss of ideals and enthusiasm caused by his years of newspaper experience. "Every sort of passion and situation had so long ceased to mystify, charm, repell [sic], or awe him," Williams writes, "that now he was forgetting how other people who had not lived so fast were mystified, charmed, repelled, or awed." When the copy desk complains that his stories lack their old sparkle, he tries to pour the sparkle back into them by "means of a few more drinks, hurriedly snatched on the way to the office."[13] He is moving along the downward path of the drunkard in the typical nineteenth-century temperance tale.

Even then, Billy still has a chance to avoid landing in the gutter. Sometimes a temperance tale ended with the return of one of the drunken characters to health and prosperity. A faithful wife was usually a great help during recovery, providing love, a safe home, and encouragement to the drunkard in his battle against drink.[14] Williams suggests that Billy also might have been saved by wifely or womanly support. "But she died."[15]

Thus Billy's disintegration proceeds apace. Soon his work is no longer in demand, and he begins to look the classic skid row bum, godforsaken and seedy. Former colleagues laugh behind his back. He gets an occasional job, "often on some poor little paper of small importance," but can't hang onto it. "How do you live," Williams rhetorically asks, "you ghosts of Printing House Square, that walk up and down the Row and stand in certain hallways and bar-rooms, talking of the story of the day and the trouble with the *Times*'s policy—and Lord knows what—most intelligently; how do you manage it, I wonder?"[16]

Although Williams draws out the ending as long as possible, Billy finally goes all to pieces, collapsing on the street with hallucinations and the shakes. He is taken to Bellevue by ambulance, a big policeman sitting on his legs. "Every paper wanted that fellow once," an onlooker remarks; "none of 'em will have him now. . . . Too bad he couldn't leave whiskey alone."[17] The irony, of course, is that whiskey had less to do with it than the newspaper business did.

"The Old Reporter" points to—if it isn't directly responsible for— a number of important themes in newspaper fiction. Besides reinforcing the stereotype of the drunken reporter that had been around since at least the 1870s, Williams's story introduced the notion that journalism was a good training ground for literature or politics, but a bad choice of profession. David Graham Phillips has a reporter in his 1901 novel, *The Great God Success*, explicitly say: "Journalism is not a career. It is either a school or a cemetery. A man may use it as a stepping-stone to something else. But if he sticks to it, he finds himself an old man, dead and done for to all intents and purposes before he's buried."[18]

Characters in later newspaper novels take the same dim view. "Business'll kill you if you keep on," the city editor in Henry Justin Smith's *Deadlines* (1923) tells a cub. "Look at me, hauled out of bed at five every morning; rush to my desk, stay there till the last dog's hung. Fight, fight, fight, all the time. Fight with the staff, with the readers of the paper, with the town itself. . . . Get a quieter job, where you can write those poems of yours."[19] In *Splendor*, a 1927 novel by Ben Ames Williams, a veteran reporter observes: "There's no future for a man in the newspaper business. Nothing but a lot of work and a sanitarium when your nerves play out. Late hours, long hours, dull scratching at things."[20] Another in Gene Fowler's *Trumpet in the Dust* (1930) says,

"I don't want to burn out in this business. They use you until you are all consumed and then toss you aside like a handful of wet ashes."[21]

Williams also helped launch the idea that newspaper work, despite its many drawbacks, is strangely addicting. About ten years after Billy Woods was carted off to the hospital with DTs, the title character of Edna Ferber's first novel, *Dawn O'Hara* (1911), declared:

> After you have been a newspaper writer for seven years—and loved it—you will be a newspaper writer, at heart and by instinct at least, until you die. There's no getting away from it. It's in the blood. Newspaper men have been known to inherit fortunes, to enter politics, to write books and become famous, to degenerate into press agents and become infamous, to blossom into personages, to sink into nonentities, but their news-nose remained a part of them, the inky, smoky, stuffy smell of the newspaper was ever sweet in their nostrils.[22]

An old, broken-down editor in *Ink*, a 1930 novel by John C. Mellett, offered an even more elaborate description of printer's ink as a kind of intoxicant: "It rushes through your arteries, and hastens your lagging veins. Unlike other drugs, the dose need not be increased to maintain the effect. The same amount taken daily produces the same old thrill. Once inhaled ink knows no cure but ink. The hair of the dog is not merely the best, it's the only thing for the bite."[23]

Early twentieth-century authors of newspaper fiction conceived of journalism in much the same terms that nineteenth-century temperance writers and speakers had conceived of alcoholism—as "a disease with a symptomatic progression of phases leading eventually from psychological to physical addiction."[24] It isn't all that hard to understand how journalism, with its overwhelming interest in sex and crime and scandal, could be compared to a disease. The question is, How did the downward spiral of alcohol addiction become the prototype for portraying the downward spiral of newspaper life?

Part of the answer may lie in the fact that the temperance movement was once the biggest reform movement in America.[25] From the early 1800s to national Prohibition in 1920, temperance was preached from the pulpit, dramatized on the stage, and advocated in pamphlets and books. The movement's disease model became well known, and as a piece of common cultural property, was available to be adapted to issues far removed from temperance—even the issue of reporter burnout.

Then, too, journalists had already established their reputation for dissolute living by the time newspaper fiction emerged as a distinct genre. Back in the 1860s, the younger members of the New York press corps frequented Pfaff's Cave, a subterranean restaurant-bar at 633 Broadway, where they drank, smoked, and otherwise cultivated a bohemian image.[26] "The term Bohemian," *Galaxy* magazine told its readers in 1867, "belongs exclusively and peculiarly to reporters."[27]

To be a bohemian afforded license for all kinds of youthful hijinks. Louis M. Starr recounted in *Bohemian Brigade*, his delightfully written history of Civil War-era journalists, how Mortimer Thomson of the *Tribune* and George Forrester Williams of the *Times* spirited the Prince of Wales from the Fifth Avenue Hotel to a bar on 25th Street. While tumult reigned in the royal entourage at the prince's disappearance, the two introduced His Highness to a mint julep.[28] The story has a mythic air, but is accurate enough in its casting of reporters as lighthearted scamps.

In 1889 a group of young Chicago reporters, copy editors, and cartoonists founded the Whitechapel Club for "no other purpose than the promotion of good fellowship, with good liquor on the table and a good song ringing clear." The club first occupied rooms at the back of Kosters' saloon, but in 1892 moved to larger, more luxurious quarters farther down "Newspaper Alley." Elmer Ellis, biographer of Finley Peter Dunne ("Mr. Dooley"), one of the club's original members, described its atmosphere as "Bohemian, Rabelaisian, and macabre."[29] A beer keg stood in a corner on the first floor, while at the bar were corked bottles for those who preferred something stronger. Upstairs, drinkers sat around a coffin-shaped table, keeping time to "their own dreadful singing by hammering with their beer mugs" on the top.[30] The club entertained many distinguished visitors. Rudyard Kipling, a favorite author of its members, showed up during an American tour. "Having seen Chicago," Kipling would later write, "I urgently desire to never see it again. It is inhabited by savages."[31]

Given that the younger generation of journalists liked to carouse in defiance of middle-class norms and values, and also that the disease model of alcoholism was widely accepted, the application of the model to journalism itself was perhaps inevitable. By the turn of the century, a journalism career was being described in terms of a degenerative disease—as a strange malady that gradually reduced the journalist to a kind of ghost. The long haunting was underway.

5

Hello Darkness

Love is a better drug than drink.

—Natalie Barney

For most of the silent era, alcoholism films reflected the dry values of the temperance movement. The films stressed the ill effects of drink, punished drinkers, and equated happiness with abstinence.[1] "Who," a liquor industry journal asked in the 1910s, "has seen liquor portrayed in any but the most unfavorable light by the movies? The films accept every chance to link liquor with the drug habits. What makes the rural lover go wrong? Liquor, always liquor. And hooked up with liquor must be evil women. The movies have made a goat of liquor."[2]

It has been estimated that between 1908 and 1989, Hollywood made at least 600 alcoholism films—that is, films in which the drinking of "one or more major characters is presented as a problem which the character, his or her friends, family, and employers, and other members of society self-consciously struggle to resolve."[3] Although the *American Film Institute Catalog* lists a combined total of more than 100 feature films under the subject headings "Alcoholism" and "Drunkenness" for just the decade 1911–20, very few of these films survive. And when one takes a specialized approach to the surviving films—by focusing, for example, on the hard-drinking journalist—the chance of locating viewing copies, already extremely slim, becomes almost nonexistent.

There is a solution of sorts, and it is to rely on the synopses of films in the AFI catalogs for the decades 1911–20 and 1921–30, supplemented, where possible, by contemporary reviews. Of course, this has its own drawbacks, as Denise Herd, who followed a similar procedure for a 1986 article, discovered:

> First, there were no uniform criteria of "alcoholism" employed to index the films. . . . we have only a rough idea that some form of deviant or problem drinking played a significant role in the film's plot. Second, plot summaries alone cannot capture the rich texture of visual imagery and auditory cues that impart meaning in film. The manifest content of the film plot can be subverted to another level of meaning through other dimensions of the film's text.[4]

Even so, we may still learn something useful from the catalogs, if it is only the extent to which the drunken journalist was portrayed in the silent era. By checking the titles listed under the subject headings "Alcoholism" and "Drunkenness" against those listed under the headings "Reporters" and "Newspapers," I was able to identify eleven relevant films. Reading the film synopses was nothing like watching the actual films, but, then, watching the films today would have been nothing like watching them in their original context. In the final analysis, we are always somewhat in the position of Dashiell Hammett's existential detective, hunting in a dark room for a black hat that isn't there.[5]

The fate of the romantic couple is a major—if not *the* major—concern of the early films that mix journalism with alcohol. By the mid-1910s America had entered a new sexual era. One sign of this was the popularization of Freudian psychology, specifically the notion that it was better to indulge sexual impulses than risk the consequences of suppressing them. *Good Housekeeping* told its readers that the sex instinct sought "every kind of sensory gratification. . . . If it gets its yearning, it is as contented as a nursing infant. If it does not, beware!"[6]

In another sign that American sexual mores were changing, cultural radicals rebelled against old patriarchal forms of marriage. Floyd Dell and other Greenwich Village bohemians argued for unions based on sexual attraction and emotional compatibility rather than on duty and personal sacrifice. They believed that these so-called "companionate marriages" didn't need the approval of church or state and ought to be dissolved at the wish of either member.[7] The belief marked a shift from nineteenth-century prescriptions about continence and self-control to a new ethic of consumption, self-gratification, and pleasure.

Historically, Hollywood has "promoted the ideal of monogamous marriage to a 'suitable partner.' "[8] The films of the teens and early twenties promoted it despite—or, perhaps, even because of—the fact that "opportunities for nonprocreative, nonmarital sexual behavior" were rapidly expanding, throwing traditional gender roles into disarray.[9] Drunkenness was often a metaphor in the films for the sexual tensions of the modern young couple.

The Rummy (1916), for example, tells the story of a reporter who marries a woman brought in on a prostitution charge while he is covering night court. He later finds her in a "rather compromising position" with his publisher. Although he had always believed her innocent of soliciting, he now turns her out into the street. "To drown his sorrows," *Variety* said in its review, "he becomes the rummy" of the title.[10]

Another 1916 film, *The Fringe of Society*, has a very similar plot. Here Martin Drake, the publisher of the *Record*, finds his wife, Esther, in the arms of Ned Medford, a powerful politician who represents the liquor interests. Martin mistakenly believes that Esther has been unfaithful and goes on a drinking spree.[11]

Don't Neglect Your Wife (1921), which was trumpeted by Goldwyn Pictures as novelist "Gertrude Atherton's First Original Screen Story," also presents a romantic triangle. Neglected by her club-going husband, San Francisco socialite Madeline Talbot falls in love with brilliant young newspaperman Langdon Masters. Gossip about them causes Masters to abandon his career and leave town. He drifts to New York's notorious Five Points, where he tries to drink himself to death.[12]

In *His Parisian Wife* (1919), the woman is the journalist, but the man is still the one who is sexually insecure and gets drunk. While visiting Paris, American lawyer Martin Wesley shares an umbrella with Fauvette, a reporter, in a rainstorm. Martin takes her to tea, then dinner, and by 11 that night has asked her to marry him. He brings his bride to live with his parents, a staid New England couple who hate all things French. Their disapproval gradually infects Martin. When his friend Tony Rye comes to dinner and Fauvette appears in a low-cut gown, Martin reprimands her. She moves out. A broken-hearted Martin turns to the bottle for solace.[13]

If sexual tensions aren't causing drinking in a film, then drinking is usually causing sexual tensions. Over a period of ten years, Clyde Manning, the protagonist of *The Night Workers* (1917), rises from copy boy to star reporter on a big-city daily, even though, in *Variety*'s words, "he proves himself a constant devotee of the spirits that come in a bottle."[14] Clyde drinks to cope with the strain of working late into the night—a motive sometimes cited in newspaper fiction as well.[15] Eventually, a new female reporter, or "sob sister," joins the staff, and she and Clyde fall in love. But the early stages of their relationship are bittersweet at best. She must save Clyde from several drunken debauches.[16]

Variety described *The Night Workers* as "just a cheap melodrama that can play the smaller houses."[17] It vastly preferred *Deadline at Eleven* (1920), calling the Vitagraph production "one of the best that has ever been shot out of the nose of a camera."[18] Yet the newsroom romances in the two films bear a strong resemblance. When socialite Helen Stevens takes a job on a New York paper in *Deadline at Eleven*, she is befriended by heavy-drinking reporter Jack Rawson. One night she is assigned to a missing-girl story, and Jack promises to accompany her. Instead, he gets drunk, stumbles onto the body of a murdered woman, and passes out. He wakes up the next morning to find himself accused of the crime. With the aid of a letter to her advice-to-the-lovelorn column, Helen catches the real killer. A relieved Jack swears off booze, and Helen brings him home to meet her mother.[19]

Almost all the drunken reporters and editors in silent films ultimately reform. The one major exception is Adrian Brownwell in *A Certain Rich Man*, a 1921 film based on a novel by Pulitzer Prize-winning journalist William Allen White. Brownwell, once a respected newspaper editor in the small town of Sycamore Ridge, dies in a train wreck after twenty years of alcoholism, thus freeing his long-suffering wife to marry her childhood sweetheart.[20]

The high rate of recovery in films distinguishes them from nineteenth-century temperance tales, which typically ended with the drunkard in the gutter or the grave. But the films are similar to the temperance tales in depicting the support of a loving woman as an essential part of a drinking cure.[21] In *Don't Neglect Your Wife*, for example, socialite Madeline Talbot tracks ex-newspaperman Langdon Masters to a dive called "The Bucket of Blood" and reclaims him from liquor and degradation by her "gentle presence."[22]

Even when the girlfriend of the drunkard holds down an untraditional job, she can still serve the traditional female function of being a positive influence. Both sob sister Ethel Carver in *The Night Workers* and advice columnist Helen Stevens in *Deadline at Eleven* inspire their reporter boyfriends to become sober—and, not incidentally, marriageable.

The Foolish Matrons (1921) makes the same point about the importance of a woman's love and support by presenting a woman who withholds hers. Although married, Sheila Hopkins is concerned only with her newspaper career. Her lack of sympathy for her sensitive husband drives him to drink. Returning to his hometown, he dies of alcohol poisoning, and she realizes too late her foolishness.[23]

Thus early alcoholism films do more than just preach temperance; they also reinscribe gender stereotypes. In them, the cure for alcohol abuse is simultaneously a cure for modern sexual upheaval. When the man stops drinking, he assumes his "rightful" position as lawgiver and breadwinner, while the woman falls back to a domestic role.

As for journalism, it emerges from the films with an ambiguous moral profile. At times it is shown as potentially corruptive, exposing the journalist to the awful temptations of drink. In *A Case at Law* (1917), for example, Jimmy Baggs moves west with his wife to the little town of Sago, where he has found a job as a reporter. Jimmy has promised to give up drinking, but gets crocked at his first meeting with the newspaper staff, held, significantly, in Art's saloon. His wife appeals to the town doctor (who, as it happens, is also her long-lost father) for help. After Doc takes the couple in, Jimmy reforms. Then one day he is sent to the saloon for a statement on the liquor question. Once again, he returns home drunk.[24]

But while journalism contributes to excessive drinking in some instances, it contributes to its abatement in others. In *The Rummy*, the title character, though fired from a newspaper for drunkenness, receives a tip that the publisher is taking graft. The rummy not only gets the story, but in the process also uncovers proof that his wife is innocent of any hanky-panky. He reconciles with her, takes the pledge, and wins back his old job—all, *Variety* wryly noted, "without even showing he has passed through the Keeley cure."[25]

The Fringe of Society ends somewhat similarly. Newspaper publisher Martin Drake acquires information damaging to politician

Ned Medford, but is kidnapped by Medford's henchmen to prevent him from running it. Reporter Tip O'Neill rescues Martin and writes up the exposé. Martin goes to Medford's apartment, arriving just as Medford is about to attack Martin's wife, Esther. After Martin trounces Medford in a fight, Esther explains everything to her husband, and his doubts about her fidelity disappear.[26]

Journalism historian Louis M. Starr once pointed out that the reporting of sex and crime in America's first mass medium, the penny papers of the 1830s, left a lingering impression that reporters were disreputable.[27] Alcoholism films did little to dispel that. Even when reporters in the films serve truth and temperance, they are still deeply involved with the seamier side of life: graft, saloons, prostitution, murder. Small wonder Clyde Manning, the star reporter in *The Night Workers*, needs a drink or three to help him make it through the night.

To the extent that the films offered a quasi-scientific explanation of drinking problems, they reflected future trends. Arnold S. Linsky, who analyzed the image of the alcoholic in popular magazines, found that the tendency to blame alcoholism on moral weakness "declined steadily" from 1900 to 1966. Instead, articles showed alcoholism as being caused by a combination of internal and external factors—the genetic, biochemical, and psychological makeup of the alcoholic and his social and cultural conditioning.[28]

Mike Lewington saw in twentieth-century cinema the same trend away from a moralistic model of alcoholism to a biological, psychological, or sociological model. Both he and Linsky observed that the changing models were part of much larger changes in popularly accepted theories of human behavior. Over the past century, the traditional image of man as possessing free will had given way, they said, to the view that man is a victim of his heredity and environment.[29]

This shift from a "free-will position" to determinism broadened public attitudes toward deviants, including the alcoholic.[30] Beginning with the films of the 1910s, the drunkard or heavy drinker was no longer portrayed as entirely responsible for his drinking. Chronic excessive drinking was now pictured as at least partly the result of forces beyond the drinker's control, from sexual insecurity in *The Rummy* to hereditary disease in *The Fringe of Society* and *A Case at Law* to a stressful job in *The Night Workers*.

Where the films were out of sync with long-range trends was in promoting total abstinence. "'The Fringe of Society,'" said a reviewer for the *New York Dramatic Mirror*, "is essentially a propaganda play for prohibition, and as such should have a strong appeal to right-thinking people."[31] A reviewer for *Variety* likewise said of *A Case at Law*, "Its gist is that if there are laws against the sale of dope[,] why not laws against the sale of liquor to youths and others [with] a weakness to excesses in the matter of John Barleycorn." The film, he added, "will doubtless prove an extra draw in the dry states."[32]

Perhaps the bluntest expression of prohibitionist sentiment occurs in *Truthful Tulliver*, a William S. Hart western from 1917. Hart plays Truthful, a cowboy-turned-newspaper editor who sets up shop in the lawless border town of Glory Hole. Truthful runs an editorial condemning the 40 Red Saloon after he sees its drunken customers insult two women. Later, he takes even stronger measures, riding his horse into the saloon, lassoing its manager, and dragging him out of town.[33]

No matter how temperance-minded a film seems, the issue of sexual identity usually lurks just below the surface. In *The Tomboy* (1921), Minnie comes home one day from playing ball to find her father insanely drunk. Swearing revenge against the local bootleggers, she joins a newspaper as a sportswriter so as to expose their activities. Pike, leader of the bootleggers, spreads a scandal about Minnie after she rejects his sexual advances, but everything is finally cleared up with the help of a handsome stranger.[34]

The advent of Prohibition would provoke a backlash against dry values, and by the late 1920s, the drinking climate of films would be predominantly wet. When legendary director D.W. Griffith released his temperance melodrama *The Struggle* in 1931, it was seen as "an outmoded testimony against drink" and withdrawn from theaters within a week.[35] In the decades ahead, there would still be films in which drinking was problematized, but there would be many more films in which drinking was presented as a normal social activity.[36] The time would actually come when audiences would be able to recognize the hero by how much he drank and how little he felt it.

To the critical fraternity, the drunken-newspaperman films of the teens and early twenties seemed to offer, within limits, realistic depictions of newspaper life. E. S., reviewing *The Rummy* in the *New*

York Dramatic Mirror, said, "The majority of 'Four[th] Estate' pictures are artificial and the characters are far from realistic, but it is just the opposite in this production. . . . Seldom do we see the interiors of a newspaper office shown in such a realistic effective manner."[37] *Wid's Film Daily* was so impressed with the "many fine bits of newspaper atmosphere introduced" in *The Rummy* that it suggested exhibitors "invite all newspaper men, and try to have a special performance at which most of the newspaper men would be present as guests of the management."[38]

Critics pretty much took it for granted that newspaper life was an inherently compelling screen subject. "The many sided and always interesting newspaper profession," began a review of *The Night Workers* in *Motorgraphy,* "provides the material for this story."[39] *Deadline at Eleven* brought a similar comment from *Wid's Film Daily,* which told exhibitors, "By presenting this as a melodrama of newspaper life you should be able to attract considerable attention inasmuch as this type of story or picture is usually fascinating to the public."[40] Meanwhile, *Moving Picture World* recommended that the film be promoted with the catchline: "Do You Know How a Newspaper Office Operates? How 'Beats' Are Scored? See Corinne Griffith in 'Deadline at Eleven.' "[41]

Although the critics tended to like *The Rummy, Deadline at Eleven,* and the rest, there was one thing about the films that seriously bothered them—the close identification of newspaper life with excessive drinking. Being members of the press themselves, they had a vested interest in denying that modern newspapermen were a bunch of drunks. Thus Fred., in a review of *The Rummy* in *Variety,* wrote, "As a picturization of newspaper life the story rings true, with the possible exception that it pictures all reporters as rummies more or less. The day has passed when the star man on any paper is the 'rummy,' for nowadays rummies do not usually get the chance to prove whether they are star men or not."[42]

The following year, 1917, Fred. predicted that critics would slam *The Night Workers* "because it makes souses of the entire 'Fourth Estate.' " He repeated that while drunkenness "existed years ago in the newspaper field the man that drinks to excess in the game at present is rather the exception than the rule."[43] A. G. S. of the *New York Dramatic Mirror* agreed, noting that "the news gatherers [in the film] are depicted as a very thirsty crew, which is not invariably the case."[44]

Such objections had little, if any, effect on the subsequent development of the newspaper-film genre. In a 1992 article in *Washington Journalism Review,* Chip Rowe asked, "What's the source of those loathsome misconceptions that journalists are hard-drinking, foul-mouthed dim-witted social misfits. . . ?" And he gave a one-word answer: Hollywood.[45]

6

Bottoms Up

Alcohol is easy to make and simple to sell and pleasant to consume, and few men will refuse so facile a method of escaping from the miseries of living.

—Andrew Sinclair

The Depression was, by almost any measure, the golden age of newspaper films.[1] Never again would there be so many newspaper films in theaters, and never again would they exude so much energy.[2] On the screen in the thirties, the newspaper office became "a great place," where star men traded humorous insults with their editors, and brash girl reporters rushed in with murder clues.[3]

Several factors contributed to this renaissance. First was the belief, supported by headlines and the best-selling memoirs of very roving reporters, that journalism was inherently dramatic, and that journalists were involved in important, or at least colorful, events.[4] Second was the related belief that journalists were quick and clever conversationalists, and thus ideal characters for the new medium of talking pictures. One observer went so far as to claim that the newspaper-film genre only began with the advent of sound.[5]

A third factor was the Depression itself. Nick Roddick noted that the classic Hollywood style "rested upon the individualising of social issues."[6] During the early thirties, what Andrew Bergman dubbed "shyster films"—films revolving around the activities of mouthpiece lawyers, corrupt politicians, or amoral newspapermen—kept faith in the American dream alive by finding scapegoats for the Depression.

Like the gangster films they strongly resembled, the shyster films transformed social evil into personal evil, "substituting crooks for economic short-circuits."[7]

Most important to the development of the newspaper-film genre, however, was the fact that from the mid-twenties into the thirties ex-newspapermen flocked to Hollywood. Ben Hecht, a Chicago newspaperman who would become a $1,000-a-day script doctor, headed west after receiving a telegram from reporter-turned-screenwriter Herman Mankiewicz: WILL YOU ACCEPT THREE HUNDRED PER WEEK TO WORK FOR PARAMOUNT PICTURES? ALL EXPENSES PAID. THE THREE HUNDRED IS PEANUTS. MILLIONS TO BE GRABBED OUT HERE AND YOUR ONLY COMPETITION IS IDIOTS. DON'T LET THIS GET AROUND.[8]

But get around it did. "No single profession," Deac Rossell said, "provided a larger or steadier stream of workers" for the film industry than journalism. Many of the former journalists wrote, directed, or produced newspaper films. Between 1928 and 1935, 70.8 percent of all newspaper films—fifty-six of seventy-nine titles—had at least one former journalist involved in the production.[9] Whenever Hollywood was criticized by the press for portraying newspapermen as drunk or unscrupulous, its standard defense was to point out that the writing or direction of newspaper films was often in the hands of ex-newspapermen.[10]

The former journalists based many of their films on their own experiences or those of colleagues, and these experiences increasingly had in the twenties and early thirties a questionable moral tone.[11] A major reason was the spread of tabloid journalism, also called "jazz journalism" and "gargoyle journalism."[12] Introduced in the United States via Fleet Street shortly after World War I, the tabloid brought sensationalism to new heights—or depths. By 1927 press critic Silas Bent was remarking that it must seem to a newspaper reader that freedom of the press was freedom for the press to "invade his personal privacy, print his picture without his consent, dump onto his doorstep filth collected from the courts, and ballyhoo . . . prize fighters, channel swimmers, football players, chorus girls, and aviators."[13]

Not all thirties films took Bent's severe view. As Rossell said, "The newspaper remained in most cases an extraordinarily flexible setting for comedy, romance, and action melodrama."[14] If a composite image of the journalist emerged on the screen, it was that of a tough, sardonic man in a snap-brim hat who, between wisecracks and dead-lines, would drink just about anything put in front of him.

The earliest newspaper films with sound continued the temperance tradition of the silent era, portraying alcohol as not only prevalent among newspapermen, but also destructive. *Gentlemen of the Press* and *Big News,* both from 1929 and based on stage plays, are good examples. In *Gentlemen of the Press,* star reporter Wickland Snell (Wal-ter Houston) gives up everything for journalism—everything, that is, except women and booze.[15] Snell is away from home when his daugh-ter is born, not around when she is married, and putting out an extra when she dies in childbirth. As Snell sits at his desk, stunned, a col-lege boy humbly asks for some advice on newspapering. The great Snell tells him to get out of the business before it poisons him.

This was a warning long familiar from newspaper fiction, as was an incident where a drunken reporter forgets for which paper he works. Although Mordaunt Hall, reviewing the film in the *New York Times,* said the incident recalled Richard Harding Davis's story "A Derelict," it was actually from Jesse Lynch Williams's "The Stolen Story."[16]

Hall found the entire characterization of newspapermen as a shift-less and cynical breed overly familiar. "Of course," he wrote, "no newspaper man [sic] by any chance ever refers to a 'death watch' without cracking jokes about the dying individual." He also com-plained that the actors, who were just learning to work with sound-recording equipment, often appeared to be waiting for a signal before they spoke their lines. "These hushed interludes," he noted, "brief though they may be, cause some discomfort, for it is evident that the characters are not thinking of what they are going to say."[17]

The film nonetheless won occasional laughter from its audience. Most of the laughs involved Charles Ruggles, who played "the stew [short for 'stewed'] reporter," a role he would reprise in *Roadhouse Nights* (1930), *Young Man of Manhattan* (1930), and *The Friends of Mr. Sweeney* (1934).[18] Ruggles scored his biggest laugh in *Gentlemen of the Press* with the drunken invitation he hands out to a secretary: "Come up to my apartment some time and fight for your honor."

Overall, *Gentlemen of the Press,* adapted by Ward Morehouse of the *New York Sun* from his own play, was a somber—and, according to

Variety, accurate—portrayal of newspaper life.[19] *Big News* would also be hailed for its accuracy when released later the same year. Its director, Gregory La Cava, had been a cartoonist for the *New York Evening World* and the *Sunday New York Herald*.[20] *Variety* opined that La Cava "remember[ed] his own daily days sufficiently" to be able to impart a true-to-life feeling to the film's newsroom sequences.[21]

La Cava was a chronic alcoholic as well as a former newspaperman. One student of his films has claimed that they "presented a particular kind of absurdist view of the world—the delightfully distorted perspective of the whiskey bottle."[22] At the very least, drinking affects the lives of many of his protagonists. In *Stage Door* (1937), for example, Ginger Rogers gets drunk on her first visit to Adolph Menjou's luxurious apartment, while in *Primrose Path* (1940), Rogers's father drinks himself to death.[23]

Alcohol figures vitally in *Big News*. The film opens with star reporter Steve Banks (Robert Armstrong) sleeping off, in *Variety*'s phrase, "a stew in the editor's chair."[24] Precisely because he was out all night drinking, his wife, Marge (Carol Lombard), a sob sister on a rival paper, has scooped him on a front-page story. In the morning, she stops by his office to give him a temperance lecture—and ask for a divorce:

> For two years, I've been trying to make a home for us, and last night he was coming home to his favorite dish, liver and onions, and his faithful little wife sits like a dumbbell until 11 o'clock entertaining herself with a plate of cold liver. If this were the first time, I wouldn't say anything, but it's been going on for two years, and I'm through this time. If I'm going to be a widow, I might as well make it official. . . . You're always blaming something beside yourself, you're always making excuses, and I'm always forgiving you. Well, last night I thought it over, and said to myself, what's the use?. . . You're not really a bum, you're just irresponsible. You'd be the best newspaperman in this town if you'd only quit drinking.

Marge isn't as ready to leave Steve as she thinks. She may sarcastically refer to herself as "his faithful little wife," but she will turn out to be just that. She conforms to the old temperance-tale stereotype of the self-sacrificing woman who "holds on through the roller-coaster of her man's drinking."[25] When Steve becomes the prime suspect in the murder of Mr. Addison, his editor-in-chief, she alone provides him with support. Beneath her liberated jazz-baby appearance—short dress, close-fitting, helmet-like hat, blonde bob—she fulfills the traditional female role of care-giver. "You know, Marge," Steve's city editor even says, "I think you've been miscast. You should've been his mother."

Although Steve, as Marge remarks, isn't "really a bum" yet, Deke Thomas, his favorite drinking partner, definitely is. Deke has the shambling gait, disheveled clothes, watery eyes, and slurred speech of the typical drunkard of temperance tales. A reporter who drank himself out of journalism, Deke represents the skid row derelict Steve will become unless he lets up on the booze. This is made explicit when Marge asks, "Where did drinking get [Deke]? There isn't a newspaper in this town that will hire him back, and you're getting just like him."

Significantly, Marge also has a nightmarish double—Vera (Cupid Ainsworth), a colleague of Steve's and the only other newspaperwoman in the film. Vera is grotesquely fat, circus-freak fat, and, with her butch haircut and masculine suit and tie, of indeterminate sexual orientation. Steve treats her with a kind of affectionate disdain, calling her "Big Girl" and "Tubby," and cracking jokes about her weight; for example, "If ya start to waste away, save me the slow-motion movie rights, will ya?"

Thomas Schatz, author of *Hollywood Genres: Formulas, Filmmaking, and the Studio System*, noted the capacity of genre films to "'play it both ways,' to both criticize and reinforce the values, beliefs, and ideals of our culture within the same narrative context."[26] In *Big News*, the doubling of the central characters allows the film to simultaneously occupy contrary sides on issues ranging from proper gender roles to Prohibition. Thus the female professional emerges as both a Marge and a Vera, as both feminine and unfeminine, as both attractive and repulsive.

The film exhibits a similar duality in relation to alcohol. For the most part, drinking is associated with negatives, such as marital trouble, unemployment, and crime. The police suspect Steve of killing Mr. Addison largely because he is, in one character's words, "notorious for getting into drunken brawls and abusing people when intoxicated." Moreover, the actual culprit turns out to be a bootlegger and speakeasy owner, Joe Reno (Sam Hardy).

Yet drinking isn't without some positive overtones. Steve, for all his incipient alcoholism, is still the hero of the film—handsome, witty, hard-boiled. His fondness for the bottle may be a flaw, but it is a glamorous flaw, a mark of his freedom from the gray and narrow confines of the Protestant work ethic. The audience is meant to enjoy his contempt for old fogies like Hansel (Louis Payne), the business manager who finds him, at the outset of the film, still recovering from last night's spree.

> **Hansel:** Banks, you're a disgrace to the newspaper profession.
> **Steve** *(yawning):* It isn't a profession, it's a game. Now run along because I don't want to play with you.
> **Hansel:** The same thing after every payday, drunk and disorderly.
> **Steve:** You know, Hansel, you're not really as bad as you seem. Nobody can be that bad. Here, *(he waves a flask in Hansel's face)* have a little drink. It might put new life in an old body.
> **Hansel:** That'll cost you your job.
> **Steve:** Phooey.
> **Hansel:** I'll see that you're fired from this paper as soon as Mr. Addison arrives.
> **Steve:** Phooey. . . . Listen, Hansel, there are 1,790 newspapers in the United States, and I've only worked on 16 of them.
> **Hansel:** Tomorrow you'll be free to connect with your 17th.
> **Steve:** Yeah? Well, if the old man does fire me, I promise to come into your office and kiss you goodbye.

Big News's ambivalence about alcohol extends to its explanation as to why Steve drinks. On the one hand, the film refers to drinking as an addictive behavior; on the other, it suggests that Steve could overcome his chronic excessive drinking if he so chose. "I was talking to Dr. McCoy yesterday," Marge mentions. "He says drinking is a mental habit. He says you actually get more stimulation out of tea." To which Steve, ever the smart aleck, replies: "Yeah, then you turn into a Chinaman and open a laundry."

Later, Steve compares journalism itself to a disease-like addiction, a motif dating back to Jesse Lynch Williams's novella "The Old Reporter" (1898). "I'm sick of this bum racket," he grouses. "It isn't even a racket, it's a disease that gets in your blood and wrings you out like an old mop. What are newspapers good for? . . . Something to put under carpet, plugs for ratholes, wrapping paper for bootleg-

Steve Banks (Robert Armstrong) may be a borderline alcoholic in the early talkie **BIG NEWS** *(1929), but he is also the hero—handsome, witty, and hard-boiled.*

gers, bed quilts for bums in the park." The implication is that journalism, like alcohol or drugs, eventually destroys its slaves.

Just not this slave. Steve exposes Reno as Mr. Addison's killer and thereby wins back his wife and reporting job. He also changes the contents of his flask from whiskey to tea without suffering even the slightest withdrawal symptoms. When, in the final shot of the film, a drunken Deke drops by the newsroom, Steve throws him out the door while Marge looks on approvingly. "Whaddya trying to do," he shouts after his old drinking buddy, "break up a man's home?" As was often the case in pro-temperance silent films, alcohol serves as a metaphor in *Big News* for sexual tension. Once the tension abates, so does the need to drink.

Young Man of Manhattan (1930) presents an almost identical mixture of big-city journalism, marital stress, and bootleg booze. Adapted from a best-selling 1930 novel by Katharine Brush, the film starred Norman Foster as sportswriter Toby McLean and Claudette Colbert as film columnist Ann Vaughn.[27] Charles Ruggles was

Toby's reporter friend Shorty Ross, a serious drinker with a droll sense of humor.

"There is a tradition," *Variety* remarked in its review, "that a newspaper play has all the odds against it for commercial success." But *Young Man of Manhattan* looked to be an exception. *Variety* praised the film for striking a "happy medium between the savage cynicism of 'Front Page' and those very terrible star-reporter-who-solved-the-murder romances." It gave most of the credit for this to director Monta Bell, who "served his own apprenticeship in the city room and knows his journalistic atmosphere."[28]

The *New York Times* wasn't nearly so impressed. "The first third of the film," its anonymous reviewer said, "lacks continuity. It follows Toby from press table to press room, dragging in all of the alcoholic sequences popularly associated with newspaper yarns." The reviewer described Toby as "one of those newspaper men who are always on the point of writing something 'big,' but never get around to it."[29] He meets Ann while covering the Dempsey-Tunney fight in Philadelphia, and they fall in love and marry. Soon tension develops between them. Ann thinks Toby drinks and plays too much; he resents her earning more money at writing than he does. The marriage blows up after he returns home drunk from a night on the town with Puff Randolph (Ginger Rogers), a dizzy young socialite.

Drinking signifies in *Young Man of Manhattan* what it had generally signified on the screen since the silent era—anxiety caused by shifting gender roles. The film restores a kind of equilibrium between the sexes, not by directly addressing the gender issue, but by displacing it with the neater and simpler alcohol issue. Toby is reporting spring training in Florida when he gets word that Ann has been stricken blind after drinking tainted liquor he left in their apartment. Horrified, he gives up his carefree ways and sets to work on a novel, which he succeeds in selling to pay for Ann's medical bills. He regains his self-esteem, and Ann regains her sight. The film ends with the couple reunited in love.

When *Variety* commented on the "savage cynicism" of *The Front Page* in the midst of its review of *Young Man of Manhattan*, it was referring to the popular 1928 play by Chicago newspapermen Ben Hecht and Charles MacArthur. The film version of *The Front Page*, directed by Lewis Milestone and starring Pat O'Brien as ace reporter Hildy Johnson and Adolphe Menjou as unscrupulous managing editor Walter Burns, didn't appear until March 1931, a full eleven months after *Young Man of Manhattan* was released. Although not the first newspaper film by a long shot, *The Front Page* would crystallize the newspaper-film genre. Chip Rowe called it in 1992 "the blueprint for press films," while Jane Gross said in 1985 that it "set the standard for all the cynical journalism movies that followed."[30] As Hecht biographer Jeffrey Martin Brown pointed out, "*The Front Page* created a new strain of newspaper films in which melodrama and suspense were used as a backdrop for comedy. The infighting between editor and newsman or between newsman and his fellows, already irreverent and tough, became the arena for exuberant comic badinage."[31]

Critics recognized immediately upon its release that *The Front Page,* which would be nominated for the Academy Award for best picture of 1931, represented something new in newspaper films, and perhaps in film in general. "Movies have been made from plays before," a critic for the comedy magazine *Judge* observed, "but seldom have they retained such raucous humor as that supplied by Ben Hecht and Charles MacArthur."[32] Mordaunt Hall of the *New York Times,* after describing *The Front Page* as a "witty and virile talking picture," added that the "censor is in more than one instance virtually defied through ingenious ideas," including resort to the "ding!" of a typewriter to drown out the offending word in the famous last line, "The son of a bitch stole my watch."[33] According to the *New Republic,* leading critics had argued for some time that with the advent of talkies, Hollywood would have to begin producing more sophisticated works—that audiences would no longer sit still for "the vapidities which were the normal diet of the silent screen." Now *The Front Page* offered "startling support of this thesis" by presenting, almost verbatim, "the dialogue which was regarded as going nearly too far for Broadway."[34]

Apparently, ordinary filmgoers enjoyed the rapid-fire, irreverent jokes of the reporters in *The Front Page* just as much as the critics did. Hall wrote in the *Times* that "while its humor is frequently harsh, it assuredly won favor with the audience yesterday afternoon."[35] And the anonymous critic for *Judge* noted, "I have seen several thousand movies in my day, but I never saw an audience laugh and cheer as it did on this occasion, and even the ushers caught the infection and assumed a sort of hell-with-you attitude that was nothing short of shocking."[36]

In a 1974 essay on *The Front Page* that would be anthologized, Richard Corliss of *Time* magazine asserted, "Only in retrospect does this delightful comedy reveal itself as possibly the most subtly cynical film Hollywood has produced."[37] But, as the reaction of thirties audiences and critics to the film indicates, its cynicism was actually quite blatant. In fact, Alexander Bakshy, reviewing *The Front Page* for the *Nation*, wondered whether the smart alecks of the Criminal Courts press room weren't a trifle too hard-boiled to be wholly credible. "If the authors are right in their characterization," he said, "aren't they guilty of treating this hard-boiled cynicism as standing for some superior knowledge and understanding of life. . . ?"[38] You bet they were. Hecht and MacArthur (as well as Bartlett Cormack, who adapted their play to the screen, and Charles Lederer, who was brought in to polish the dialogue) indulged in the notion that "personal corruption was a viable response to a corrupt social environment."[39]

Film scholars have attributed the cynicism that cheerfully bubbles through *The Front Page* and other so-called "shyster films" to the psychological dislocations caused by the Depression. "As the American Dream and the attendant myths were shattered," a typical explanation goes, "the public felt more and more as if they'd been suckered and adopted an increasingly cynical stance toward the country's leaders and institutions."[40] It should be pointed out, however, that while the film version of *The Front Page* was released at the bottom of the Depression, the play on which the film was very closely based debuted on Broadway in 1928, a year before the stock market collapsed. This suggests that *The Front Page*'s renowned cynicism—its sardonic view that everyone, including its protagonists, is completely and gloriously corrupt—perhaps stemmed more from the culture-wide backlash against Prohibition than from any other source.

The Eighteenth Amendment to the Constitution, outlawing the "manufacture, sale, or transportation of intoxicating liquors," was approved by Congress in 1917, and ratified by the states in 1919. No previous amendment had ever passed so quickly or, once passed, stirred so much controversy.[41] The Volstead Act, which provided for enforcement of the amendment, went into effect in January 1920, but Americans didn't suddenly stop drinking. Rather, their demand for liquor was met by rum-running and bootlegging, most of which was controlled by organized crime. What Indianapolis humorist Kin Hubbard said about Prohibition was true: it was "better than no liquor at all."[42]

A law can only be enforced in a democracy when the majority of people support it. "And," as Andrew Sinclair remarked, "the majority of people did not support the Volstead Act."[43] Although middle- and upper-class Americans thought Prohibition was a good thing for blue-collar workers and blacks, they opposed it for themselves and continued to carouse. Far from ending drinking in America, Prohibition had the unintended effect of transferring about $2 billion a year from the hands of brewers and distillers to those of gangsters. This was more than enough loot to buy judges, district attorneys, and whole police forces.[44] Small wonder Hecht and MacArthur, emerging from 1920s Chicago, "the breezily medieval Gun City of Al Capone," portrayed corruption with amused resignation, not moral outrage.[45]

The Front Page contains one lengthy drinking scene, added by Cormack in adapting the play.[46] It occurs in a speakeasy early in the film. To grasp all the implications of the scene, we must remember that a visit to a speakeasy—an illegal saloon offering nightclub acts, liquor, and indifferent food at inflated prices—was considered fashionable among the middle class, a sign of advanced attitudes. Moreover, unlike the old-time saloon, the speakeasy welcomed female as well as male drinkers.[47] Columnist Heywood Broun even complained that however bad the old saloons were, at least a man didn't have to fight his way through a crowd of schoolgirls to the bar.[48]

In the Cormack-created scene, Walter drags a reluctant Hildy to a speakeasy called Polack Mike's. The editor intends to fill his star reporter with cheap booze so as to prevent him from quitting the *Post* for marriage and a cushy job in a New York ad agency. That they are locked in a power struggle is apparent from the moment they step into the speakeasy, dressed masculinely in big overcoats and snap-brim hats.

Walter *(to the bartender):* Set 'em up.
Hildy: None for me.
Walter: He'll have the same.

Walter seems to be drinking, but through sleight of hand is actually giving extra shots to Hildy, who tosses them down one-two-three. When Hildy realizes that he is being tricked, he goes to the men's room and escapes out the window. Meanwhile, Walter pulls a flask—known during Prohibition as the "peripatetic bar"—from under his coat and, in his usual selfish manner, pours himself a shot of the good stuff.[49]

Even though this scene is played largely for laughs, it has a kind of

totemic significance. Walter and Hildy's obvious familiarity with the
speakeasy marks them both as experienced and tough and as connected to all the crazy excitement in town. Their drinking symbolizes
their privileged position, the romance and glamor of newspaper life.
And yet, because speakeasies were practically synonymous with
organized crime, their drinking also suggests that newspaper life is
unsavory, even corrupt—an impression reinforced by the fact that
Walter keeps an Italian mobster, Diamond Louie (Maurice Black), on
the *Post*'s payroll.

This by no means exhausts all the implications of the scene, which
reflects, for example, the conflict between freedom and domestica-
tion that runs through the entire film. Drinking establishments have
traditionally been male preserves, far removed from women and the
domestic regime.[50] Thus when Walter marches Hildy into the
speakeasy—they are the only customers in the place—he is hoping
to reaffirm solidarity among men, threatened now that Hildy is about
to marry and move away. As Walter pours the drinks, they fondly
reminisce about their boyish adventures in yellow journalism. "Ah,"
sighs Hildy, "those were the days."

The speakeasy becomes in *The Front Page*, as in several newspaper
films from the first years of talkies, an adjunct to the newsroom. Both
the newsroom and the speakeasy represent a rugged notion of manhood, antagonistic to marriage, home, and family. "Marriage," Walter tells Hildy in Polack Mike's, "does make a respectable citizen out
of a man," then adds with false sincerity, "It must be grand." Hildy
takes this as his cue to flee. He is defecting from the male world, symbolized by newspapering and drinking, to the female world, symbolized by romance and marriage.

But, alas, Hildy isn't destined to escape so easily. He proves just
the latest in a long line of fictional journalists, going back to "The Old
Reporter," who are addicted to journalism in the same way alcoholics are addicted to alcohol.[51] Hildy labors under the delusion that
he doesn't crave scoops and front-page bylines anymore; that he can
take or leave the thrills of smash-mouth journalism; that he, unlike
his colleagues, is in complete control of his reporting habit. "You'll
all end up on the copy desk," he warns the boys in the press room,
"gray-haired, humpbacked slobs dodging debt collectors when
you're 90." Then cop killer Earl Williams (George E. Stone) breaks
out of jail on the eve of his hanging, and Hildy forsakes conventional
dreams of domestic bliss to chase after the story.

We are introduced to the other police reporters in *The Front Page*—variously referred to as "tramps," "crumbs," "wise guys," and "hoodlums"—when one of them throws an empty whiskey bottle out the press room window, nearly hitting a deputy walking below. This image of rowdy reporters drinking on the job raises interesting questions about the status of journalism within the overall social order.

Joseph R. Gusfield, in a sociological essay titled "Passage to Play: Rituals of Drinking Time in American Society," noted: "Before the 1830s, while drunkenness was observed and condemned, it had an accepted place in American life in both work and play. With the emergence of industrial organization, the separation of work as an area of sobriety and play as an area of permissible insobriety became more common. The development of leisure as a contrast to work did much to reinforce the disapproval of drinking as a daytime activity."[52] What the urban-industrial order has demanded, in other words, is that the playful, the irresponsible, the hedonistic not be permitted to enter the serious domain of making a living.[53] To mix the two areas, as the reporters in *The Front Page* do by drinking on the job, implies opposition to, or at least misunderstanding of, the structure of modern life. Insofar as alcohol is believed to relax inhibitions, dissolve hierarchy, and facilitate pleasure, it is a threat to the workaday world.

Gusfield pointed out that some occupations—he was thinking in particular of the construction industries—"have only partially 'surrendered' to the routinized and controlled arenas of bureaucratic organization and factory discipline. Here the idea of a regulated order of space and time has not fully been institutionalized. Work and play are not yet impermeable."[54] One possible interpretation of the on-the-job drinking of the reporters in *The Front Page* is that it is a vestige of traditional work habits, a carry-over from the days when journalism was more a craft than an industry and the journalist more a wandering minstrel than a wage slave.[55] Or, alternatively, their drinking can be seen as a protest against the modern corporate newsroom, with its rationalistic, hierarchal system of legmen, rewritemen, and other specialists. *The Front Page* reporters rarely, if ever, flop down at a typewriter and bang out a story. Rather, they rush to the phone and bawl highly embellished facts and outright fabrications to their respective rewrite desks. They aren't autonomous artists, but assembly-line workers, minor parts in a complex news machine.

Their indiscriminate drinking (and desultory poker playing) may be their subversive response to the growth of mind-numbing, soul-killing bureaucracy.

As much as this casts a romantic halo around the reporters, making them seem the last of the rugged individualists, there is a potential dark side to their boozing it up. "While drinking can promote fellow-feeling," Gusfield said, "it can also be a catalyst for angry words, denunciations, and the exposure of those secrets by which social organization is held in place. *In vino veritas,* but social order cannot stand too much *veritas.*"[56] The reporters, when in their cups, mock the sheriff, the mayor, and the court-appointed psychiatrist, exposing authority as hollow and corrupt. If their mockery stopped there, it would be liberating. But they mock those at the bottom of the social order as well, badgering prostitute Molly Malloy (Mae Clarke), for example, until she jumps out a window. At such moments, their boozy humor lacks all compassion, and becomes merely nihilistic and callous, a form of urban barbarism.

Other newspaper films of the thirties contain drinking sequences very similar to those found in *The Front Page,* but generally give them a more conservative meaning. A good example is *Five Star Final* (1931), an exposé of gutter journalism based on a play by Louis Weitzenkorn, who had worked for the *New York Graphic,* also known as the "Pornographic" because of its lurid coverage of sex and crime. Directed by Mervyn LeRoy and starring Edward G. Robinson, *Five Star Final* belonged to Warner Brothers' "social consciousness" period, approximately 1930–33, during which the studio specialized in topical films that reflected the upheaval of the Depression.[57]

Perhaps the most memorable motif in *Five Star Final* is its repeated closeups of Robinson, playing tabloid editor Joseph Randall, obsessively washing his hands as if tarnished by his "dirty job." We are introduced to Randall in a speakeasy, where, significantly, his first hand-washing occurs. Speakeasies aren't associated with fun or freedom here, but with filth, corruption, and evil. *Five Star Final,* for all its references to contemporary celebrities and events (Peaches Browning, breadlines, etc.), remains rooted in Victorian standards. Drinking is viewed as a sign of moral weakness; ergo, the yellow journalists in the film drink. George E. Stone plays a contest editor who supplies his superiors with bootleg hooch on the side, while Boris Karloff plays an unfrocked clergyman-turned-reporter, T. Vernon Isopod, who offers platitudinous excuses for his drunkenness.

What's more, when Randall suffers pangs of conscience about being a scandalmonger, he anesthetizes himself by going on a spree.

The Famous Ferguson Case (1932) also portrays chronic excessive drinking as a symptom of unethical journalism. Produced by First National, the B-picture unit at Warners, the film was supposedly based on the Hall-Mills murder case.[58] In 1922 the Rev. Edward Hall and Mrs. James Mills, a choir singer, were found shot to death under a tree in New Brunswick, New Jersey. Despite an intense investigation, the police never solved the killings. Then, in 1926, the *New York Mirror* launched its own investigation. The Hearst tabloid's dramatic findings led to the indictments of Hall's widow, her two brothers, and a cousin. After a four-week trial conducted in a circus atmosphere—the low point came when a witness dubbed the "Pig Woman" was carried in dying on a hospital cot—the defendants were acquitted. Stanley Walker, city editor of the *New York Herald Tribune* at the time, said coverage of the trial "disgusted the public with the sensational press generally, and even affected the esteem in which all the press was held."[59]

Except for a passing reference to the Pig Woman ("Go see that Pig Woman, kid," one reporter suggests to another. "She might talk to you."), the actual details of the Hall-Mills case don't make it into *The Famous Ferguson Case*. The film does, however, reflect the mood of disgust with the press. Not that this improved it in the eyes of reviewers. In fact, the reviewer for *Variety* took the film's release as a perfect opportunity to question the value of newspaper films in general:

> "Five Star Final" was the exception to the rule that newspaper stories start off with a handicap for the reason that the story tries to trick the auditor into thinking the newspaper people are more interesting than the events they chronicle, which isn't true inside journalism or outside. "Final" and "Front Page" turned the difficult trick, but before and after the two plays mentioned there have been a long, long series of stage and screen flops dealing with the Park Row locale.[60]

The reviewer called *The Famous Ferguson Case* "one of the most glaring failures of the whole series," adding that it "hasn't even the merit of those shoddy star-reporter-hero affairs that preceded the tab expose type of story. It hasn't even the phony glamor of the old style. Instead a lot of rather cheap people argue and debate a murder trial which concerns people much more interesting than themselves."[61]

The film follows what happens when big-city reporters descend on the small town of Cornwall, where a millionaire banker has been mysteriously shot to death in his summer mansion. It contrasts the razzmatazz of the tabloids with the propriety of the older, more established papers. The yellow journalists are identifiable not only by their shameless tactics—hounding relatives of the principals in the case, browbeating officials, fabricating stories—but also by their heavy drinking. One of them, a reporter for the *New York Bullet,* is even nicknamed "Jigger" (a jigger, of course, being either a small whiskey glass or a one-and-a-half ounce measure used in cocktail recipes).

If that isn't bad enough, the leaders of the tabloid crowd, Bob Parks (Kenneth Thomson) and Jim Perrin (Leslie Fenton) of the *New York Globe,* arrive in town drunk and stay that way for most of the film—this despite not being able to get "any real booze," only the stuff sold under the counter at the drugstore. As Jigger says of Parks during a party in a hotel room, "decadent" jazz pouring from the Victrola: "That's his one real talent. He can make a martini out of cockroach paste and turpentine."

Parks takes a fatalistic attitude toward his drinking. "In the first place," he tells Toni Martin (Adrienne Dore), a reporter for the local daily whom he is trying to seduce, "I'm what's laughingly known as a chronic alcoholic. I seldom develop the yellow spot and staggers, and I can talk at all times, but I do get awfully drunk now and then. And it's more often now than then." When Toni responds, "Well, you have to drink to keep up such a terrific pace, I guess," Parks demurs: "No, it's more than that. A drunkard never gets a day off. He's up for life." Unlike the vast majority of fictional journalists, Parks blames his own nature, not the nature of journalism, for his drinking problem. The same weak, unstable personality that causes him to sensationalize also causes him to drink.

With Toni, *The Famous Ferguson Case* presents one of the most oppressive stereotypes in American film: the female drinker. Judith Harwin and Shirley Otto, in an essay on "Women, Alcohol and the Screen," noted that there is a clear gender differentiation in the portrayal of alcoholics. "The spectacle of male drunkenness," they wrote, "is often humorous or physically commanding. When women are drunk, it is nearly always degrading," a sign of "easy virtue."[62] Alcoholism expert Robin Room agreed, concluding from her extensive research that films "had long given a special meaning to a liquor glass in the hands of a woman: it served as a visual code for sexual license."[63]

As *The Famous Ferguson Case* begins, Toni is the girlfriend of Bruce Foster (Tom Brown), the young editor of the *Cornwall Courier* ("Covers Cornwall County Like the Dew") who is so enthusiastic about his work that he seems demented. "Oh, boy!" he exclaims in a typical speech. "Shooting at the Ferguson's! This sounds like a real story! I'm going to give this town its first extra!" Then the tabloid reporters show up, and Toni finds their drunken cynicism immediately appealing. "This is as good as a school of journalism for me," she says, sitting in their hotel room, a drink in one hand and a cigarette in the other. Even though Parks and his crowd turn out to be base and irresponsible—according to one reviewer's tally, their scheming causes one death, one miscarriage, and immeasurable heartache— Toni boards the New York train with them at the end of the film, a blonde floozy deserting Cornwall and the virtuous life traditionally associated with small-town America.[64]

Scandal for Sale sends its protagonist, editor Jerry Strong (Charles Bickford), in the reverse direction, from the corruption of the big city to the innocence of the small town. This 1932 film, based on *Hot News*, a novel by Emile Henry Gauvreau, ex-managing editor of the sleazy *New York Graphic*, was described in a *New York Times* review as "one of those popular stories, with a dash of sentiment, a generous amount of drinking, and a final return to calmer fields."[65] Strong will earn a $25,000 bonus if he can raise the readership of the *New York Comet* to the million mark. He neglects his family in his zeal to increase circulation, even losing his son because he is too absorbed by work to get a doctor for the ill boy.[66]

Strong's star reporter, Waddell (Pat O'Brien), is a heavy drinker, never going anywhere without a bottle. As was often the case in silent films, drinking here signifies sexual upheaval, for Waddell loves Strong's wife (Rose Hobart), who returns the compliment. To get Waddell out of the way, Strong assigns him to accompany a German pilot on a risky transatlantic flight. The plane crashes, killing both men. Strong, with his wife in tow, retreats to the sanctuary of a small-town newspaper, but only after he exploits the crash in big, black, apocalyptic headlines and wins the bonus.

The triumph of small-town values in *Scandal for Sale* was more apparent than real. This reflected general social trends: a secular urban culture was on the rise; the old rural morality was increasingly irrelevant. Within a year, Prohibition, the attempt by the countryside to force its narrow standards on the city, would be over.

The Twenty-first Amendment to the Constitution, adopted in 1933, became the only amendment to repeal an earlier amendment—specifically, the Eighteenth, which had proved a legal and moral failure. In 1920, the first year of Prohibition, there were already signs that the law might not live up to expectations: the refusal of state legislatures to allocate money for enforcement; the huge rise in the number of illegal stills; the reopening of old saloons and blind pigs as speakeasies; and the flagrant drunkenness of many delegates at both the Republican and Democratic national conventions.[67]

Moreover, the media provided little support for the Eighteenth Amendment. The opposition to Prohibition in bourgeois magazines increased fivefold between 1914 and 1931. A similar shift took place in the nation's newspapers. While more than half of the press supported the drys in 1907, hardly a major paper backed them twenty years later. A 1931 survey showed that the circulation of wet papers outnumbered that of dry papers by two to one.[68]

Films were also quite wet. Clarence Brown, a director at MGM, even claimed that "it was the motion picture, showing that in spite of Prohibition liquor was an immense factor in American life, that had a great deal to do with changing sentiment on the question."[69] A 1935 study found that drinking was depicted in about 66 percent of films, and that drunkenness was depicted in 43 percent. Oddly enough, most of the drinking was done by the hero and heroine, not by the villain. The hero drank in two out of five films, the heroine in one out of five, and the villain in only one out of ten. The study's author, Edgar Dale, concluded that films set "the standards of approved drinking."[70]

Platinum Blonde (1931) is an example of a late Prohibition-era film in which drinking was largely regarded as congenial, attractive, and fun, a stimulus to good times. Directed by Frank Capra and with dialogue by Robert Riskin, it starred Robert Williams as reporter Stew Smith, Jean Harlow as the heiress he marries, and Loretta Young as the sob sister he leaves behind, though not forever. *Variety* praised the newspaper background, declaring, "For once it's 100% natural. A paper's office looks like the McCoy, as do the newsmen in and out of their working hours, from good reportorial work down to serious drinking."[71] *The New York Times*, while also liking the film, struck a more ironic tone in its review:

> When a newspaper man [sic] sits down to do a piece of fiction about his craft he is likely to produce a reporter like Stew Smith, the hero of "Platinum Blonde." A cynical fellow is Stew, and a gallant one, as much at home in a speakeasy as in a flower arbor, careless in a neat way about his dress, perpetually writing a play that never gets beyond the title, shrewd in the ways of life and fast with his talk.[72]

The reporter's very name is associated with drinking. "My friends all call me Stew," he observes early in the film. "It's an injustice, too, 'cause I hold my liquor all right." His drinking isn't immoral or neurotic, but celebratory. He goes to Joe's, a speakeasy with a peephole in the door (through which he comically sticks his finger, nearly poking the lookout in the eye), after he scoops the rival *Tribune* and again after he elopes with the rich and beautiful Anne Schuyler (Harlow). "Have a drink on the house!" Joe welcomes him. "I'm going to have a lot of drinks," Stew replies. When he drinks, it is because he is happy and wants to intensify and prolong his happiness.

Young's character, a reporter known only by her surname, Gallagher, has a more ambiguous relationship with alcohol. "The arrival of nightclub culture in the 1920s," Denise Herd and Robin Room of the Alcohol Research Group pointed out, "brought mixed-sex drinking in public places. . . . Many movies of the late 1920s and early 1930s focused with fascination on the new phenomenon of more-or-less respectable women drinking in public."[73] Gallagher drinks at Joe's with the rest of the journalists, but only she is de-sexed by it. "We never look at Gallagher as a girl," Stew explains to Anne, while Gallagher herself adds, "Down at the office, they consider me just one of the boys." This equality becomes a source of frustration and pain for her. She loves Stew in a way that Anne, who wants to remake him into a gentleman, never can. But Stew is so used to Gallagher being his drinking buddy that he can't imagine her as his sweetheart or wife. It takes him the whole film to finally recognize her feminine charms.

If drinking by women represents an abuse of their femininity, drinking per se still has a generally positive meaning in *Platinum Blonde*. Capra is famous, of course, for celebrating the virtues of "little people," particularly in the five films he made from 1936–46: *Mr. Deeds Goes to Town, You Can't Take It with You, Mr. Smith Goes to Washington, Meet John Doe,* and *It's a Wonderful Life.*[74] The theme is also in evidence here, with alcohol serving as a solvent of class distinctions. One night the newspaper gang drops in on Stew at the Schuyler mansion, a vast, cold, echoing tomb where he feels increasingly lost and alone. They proceed to get drunk and trash the place. Earlier scenes there had shown society balls with a lot of upper-crust snobs standing around trying to look superior; now we see newspaper tramps banging on the grand piano, singing, jitterbugging, wearing flowerpots and lamp shades on their heads, and sliding down banisters. Even the stiff English butler unbends and joins the drunken revelry. Drinking is antihierarchal, democratic, a joyous expression of life.

Three years later, Capra directed *It Happened One Night* (1934), another fizzy love story involving a newspaperman and an heiress, played by Clark Gable and Claudette Colbert. The film not only did outstanding business at the box office, but also swept all five major Academy Awards, a feat unduplicated until *One Flew over the Cuckoo's Nest* in 1975. At least some of the credit for the film's success belonged to Capra's friend Myles Connolly, who suggested improvements in an early version of the script, including changing the hero from a vagabond painter to a reporter so that audiences could better identify with him.[75]

The reporter, Peter Warne, was himself initially identified by his drunkenness. We first see him in a phone booth at the Miami bus station, telling off his boss in New York. "Hey listen, monkey face," he says with drunken bravado, "when you fired me, you fired the best newshound your filthy scandal sheet ever had." He has been let go for submitting his copy in free verse—a sign that he isn't just any reporter, but a creative type, "a poet at heart."[76] Since a popular cultural myth holds that creative types abuse alcohol and drugs ("Drinking is a writer's vice," alcoholic F. Scott Fitzgerald once said), Warne's drunkenness is further proof of his special status.[77]

It is also proof that drunkenness was often treated comically in thirties films. Brooks Robards, after noting in a 1990 essay that a snap-brim hat was mandatory wear for newspaper characters, added: "Snapped down, it meant serious business; left up, it signaled comedy."[78] Warne leaves his brim up throughout his first scene. Despite being out of a job at a time of mass joblessness, he isn't out of humor or optimism. The power of drink protects and sustains him.

In a good-natured parody of a royal procession, drunken acquaintances lead him from the phone booth to his bus, chanting, "Make way for the king, make way for the king," while sprinkling torn newspaper at his feet.

There has been some disagreement among film scholars about whether *It Happened One Night* qualifies as "screwball comedy," even though it features an eccentric heiress, a prime ingredient of the genre.[79] No such doubt has arisen in connection with *Libeled Lady* (1936), which *Variety* described as "a sockeroo of a comedy," "a holiday for gag-writers."[80] At any rate, drinking is integral to journalistic identity in both films. The libelous news story that kicks off the plot of *Libeled Lady* comes from the typewriter of a drunken reporter. "Why, that thing fairly reeks of alcohol," says managing editor Warren Haggerty (Spencer Tracy), glowering at an assistant who allowed the story into print. "Jackson was drunk. You got to smell things like that. You don't need any brains. All you need is a nose."

Yet the film by no means suggests that journalists shouldn't drink on the job, only that they shouldn't get drunk. This distinction becomes clear when Haggerty's tirade is interrupted by a ringing phone. His assistant answers it, listens a moment, then grimly hangs up.

> **Assistant:** Boss is here. He wants you right away.
> **Haggerty:** He want me or my job? You got a drink?
> **Assistant:** Yes, there's a fresh bottle on your desk. I thought you'd need one.
> **Haggerty:** I'll need it and how.

In addition to being an acceptable coping mechanism, drinking is presented in the film as a normal social activity. An international playgirl (Myrna Loy), her millionaire father (Walter Connolly), and a suave troubleshooter for the newspaper (William Powell) are repeatedly shown inviting each other to cocktails, ordering cocktails, and sipping cocktails, all in the midst of glamorous settings—hotels, cruise ships, mansions. Drinking becomes a metaphor for a fashionable lifestyle, for urbanity and sophistication. It is what the leisure class does and, by implication, what ordinary filmgoers who desire to taste the life of the rich might do.

Ironically, at about the same time *Libeled Lady* was normalizing drinking on the screen, Alcoholics Anonymous was re-problematizing drinking off it. Founded in 1935 by stockbroker Bill Wilson and Dr. Bob Smith, two alcoholics who met on a business trip, AA preached "a less extreme version of the old temperance creed."[81] Among its basic tenets were: (1) some people have a biological vulnerability to alcohol, a special kind of "allergy"; (2) alcohol triggers in these at-risk drinkers, or alcoholics, an uncontrollable craving for more alcohol; (3) the only cure for the disease is total abstinence; and (4) alcoholics who continue to drink will, stage by stage, succumb to insanity or death.[82]

It would be almost a decade before AA ideology would begin to noticeably influence film portrayals of alcoholism and alcoholics, and even longer before the release of the first AA-influenced newspaper film, *Come Fill the Cup* (1951), directed by Gordon Douglas and starring James Cagney. Until then, journalists would go on drinking in films for all the familiar reasons—to relax their nerves, to drown their conscience, to confirm their manhood, to heighten their fun.

Nothing Sacred (1937), for example, opens with a banquet for the Sultan of Marzipan at which star reporter Wallace Cook (Frederic March) is obviously, if morosely, drunk. As we soon find out, the sultan is actually a bootblack, a fake foisted on the public by Cook. The reporter's drunkenness marks him as a typical shyster, callous, corrupt, and conniving.

Cook, however, isn't the only character with these shyster qualities. Adapted by Ben Hecht (who, as the *New York Times* noted, must have been squinting at *The Front Page* again) from a James H. Street short story, *Nothing Sacred* is "one of the most cynical of all Hollywood films."[83] Its cast is a collection of swindlers, suckers, phonies, and drunks. Indeed, the whole premise of the film is that a small-town girl, Hazel Flagg (Carole Lombard), can be just as devious as—or even more devious than—any big-city newspaperman.

Nothing Sacred contains some choice swipes at journalism. "I'll tell you briefly what I think of newspapermen," Hazel's doctor, Enoch Downer (Charles Winninger), says. "The hand of God reaching down into the mire couldn't elevate one of 'em to the depths of degradation." But Downer, despite fitting the physical stereotype of the white-haired, twinkly-eyed country doctor, is hardly a moral paragon himself. Drunk throughout the film, he first misdiagnoses Hazel as having six weeks to live and then, at her insistence, covers up his misdiagnosis so as not to spoil her trip to New York as a guest of Cook's paper. "Enoch," Hazel cries when their scam begins to unravel, "why did you let me come to New York? If you were only as honest as you look!"

Besides signaling character defects, drinking in *Nothing Sacred* stimulates comedy. When Hazel and Cook attend a party in her honor at the Casino Moderne, an art deco nightclub featuring "Tootsies of All Nations," she gets so drunk that she behaves in a slapstick manner—slurring her sentences, hiccupping, bumping into things. And when Dr. Downer, at the end of the film, wakes up hung over on a cruise ship, he takes one look out the porthole and yells, "Run for your life, run for your life, the hotel is flooding!" This sort of comic befuddlement is no less a response to the collapse of the old moral order than is Cook's journalistic cynicism. They are two sides of the same insight that the world, unvarnished by alcohol, has become too difficult to bear.

The Sisters (1938), in contrast to *Nothing Sacred*, is a sumptuously mounted period piece. Set for the most part in San Francisco at the turn of the century, it starred Errol Flynn as a hard-drinking sports reporter and Bette Davis as his new wife. Graham Greene, reviewing the film for the *Spectator*, praised Anatole Litvak's adroit direction and Davis's "fragile, pop-eyed acting," but found the main situation to be "as old as the cinema." "The pathos is very familiar —" he wrote, "the husband returns drunk on the evening when his wife intends to tell him she is pregnant: they quarrel on Christmas Day beside the Christmas-tree."[84]

Familiar, too, was the heavy drinking of Frank Medlin (Flynn). He is introduced as a newspaperman who "likes prize fights better than dances" and "a drink better than pretty young girls." A few scenes later when he proposes to Louise Elliott (Davis), the oldest daughter of a druggist in Silver Bow, Montana, she is fully aware of his potential drawbacks as a mate. "I know he hasn't the kind of ambition we're brought up to expect in a man," she tells her two sisters. "I know he's irresponsible and restless. Oh, but he makes me feel alive!" Once married to him, she might as well be dead, for he is reluctant to give up his freedom, still preferring the male camaraderie of the sports arena and the saloon to the quiet of the domestic circle. "I'm the kind of husband," he admits with a bitter laugh, "that makes everybody feel sorry for his wife."

He is also the kind of aspiring novelist who spends more time talking about his novel than actually writing it. Even so, he exhibits many of the traits culturally identified with creative writers—instability, immaturity, selfishness, and, of course, excessive drinking. Louise tries to keep him on task, to be his muse, but he lacks the necessary confidence and discipline to see the book through to completion. "My work!" he howls during one of his periodic depressions, crumpling pages in his fist. "It's rotten. It smells to high heaven it's so rotten." He grabs his coat and hat, and hustles to the nearest saloon.

The Sisters exemplifies the women's pictures popular in the thirties and forties, a genre that touted the image of the self-sacrificing wife or mother. In the course of one hour and thirty-nine minutes, Louise patiently endures a ne'er-do-well husband, a miscarriage, and the San Francisco earthquake of 1906. Her defining quality is stoicism. When Frank deserts her to go in search of himself, she simply says, "He'll come back. . . . All I have to do is wait."

Although journalism is peripheral to the main plot, it does serve to justify the film's negative view of male culture. Milton Krimms, who adapted *The Sisters* from a best-selling novel by Myron Brinig, was a former newspaperman, but evidently no sentimentalist about newspapers. In the only scene set in a newspaper office, Frank braces the grizzled city editor for a raise.

> **Frank:** I'm a married man with responsibilities, and all I'm asking you for is enough money to live like a human being.
> **City Editor:** You can't come around here complaining about hard times when you smell like a saloon most of the time.
> **Frank:** Ha! You're a fine one to preach. Why, you've had your nose in a whiskey bottle so long it looks like a cork.
> **City Editor:** I've had enough out of you, Medlin. You're fired.

Whether reporter or editor, young or old, getting fired or doing the firing, here journalists are drunken hacks at best and chronic drunks at worst. And they are usually at their worst.

From the late twenties through the thirties, roughly the first decade of talking pictures, journalistic drinking had a wide range of metaphorical functions on the screen. It symbolized the unscrupulousness of particular types of journalism or the corruption of journalism as a whole; represented sometimes the cause, sometimes the consequence of marital strife; described the spreading stain of urban anomie. In all these instances, the films were drawing on the ideology of the old temperance movement, which condemned drinking as sinful and socially destructive.

Yet journalistic drinking also had positive associations in films. It served as a leveler of hierarchal organizations; an unambiguous masculine gesture; a sign of worldliness and urbanity; a trigger for comic action.

The existence of such diverse meanings suggests that American attitudes toward drinking were still open-ended, still evolving. Continuously replenished by culture-shaking events—from the bourgeois revolt against Prohibition to the onset of the Depression—the shot glass in the hands of a journalist (or the flask on his hip) retained enormous vitality as a film metaphor. Drink wasn't yet just drink, but a liquid dream.

7

The Dog That Bit You

If we had talking livers, we wouldn't need AA.
                                        —Charles Bukowski

The contradictory array of alcohol images that were parading across the screen at the end of the 1930s can be analyzed and explained in terms of colliding ideologies. Russian linguist V. N. Volosinov, one of the founders of modern semiotics, observed, "Wherever a sign is present, ideology is present." He further noted that class "does not coincide with the sign community. . . . Thus different classes will use one and the same language. As a result, differently oriented accents intersect in every ideological sign. Sign becomes an arena of the class struggle." This inner dialectic quality of the sign—what Volosinov called its "social multiaccentuality"—comes out in the open "only in times of social crisis or revolutionary change." Under most circumstances, the contradictions imbedded in every sign can't emerge fully because the dominant ideology is "always somewhat reactionary" and strives to "extinguish or drive inward the struggle between social value judgments which occur in the sign, to make the sign uniaccentual."[1]

From the perspective of Volosinov's theories, the fact that drinking generated such a wide range of meanings in thirties films would indicate that social consensus about alcohol use had broken down and that various concepts of drinking and drunkenness were now competing for dominance. Eventually, one would triumph, though it would occasionally be disturbed by contradictions (the remnants of the old temperance creed, the hedonism of the modern consumer culture, and so on). The dominant ideology for years to come would be that of Alcoholics Anonymous, sometimes summarized as "drunks helping drunks."[2]

Its ideology actually rests on more than the belief that alcoholics somehow are able to stay sober by helping each other. AA members also believe that (1) alcoholism is a treatable disease, not a moral weakness, and (2) the only successful treatment is total abstinence. The generally accepted position is that a reformed alcoholic can never safely return to social or controlled drinking.[3]

Launched in 1935, AA remained a relatively small sectarian movement for the next decade or so, with groups of reformed alcoholics meeting in several cities.[4] A turning point came in 1946 when E. M. Jellinek, a research professor in applied physiology at Yale University, published an article that seemed to confirm major elements of AA ideology.[5] Jellinek's findings were reproduced in popular national magazines, helping create a new consensus about alcoholism—so much so that in the mid-fifties both the American Medical Association and the American Hospital Association passed resolutions recognizing the disease concept.[6]

AA ideology began to be reflected in films as early as *The Lost Weekend* (1945), based on a novel by Charles Jackson, who once quipped that an alcoholic was a "person who could take it or leave it, so he took it."[7] *The Lost Weekend,* which won Academy Awards for best picture, best director, best screenplay, and best actor, kicked off a series of AA-influenced films, including *Smash-Up* (1947), *Come Fill the Cup* (1951), *Come Back Little Sheba* (1952), *I'll Cry Tomorrow* (1955), *The Voice in the Mirror* (1958), *Too Much, Too Soon* (1958), and *Days of Wine and Roses* (1962).[8] For some of the films, AA organizers provided technical advice and even plot ideas.[9]

The reintroduction of the disease concept by AA and Jellinek—Dr. Benjamin Rush had originally introduced it in 1784—softened the social stigma that had long surrounded alcoholism. By the forties, as more middle-class families were affected by alcohol abuse, the public became receptive to the idea that alcoholism wasn't merely a matter of weak willpower or loose moral standards. The temperance-tale stereotype of the skid row bum gradually gave way to an image of the alcoholic as the "unfortunate victim of a disease that strikes indiscriminately at every social level."[10]

It is this image that generally comes to mind when one thinks of Hollywood's portrayals of drinking over the past fifty years. Indeed, some scholars have argued that as public acceptance of the disease concept has expanded—a 1987 Gallup poll found that nearly 90 percent of Americans believe that alcoholism is a disease—the range of meanings attached to drinking in films has narrowed.[11] But though AA-influenced films may have dominated the screen, their emergence in the mid-forties didn't actually wipe out other portrayals of drinking. As we will see, many already familiar stereotypes, including the comic drunk and the supermasculine drinker, persisted.

One of the most interesting representations of drinking was also one of the most invisible—drinking as part of a "routinized," "taken-for-granted" background.[12] Scenes of casual social drinking in bars and cocktail lounges became common in postwar films, perhaps reflecting the unprecedented prosperity of the era and the upswing in jobs and status and ways of living that previously had been closed to many Americans.[13] By taking social drinking for granted, the films, in effect, defined "drinking normality."[14] Harold W. Pfautz, who found in popular postwar fiction this same tendency to treat alcohol as a "social tool" rather than a drug, pointed out, "It is in social contexts permeated by an ethos of urbanity and professionalism that alcohol's negative implications can be relegated to a narrow and disassociated 'clinical' and 'problem' status."[15] In other words, both fiction and film re-privatized drinking problems, divorcing them from general cultural patterns and turning them back into "a matter of private anguish, to be handled on an individual basis."[16]

Robert Benchley was already something of a specialist in drunk roles when he played the alcoholic journalist Stebbins in Alfred Hitchcock's 1940 spy thriller *Foreign Correspondent*. Five years earlier, in *China Seas*, Benchley had played McCaleb, a character who remained drunk throughout the entire picture. This led to alcoholic parts in *Piccadilly Jim* (1936) and *Live, Love and Learn* (1937).[17]

By 1940 Benchley had practically stopped writing the humorous magazine sketches for which he had first become known and had begun thinking of himself as primarily an actor. He would appear in forty feature films (plus numerous shorts) before his death in 1945, often providing comic relief. Originally hired to just write dialogue for *Foreign Correspondent*—fourteen writers would work at various times on the screenplay—he was encouraged by Hitchcock to create a role for himself in the film.[18] *Time* magazine observed in its review that Stebbins "is to the life what Robert Benchley would undoubtedly be if he had been a foreign correspondent in London for twenty-five years."[19] And, in fact, Hitchcock had told Benchley on the set to "be himself" and that the camera would simply "eavesdrop."[20]

Stebbins is a "broken-down bowler-and-cane type of London correspondent" who has made a career out of rewriting government handouts in the morning and drinking all afternoon.[21] Early in the film, he guides the hero (Joel McCrea, who got the part of police reporter Johnny Jones after Gary Cooper turned it down) into a pub.[22] The scene exemplifies the kind of droll humor Hitchcock routinely used to punctuate suspense.

Waddling up to the bar like a penguin with achy feet, Stebbins orders a glass of milk. "Milk?" Jones says in surprise.

Stebbins: Well, I'm on the wagon. I went to the doctor today to see about these jitters I got and he said it's the wagon for a month or a whole new set of organs. I can't afford a whole new set of organs, so. . . . (*The bar maid arrives with their drinks.*)
Jones: If I'd known you were on the wagon, I could've got along all right without this, but since it's here. . . . (*He lifts his glass.*) Good luck. (*Stebbins watches dolefully as he takes a big gulp.*)
Stebbins: Good?
Jones (*matter-of-factly*): Yes, it's just like any other scotch and soda.
Stebbins (*with a regretful shake of his head*): That's what I thought. (*He sips experimentally at his milk, makes a horrid face.*) It doesn't taste like it did when I was a baby. It's got poison in it.

Despite being on the screen only briefly, Benchley won considerable praise from the critics.[23] *The Hollywood Reporter* said he did "a great bit with his Stebbins," and *Variety* claimed that he had "one of the finest cases of the jitters ever recorded for the camera."[24] Herb Sterne wrote in *Rob Wagner's Script* that while the entire cast of the film was very good, the "real acting honors . . . go . . . to that able funnyman, Robert Benchley."[25]

The significance of Benchley's performance, outside its obvious use as comic relief, lies in its contrast to McCrea's. Where Stebbins is lazy, nervous, and effete, Jones is relentless, hard-nosed, and masculine. The differences in their personas are perhaps most clearly reflected in their different drinking styles. Stebbins has drunk himself into physical ruin, even if his jitters are presented as a kind of joke. Jones, on the other hand, is a casual social drinker ("I could've got along all right without this, but since it's here. . ."). He is in control, not the booze. This display of discipline indicates that he is hero stuff, that he has the manly qualities necessary to expose a Nazi spy ring and scoop the world with the story. The ideal man drinks, the film suggests, but doesn't get sloppily drunk or addicted to drink.

Other films of the early forties feature drunk scenes somewhat similar to the one in *Foreign Correspondent*. The scenes are like arias in an opera—that is, set pieces that test a performer's virtuosity—and critics frequently singled them out for comment. If anything ever varied from film to film, it was the particular causes and consequences of the journalist's drunkenness, rather than the flamboyance of the drunkenness itself.

The Philadelphia Story (1940), a late screwball comedy starring Katharine Hepburn as heiress Tracy Lord, Cary Grant as her former husband, and James Stewart as magazine reporter Macaulay Connor, contains numerous references to drinking, but only one full-blown drunk scene. Adapted by Donald Ogden Stewart, an alcoholic, from a hit play by Philip Barry, another alcoholic, the film treats the stereotype of the hard-drinking writer with self-reflexive irony.[26] "You drink, don't you?" Grant asks Stewart. "Oh, a little," Stewart replies. "A little?" Grant exclaims in mock amazement. "And you a writer? I thought all writers drank to excess and beat their wives. You know, at one time I think I secretly wanted to be a writer."

Grant's character, C. K. Dexter Haven, is a reformed alcoholic whose chronic excessive drinking wrecked his marriage to Tracy. As he explains to Stewart, "She never had any understanding of my deep and gorgeous thirst." Now that he is on the wagon, he wants to stop her from remarrying and win her back for himself. It proves hard work. When he unexpectedly appears at the Lord mansion on the eve of her wedding to an up-and-coming politician (John Howard), she greets him with the crack, "You haven't switched from liquor to dope by any chance, have you, Dexter?"

Thus even before the film's drunk scene, drinking has accumulated a host of contradictory associations. First, it is associated through Connor with the bohemian lifestyle of artists and writers. Second, it is associated through frequent instances of casual social drinking—"Shall we have sherry on the porch?" Mother Lord (Mary Nash) always seems to be asking—with money and breeding and the good life. Third, it is associated through the swift repartee between Tracy and Dexter with humor. Fourth and last, it is associated through their ruined marriage with the old temperance-tale concept of alcohol as "demon rum," the destroyer of home and family.

The drunk scene—it is actually more a sequence than a scene, stretching across about fifteen minutes of screen time and three different settings—is also riddled with contradictions. Connor begins drinking at a pre-wedding party, continues drinking during a middle-of-the-night call on Dexter, and finishes drinking at dawn with Tracy, who herself has gotten uncharacteristically drunk. The scene presents the culture's inconsistent valuations of drink, but without reconciling or resolving them.

When, for example, Connor barges in on Dexter, waving an open bottle of champagne in his fist, he behaves in the tradition of the comic drunk, a popular figure in American culture since the age of vaudeville. He trips over furniture, slurs his words, loses all inhibition. It is the kind of portrayal of drunkenness in which an uncontrollable case of hiccups is assumed to be funny. Yet this same drunken boor soon transforms into a man of charm. Although both he and Tracy are supposedly tipsy, they dance with perfect coordination along the top of a low stone wall, a beautiful young couple floating on music and champagne. Bosley Crowther of the *New York Times* called it "one of the most cozy drunk scenes . . . we've ever seen."[27] Certainly, it is one of the most romantic, with Connor, who earlier could barely complete a sentence, now speaking love poetry: "There's a magnificence in you, Tracy, a magnificence that comes out of your eyes and your voice and the way you stand there and the way you walk. You've got fires banked down within you, hearth fires and holocausts."

Screwball comedy is devoted as a genre to issues of courtship and marriage, the search for a suitable partner, and eventually the couples in *The Philadelphia Story* do sort themselves out.[28] Remaining confused to the end, however, is the film's interpretation of alcohol use. Is drinking a sign of weakness, a vehicle for comedy, or a normal social activity? Does it actually make the drinker more charming or just make him think he is more charming? Stewart would win an Academy Award for his performance as Connor—deservingly so when one considers how many different types of drunks he was required by the script to play.

Like *The Philadelphia Story*, *Meet John Doe* (1941) includes a drunk scene that was highly acclaimed in its own time despite what now seems an inconsistent tone. Crowther observed in his review that "James Gleason makes a forbiddingly hard-boiled managing editor whose finer instincts are revealed in a superb drunk scene."[29] Both Edwin Schallert of the *Los Angeles Times* and James Shelley Hamilton of *New Movies* magazine praised director Frank Capra for bringing out the hidden talents of actors, with Schallert adding that the "work of Gleason in a part that is genuine throughout . . . is noteworthy."[30] Even Otis Ferguson of the *New Republic*, who generally disliked the film, acknowledged that the "one scene which came through . . . with true sincerity and eloquence was Gleason's drunken talk in the bar. . . . It was just talk, with business, but he made it his, and it will remain one of the magnificient scenes in pictures."[31]

At the very least, the drunk scene fulfills an important narrative function. It is there in Jim's Bar that Gleason, playing gruff-editor-with-heart-of-gold Henry Connell, first warns John (Gary Cooper) that homegrown fascists are plotting to take over the John Doe movement and use it to catapult media mogul D. B. Norton into the White House. Although he started out as a fake, a mere hobo caught up in a newspaper circulation stunt, John has come to believe the message of neighborliness he has been preaching around the country—"the Sermon on the Mount with a drawl," in Ferguson's sarcastic phrase.[32] He also has come to love Ann Mitchell (Barbara Stanwyck), the cynical columnist who invented the John Doe character and writes his "holy hokum."[33]

The drunk scene is basically a monologue during which Connell exposes his inmost self. Jim's Bar exists as a space apart from the competitive, hierarchal world of work, a refuge where men can safely drop their tough expressions, the masks they normally wear, and confess their real feelings. "Yep, I'm hard," Connell says. "But you wanna know something? I've got a weakness. You'd never guess that, would you? Well, I have. Wanna know what it is? 'The Star-Spangled Banner.' Screwy, huh? Well, maybe it is. But play 'The Star-Spangled Banner' and I'm a sucker for it." Under the influence, Connell becomes voluble, nostalgic, sentimental. Drunkenness provides him with a kind of exemption from the harsh, close-mouthed style of the traditional American male. He reminisces, for example, about serving in the military in World War I: "Know what my old man did when I joined up? He joined up, too. Got to be a sergeant. And here's the kicker for you. We were in the same outfit. Funny, huh? Hmm? [He lifts a shot glass to his lips. His look grows distant.] He was killed, John. I saw him get it. I was right there and I saw it with my own eyes."

Meet John Doe was supposedly intended to spotlight the threat of native fascism. As Capra wrote in his autobiography, "Hitler's strong-arm success against democracy was catching. Little 'fuhrers' were springing up in America, to proclaim that freedom was weak, sterile, passé. The 'new wave' was Blood Power!"[34] Yet the serious political message contained in Connell's ramblings—"I'm a sucker for 'The Star-Spangled Banner' and I'm a sucker for this country. I *like* what we got here. . . . A guy can say what he wants, and do what he wants, without having a bayonet shoved through his belly. And that's all right, isn't it?"—is undercut by the stage business Ferguson so much admired. Three times in the course of the drunk scene Connell tries to light a bent cigarette. All three times he misses, but doesn't seem to notice. At the end of the scene, after trying to draw on his unlit cigarette, he mutters, "I, I'm smoking too much," and grinds the cigarette in an ashtray.

The old comic drunk vies with the philosophical drunk in Gleason's portrayal of Connell, creating a somewhat discordant image. It is but a small reflection of the discordance that afflicts *Meet John Doe* as a whole. Beneath the patriotic hurrahs, the film was Capra's most pessimistic to date, portraying common folks as gullible, delusive, a potential mob. So ambivalent was the film about the future of American democracy that Capra and screenwriter Robert Riskin found themselves unable to devise an acceptable ending for their story. "Why?" Capra asked years later. "Why did the hundreds of scenes integrate into a jigsaw puzzle that had greatness written all over it except for one gaping hole no last scene would plug up?" In desperation he shot and test-marketed five different endings, "setting," in his own words, "some kind of a pointless record."[35]

Critics panned the original ending, which had Norton undergo a conversion on the snowy roof of City Hall on Christmas Eve. "All that lacks in the picture," Schallert asserted in the *Los Angeles Times*,

is the spell of a great sacrifice to make the whole impression convincing. Instead we witness John Doe, willing to give his life for a cause, won over to living by the persuasions of a woman who has double-crossed him. We also behold the man who exploited him, and who never showed any previous signs of relenting in his crafty ways, suddenly showing the milk of human kindness.[36]

In the ultimate ending, the characters have at least a bit more nuance. John is persuaded by Ann *and* members of the Midville John Doe Club to not jump off the roof, and Norton remains unregenerate. Moreover, Connell delivers the film's new last line: "There you are, Norton! The people. Try and lick that!" This isn't the hard-boiled cynic who ran Norton's newspaper empire speaking, but the idealist who emerged in Jim's Bar with the help of alcohol.

Two months after *Meet John Doe* hit theaters, a film that many consider the greatest of all time—and others merely the most greatly overrated—was released: *Citizen Kane.*[37] Its protagonist, Charles Foster Kane (Orson Welles), bears more than a passing resemblance to D. B. Norton. Both Kane and Norton hide their appetite for dictatorial power behind a democratic facade. Both use the modern integrated system of mass communications to corrupt and slant public opinion. And both owe their origins to actual right-wing publishers, particularly William Randolph Hearst, an old, red-baiting reactionary who saw enough of his life reflected in Kane's that he tried to have the film suppressed.[38]

Citizen Kane, for all its reputation as a precocious work of genius (Welles, also its director and co-author, was only twenty-six), is still another early forties film with a *pro forma* drunk scene—or, rather, two. The first occurs after Kane, running as the reform candidate for governor, loses the race because of public outrage over his extramarital affair with singer Susan Alexander (Dorothy Comingore). Upset by the defeat, Jedediah Leland (Joseph Cotton), drama critic for Kane's flagship paper and his oldest friend, gets drunk and lectures him on the realities of elective politics, not unlike a soused Connell lectured John Doe. Alcohol seems to give Leland the ability to see Kane's increasing megalomania clearly and the courage to criticize it:

> You talk about the people as though you own them, as though they belonged to you. As long as I can remember you've talked about giving the people their rights as if you could make them a present of liberty for services rendered. . . . Remember the workingman? . . . You used to write an awful lot about the workingman. He's turning into something called organized labor. You're not going to like that one little bit when

you find out it means your workingman expects something as his right and not your gift. Charlie, when your precious underprivileged really get together, oh boy, that's going to add up to something bigger than your privilege.

It is significant that when Kane interjects, "I'll get drunk, too, Jedediah, if it'll do any good," Leland responds, "It won't do any good. Besides, you never get drunk." There is a coldness in Kane, a lack of bonhomie, that no amount of alcohol can erase or ease.

The second drunk scene also involves Leland, whose friendship with Kane has now broken down. Leland passes out from drink while writing an honest negative review of Susan's ludicrous performance in an opera. When he finally wakes up, Kane is finishing the review for him.

> **Kane:** Hello, Jedediah.
> **Leland:** Hello, Charlie. I didn't know we were speaking.
> **Kane:** Sure, we're speaking—you're fired.

Perhaps because the stereotype of the hard-drinking journalist was already so deeply entrenched in popular culture, *Citizen Kane* took unusual pains to point out that Leland wasn't a habitual drunk. "He ain't been drinking before, Mr. Kane," the sycophantic Bernstein (Everett Sloane) says during the second drunk scene. "Never. We would've heard." Leland drinks to excess only when faced with the task of revealing or confirming a bitter truth. This makes him very different from the newspapermen in *Woman of the Year* and *Roxie Hart,* 1942 films in which drinking is pictured as a routine journalistic activity.

Woman of the Year, the first of nine Spencer Tracy-Katharine Hepburn films that would be made over the next twenty-five years, opens in a saloon owned by former prizefighter "Pinkie" Peters (William Bendix). Sam Craig, sportswriter for the *New York Chronicle,* joins three newspapermen already at the bar. They are listening to the popular radio program "Information Please," whose celebrity contestant is a colleague of Sam's, foreign affairs columnist Tess Harding (Hepburn). "Federman says she's the No. 2 dame in the country," Pinkie notes, "right next to Mrs. Roosevelt." To which one of the newspapermen (Roscoe Karns) replies, "So they're giving 'em numbers now, like public enemies."

With this wisecrack, the saloon is clearly identified as a male pre-
serve, created and maintained in opposition to women's interests,
the matriarchal order. The gender conflict intensifies when Tess suggests on the air that baseball, a game played by millions of American
men and boys, is "a frightful waste of energy" and ought to be abol-
ished for the duration of World War II. Her suggestion gets Sam all
steamed up. "You know what that kind of thinking leads to?" he
rhetorically asks. "Say, look, we're concerned with a threat to what
we like to call our American way of life. Baseball and the things it represents is [sic] part of that way of life. What's the sense of abolishing
the thing you're trying to protect?" The thing Sam may be trying
most to protect is male hegemony. In defending the American way
of life, he is also defending the traditional male role as rule-maker
and breadwinner, challenged by the invasion of Tess's censorious
voice into the saloon and by her professional standing.

The film eventually introduces the actual person of Tess into the
saloon. After trading insults in the columns of the *Chronicle*, Sam and
Tess meet face to face for the first time and begin falling in love. One
night he takes her to Pinkie's—a breach, it would seem, of male pro-
tocol. Seated at a back table, each quickly downs a scotch and then
orders a double.

Sam *(lifts the glass to his lips):* A lot of drink in these.
Tess: Oh, I don't know.
Sam: Well, I just mean if you're not used to 'em.
Tess *(laughs):* Oh, don't worry about me. As a diplomat's
daughter, I've had to match drinks with a lot of people, from
remittance men to international spies. And, I may say, I've
never wound up under the table.
Sam: Reminds me of my year at college. I used to bet on drink-
ing. Make a contest out of it. Kid stuff.
Tess: Imagine. Silly.

Silly as it is, they nonetheless try to outdrink each other, indicated by
a dissolve to a shot of their table littered with empty glasses. While
treated humorously here, the competition between them will come
close at times to destroying their relationship. The blame will fall
completely on Tess, who will be punished in sadistic ways—for
example, by having kitchen appliances turn on her. According to
contemporary social expectations, a man was supposed to be com-

petitive; a woman, supportive. Tess will ultimately accept this, adjusting herself to a more wifely role.

Her transformation is foreshadowed on the cab ride home from Pinkie's. Half-drunk, Sam and Tess cuddle in the back seat. Alcohol has relaxed their inhibitions, heightened their intimacy—served, in brief, as a kind of aphrodisiac.

> **Sam:** I love you.
> **Tess:** You do?
> **Sam:** Positive.
> **Tess:** That's nice. Even when I'm sober?
> **Sam:** Even when you're brilliant. (*He leans his face down and kisses her.*)

"Hollywood's traditional stories of courtship and marriage," Virginia Wright Wexman reminds us in her book, *Creating the Couple,* "have typically focused on the woman's resistance to romantic attachments; therefore, the kiss often represents a significant moment of change for her and documents her surrender to the erotic will of men."[39] But Tess isn't ready to fully surrender yet. Once she sobers up, she returns to being her old intractable self. This frustrates Sam, a rumpled, salt-of-the-earth type whose easygoing manner hides a deep patriarchal streak. "You know it's too bad I'm not covering this dinner of yours tonight," he says during one of their frequent arguments, "because I got an angle that would really be sensational: 'The Outstanding Woman of the Year' really isn't a woman at all." His harsh words hit home, and Tess seems almost relieved when, at the end of the film, she capitulates. The heterosexual couple of reproductive age, forged earlier under the spell of alcohol and glimpsed in the semi-darkness of the cab, re-emerges as the basic social unit.

World War II-era audiences must have found this comforting. With millions of men going into the military, couples were being torn apart or even prevented from forming. Moreover, because of war-related labor shortages, women were entering fields of work once closed to them, including most newspaper work. If film is any clue—and, as a site for the construction of ideological processes, it is—there was a need to reconcile these traumatic changes with older social values. *Woman of the Year* did it by appearing progressive while actually reinforcing the ideology of the dominant patriarchal order.

Released within a month of *Woman of the Year, Roxie Hart* seems almost to belong to an earlier decade, no doubt because it was assembled by screenwriter Nunnally Johnson and director William A. Wellman from the bones of the popular old play (and 1927 film) *Chicago.* Its story—about a gum-chewing flapper (Ginger Rogers) who basks in the publicity spotlight when picked up on a murder charge—is presented as the barroom narrative of a newspaperman nostalgic for the wild and irresponsible days of the 1920s. But though the shadows of war didn't intrude on the film, they did intrude on some of the reviews. Bosley Crowther, for example, complained that it was "a most unsuitable time to be calling to mind the follies, the court-room circuses and vulgarities of this brashly eccentric nation during a period which might better be forgotten."[40]

In the film itself, the flow of alcohol stimulates the flow of memory. With a glass in his hand and a bottle at his elbow, crime reporter Homer Howard (George Montgomery) follows in the oral tradition of his namesake, regaling fellow drinkers with the colorful details of Roxie's rise to tabloid glory. Alcohol turns Homer into an inspired speaker—a function it served as well for other newspapermen in early forties film, most notably Connor in *The Philadelphia Story* and Connell in *Meet John Doe.* However, where they comically slurred some words, Homer remains fluent throughout.

Roxie Hart can perhaps best be viewed as an homage to Depression-era shyster films. It was fitting therefore that Adolphe Menjou, who portrayed slick managing editor Walter Burns in *The Front Page* (1931), portrays slick mouthpiece Billy Flynn here. Wellman's biographer, Frank T. Thompson, remarked that the director "had a particular affection for low-lives, frauds, criminals and sensation seekers."[41] His *Nothing Sacred* (1937) became one of the classics of the shyster-film cycle. But by the time he made *Roxie Hart,* America was at war, and the moment of the cynical shyster hero had passed. The flashback structure of the film implied as much.

Reviewers noted that *Roxie Hart* seemed to be working just a little too hard for laughs. They attributed this heavy-handedness to a lack of restraint on the part of its screenwriter, director, and actors.[42] Actually, *Roxie Hart*'s frantic, cartoonish style—Thompson compared it to "the relentless urgency of a burlesque skit"—may have had more to do with the film belonging to a cycle or genre in decline than with overacting.[43] The twilight period of a genre is generally characterized by self-consciousness or even self-parody. Having run out of new things to say, works in a moribund genre tend to offer pointed commentary on their own status as cultural items.[44]

Thus Homer, standing at the bar in the opening scene, comments on the stereotype of the hard-drinking journalist, a stereotype popularized by numerous shyster films of the previous decade. "Another thing you got to remember about newspaper work," he lectures a smooth-cheeked cub, "the public always expects a newspaperman to do a lot of drinking, and so you mustn't ever let the public down." By mocking the film journalist, or at least audience expectations of the film journalist, *Roxie Hart* was trying to freshen a character who had grown old and overly familiar.

Three years later, *The Lost Weekend* (1945) would inaugurate a new era of alcoholism films.[45] Coinciding with the "rediscovery" of alcoholism as a disease by Alcoholics Anonymous and the Yale Center of Alcohol Study, the films of this era cast alcoholism in medical terms and presented AA as an option for treatment.[46] Most scholars agree that the era ended with *Days of Wine and Roses* in 1962, at which time stories of alcoholism became "more the province of television than of films."[47]

Despite *The Lost Weekend* and its various AA-influenced spinoffs, scenes of socially acceptable drinking and drunkenness continued to appear on the screen. What's more, even when drunkenness was portrayed as problematic, the solution to it wasn't always one AA would have recommended. *Welcome Stranger* (1947), a Bing Crosby-Barry Fitzgerald vehicle intended to capitalize on the success of their Academy Award-winning *Going My Way*, offers a good example.

Crosby plays Jim Pearson, a breezy young medico who comes to Fallbridge, Maine, to fill in for old Doc McRory (Fitzgerald) while the latter takes a vacation. At a barn dance, Bill Walters (Frank Faylen) introduces himself to Pearson as "editor, reporter, copy boy of the town's leading—and only—newspaper," adding: "I'm drunk. I'm going to give you a little advice: get drunk. The town's more charming that way." Walters seems at first to be just another shabby newspaperman with his occupation's fondness for cynicism and alcohol. Our impression changes, though, when Pearson drops in on him at home.

Walters: Would you guess, doctor, that the present editor of the *Fallbridge Weekly Times* once won a Pulitzer Prize? Well, I did, back in Boston.

Pearson: Were you drinking better whiskey back then?
Walters: I wasn't drinking then. Whiskey isn't the reason I'm here. The reason I'm here is, you can't work on a daily paper and have your head splitting wide open half the time.

Walters suffers from "bustin' headaches," which he relieves with booze. Pearson determines through blood tests that the headaches are caused by a tumor on Walters's adrenal gland. Once the tumor is removed—snip-snip—so will be the root cause of his chronic drinking.

All this has little to do with AA ideology. *Welcome Stranger* may provide a medical explanation for alcoholism, but alcoholism itself isn't defined as a disease. And where AA believes that the only cure for alcoholism is total abstinence, the cure in the film is surgery, after which Walters will be able to take a drink again if he wants. In fact, Pearson brings along a bottle to the newspaper office when he goes to deliver his diagnosis. "You mean I need a drink to find out what happens to me?" a nervous Walters asks. "It's to celebrate," Pearson replies.

As if a bastardized version of the disease concept weren't confusing enough, *Welcome Stranger* also mixes in the conventions of the "drunkard's progress" from nineteenth-century temperance tales. Walters, once among the best reporters in the country, now lives on the edge of poverty with his twelve-year-old daughter, Emily (Wanda Hendrix), who often misses school because of his binges. This marginal, motherless family hanging on in squalid surroundings serves as an old-fashioned warning about the price of drunkenness.

The portrayal of drinking in *Welcome Stranger* is so contradictory as to be practically incoherent. Sometimes within the same scene, the film presents drinking as a medical dilemma, a moral wrong, and even a normal social activity. Only one thing seems clear: we are a long way from the newspapermen of *The Front Page* and other thirties films, for whom drinking was a mark of urbanity, or a rite of manhood, or a symbolic gesture of defiance.

In the fifties the hard-drinking journalist appeared in films across a wide variety of genres. He bar-hopped his way through not only alcoholism films and newspaper films, but also historical films, crime films, romantic comedies, and family melodramas. If nothing else, this illustrates the extraordinary flexibility of both the journalist as a character and drinking as a metaphor. The hard-drinking journalist was now so deeply woven into the cultural fabric that he could appear in almost any kind of film and not seem out of place.

The fifties have come down to us as a conservative decade, a somnolent decade, the "Silent Fifties."[48] "These are days," John Kenneth Galbraith wrote, "when, in minor modification of the scriptural parable, the bland lead the bland."[49] The country was enjoying an unprecedented boom, with nearly 60 percent of all American families reporting wages in the middle-class brackets, a standard of living beyond the comprehension of the rest of the world.[50]

But beneath the prosperous surface, there were problems in the making. In 1956, for example, the number of blue-collar workers was surpassed by that of white-collar workers—a milestone, William Manchester said, as important as the closing of the frontier in 1890.[51] The typical wage earner was no longer a producer of things, but a pencil pusher, a cipher working for a large, impersonal corporation. Increasingly, Americans were hemmed in by bureaucratic routines, their vaunted individualism compromised. Small wonder the dominant intellectual fashions of the decade included Freudian psychology and existential philosophy, each of which addressed in its own way the loss of personal control.[52]

Fear haunted fifties culture—fear of communist aggression abroad, fear of communist infiltration at home, fear of world-ending mushroom clouds. After the Truman administration ordered the building of the hydrogen, or "super," bomb in 1950, Albert Einstein went on TV to warn that "radioactive poisoning of the atmosphere and hence annihilation of any life on Earth has been brought within the range of technical possibilities. . . . General annihilation beckons."[53] The uneasy mood of the post-atomic era was caught by a James Thurber cartoon in which one middle-aged man wistfully asks another, "Do you remember when the only thing to fear was fear itself?"[54]

On the screen, weak men proliferated, "delivering staggering confessions of inability to maintain their self-imposed burden of male supremacy."[55] Alcoholism, particularly in *films noir* and family melodramas, served as a metaphor for defeat, stagnation, a thrown-away life. Where once characters' drinking problems were attributed to external forces, now they were often shown to stem from internal conflicts—were, in Denise Herd's image, "mapped out along the

Freudian terrain of neurosis, infantile fixations, and unresolved Oedipal complexes."[56]

Come Fill the Cup (1951) combined the older mechanistic explanation of alcoholism—the belief that alcohol is inherently addictive, at least for some people—with the new emphasis on psychological causality. Described by the *New York Times* as a "melodramatic dissertation on newspaper work and strong drink," the film features not one, but two alcoholic characters.[57] Reporter Lew March destroys his career through excessive drinking. He follows the downward spiral of the drunk in a nineteenth-century temperance tale, falling from middle-class respectability to skid row and into the alcoholic ward of a hospital. There, after a siege of DTs, he is befriended by reformed alcoholic Charley Dolan (James Gleason), whose advice and example encourage him to dry out.

This was apparently the first appearance on the screen of the AA theme of "drunks helping drunks."[58] Once recovered, Lew himself does twelfth-step work. He gets back into the newspaper game, rising to city editor and hiring several former alcoholics as reporters. The managing editor even complains that "this place is beginning to look like a branch of Alcoholics Anonymous—we're crawling with ex-drunks." To which Lew replies, "When it comes to newspapermen, give me the reformed lush every time. . . . Work takes the place of liquor."

The other big boozer in the film is the publisher's nephew, Boyd Copeland (Gig Young). Boyd started drinking heavily after marrying Lew's old sweetheart (Phyllis Thaxter), who had ditched Lew—talk about irony!—because of his drinking. "In films with two alcoholic characters," Robin Room pointed out, "a quite different rhetoric of motivation for drinking is often assigned to each."[59] And this is the case in *Come Fill the Cup*. While the film offers very little motivation for Lew's drinking, it offers a psychological explanation for Boyd's.

"Why do you do it, Lew?" the managing editor asks early in the film. "Why do you swill all that talent down the drain?" Cut to the interior of a newspapermen's bar, the Blue Pencil, where the bartender suggests an answer, but one that Lew, sitting on a stool and fondling a shot glass, ultimately rejects.

Bartender (*scanning the front-page headlines*): Another normal day—war, love-nest killing, train wreck, tax boost. No wonder I'm doing so good. People have to forget. If they were happy, I guarantee you, Lew, I'd have to close up shop.

Lew: It's about time you got to know your customers, Al. Happiness has nothing to do with it. A lush can always find a reason if he's thirsty.

The white-coated doctor in the alcoholic ward comes the closest to providing an authoritative explanation for Lew's drinking. Using standard AA rhetoric, he tells Lew: "You have an incurable disease—alcoholism. Liquor is as poisonous to you as sugar is to the man with diabetes. The only sure treatment is to quit."

In contrast, the film traces Boyd's drinking to psychological tensions caused by his dominant mother. The unnatural closeness of their relationship is symbolized by the large oil painting of her hanging over his piano (significantly, when we first meet Boyd, a gifted composer, he is blocked, impotent, unable to finish a concerto he is writing). Almost a decade earlier, author Philip Wylie had seen this kind of "momworship" as rampant in American culture and had railed against it as a model of perverted sexuality:

> Our land, subjectively mapped, would have more silver cords and apron strings crisscrossing it than railroad and telephone wires. Mom is everywhere and everything and damned near everybody, and from her depends all the rest of the U.S. Disguised as good old mom, dear old mom, sweet old mom, our loving mom, and so on, she is the bride at every funeral and the corpse at every wedding. Men live for her and die for her, dote upon her and whisper her name as they pass away, and I believe she has now achieved, in the hierarchy of miscellaneous articles, a spot next to the Bible and the flag, being reckoned part of both in a way.[60]

Pressured by the publisher to cure Boyd of drink, Lew objects that it is "a job for a psychologist." Nonetheless, he plunges in, quickly diagnosing mom as a major part of the problem. "Did it ever occur to you," he asks the publisher, "to keep her out of it?" When Boyd takes down mom's picture near the end of the film, it confirms that Lew has successfully guided him through setbacks and blowups to sobriety, that his drinking days are indeed over.

A deep strain of misogyny runs through *Come Fill the Cup*. Boyd's drinking is related not only to the smothering attentions of his mother, but also to his affair with a seductively shaped Mexican nightclub singer. The film portrays women, no matter what their shape, as emasculators. In a suggestive bit of symbolism, Boyd returns with a knife wound from a drunken weekend with the singer.

If Boyd appears somewhat effeminate—his term for being drunk is "I'm in a condition"—Lew emerges as "unqualifiedly two-fisted."[61] At first, he is a two-fisted drinker, then a two-fisted battler against drink, and finally a two-fisted hustler after news. He remains tough and intact, invulnerable to temptation, by withdrawing from emotional involvement with women. The newspaper becomes his entire world. "Can I drop you off at your home?" the publisher asks him in the final scene. "Can't you see, Mr. Ives," Lew says, gesturing at the city room. "I am home." Although meant positively, this line is, in a sense, an admission of defeat. Lew may not drink anymore, but he doesn't love anymore either.

Many old and honored newspapers were dying in the fifties, the victims of urban flight, rising production costs, and murderous competition from radio and TV. Between 1937 and 1944, there had been 362 suspensions or mergers of papers, dropping the total number of dailies to a low of 1,745. In 1959, despite an increase in population from 140 million to 175 million, the total number of dailies was still about the same—1,751. New papers in the suburbs had been almost exactly offset by those that had died in large cities. More and more cities, including even metropolises like Cincinnati and New Orleans, had either one paper or two under one ownership. Apologists argued that "responsible monopoly" reduced the need for competing papers to coddle advertisers and indulge in sensational circulation stunts. But, as Bernard A. Weisberger pointed out at the time, "it was equally true that without rivalry there was less of a spur to furnish more and better news."[62]

Two 1952 films, *Deadline, U.S.A.* and *Park Row,* were inspired by some of the sadder newspaper deaths of the previous twenty years: the *New York World* in 1931, the *Boston Transcript* in 1941, and the *Philadelphia Public Ledger* in 1942. As recently as 1950, another great name in American newspaper history, the *New York Sun,* had joined the casualty list. Once known as "the newspaperman's newspaper" because of the fine writing that filled its columns, the *Sun* was merged with the *New York World-Telegram,* whose hyphenated masthead already symbolized the new economics of mass communications.

Deadline, U.S.A., written and directed by ex-newspaperman Richard Brooks and shot largely on location at the *New York Daily News*, seemed that rare thing to reviewers, a newspaper picture that "does all right by the trade."[63] Humphrey Bogart starred as the managing editor of the *Day*, an upstanding paper about to be sold to a yellow journal. At the same time that he is trying to prevent the sale—tantamount to death for the *Day*—Bogart's character, Ed Hutcheson, is conducting a crusade against Rienzi (Martin Gabel), a mob boss whose mouthpiece lawyer has just outwitted a Kefauver-type Senate investigating committee.[64]

While the press has its share of problems in the film—from superficial readers and interfering advertisers to profit-obsessed owners—it is still presented as the only social institution with the dedication and resources to do the job the public needs done. This is the theme of most of the journalistic aphorisms Hutcheson goes around dispensing. For example: "Newspaperman is the best profession in the world." Also: "A free press, like a free life, is always in danger." And: "An honest, fearless press is the public's first protection against gangsterism, local or international."

For a man who takes the role of the press so seriously, Hutcheson does a surprising amount of drinking with his staff. Moments after learning that the *Day* will be sold, he asks copy desk chief Frank Allen (Ed Begley), an old-timer who worked on Pulitzer's *World*, what he did when it folded. "Let's see now," Allen muses. "I think I got myself a drink. Yeah, I'm sure of it." Hutcheson goes to his file cabinet, brings out a bottle, and pours Allen a tumbler of whiskey. It is an egalitarian gesture, the booze blurring their manager-worker relationship, signifying and cementing their deeper bond as fellow mourners.

The scene is repeated on a larger scale at O'Brien's, a saloon where a noisy crowd of *Day* reporters and editors hold a "wake" for their doomed paper. "Have some anesthetic, brother?" Allen asks Hutcheson, handing him a drink. But alcohol serves as more than a painkiller. It also (and somewhat contradictorily) stimulates memory and speech, creating a break in the relentless news cycle, an interlude during which drunken staff members take turns eulogizing the *Day* and reviewing their lives and careers. Mrs. Willebrandt (Audrey Christie), a middle-aged sob sister, says:

> I gave it the best fourteen years of my life. And what have I got to show
> for it? Eighty-one dollars in the bank, two dead husbands, and two or

three kids I always wanted, but never had. I've covered everything from electrocutions to love-nest brawls. I've got fallen arches, unfixed teeth. And, you wanna know somethin', I never saw Paris. But I wouldn't change those years, not for anything in the world.

Although much of the drinking in the film is connected with the imminent death of the *Day*, characters do use alcohol for other reasons—as a social tool, as a business ritual, as a kind of love potion. After the wake, for example, a drunken Hutcheson shows up at his ex-wife's door with the idea of winning her back. She lets him in, but resists his sexual overtures. "You know what's the matter with you?" he says, becoming the comic drunk of so many previous films. "You're a spectic, uh, skeptic." In a later scene, he continues his wooing of her with pre-dinner drinks at a high-class restaurant. "How do you feel?" she asks. "Amorous," he answers, making bedroom eyes at her over the rim of his glass.

No matter how often or how much a newspaperman drinks, the film suggests that he shouldn't be drinking with just anyone. It is OK for him to drink with his co-workers, and it is OK for him to drink with his ex-wife, but it isn't OK for him to drink with gangsters or other public enemies. Where and with whom a newspaperman chooses to drink is a measure of his integrity—a big change from the late twenties and early thirties films in which newspapermen unconcernedly rubbed elbows in speakeasies with criminal types. Here Rienzi, driving Hutcheson to the *Day* building in his limo and wishing to cut a deal before they get there, pulls down a mini-bar from the middle of the back seat.

> **Rienzi:** What'll it be?
> **Hutcheson:** Nothing.
> **Rienzi:** Not a drinkin' man?
> **Hutcheson:** Not in an armored car.

Part of what makes *Deadline, U.S.A.* such an interesting film is that it portrays fifties America as largely immune to the moral example of a man like Hutcheson. It is a society in which the public responsibility of a great metropolitan newspaper is sacrificed, with court approval, to private gain; in which brother turns against sister, daughters against mother, and lover against lover; in which thugs masquerade as officers of the law. Corruption is general and ingrained, a point subtly emphasized when Hutcheson visits Mrs. Garrison (Ethel Barrymore), the old widow of the *Day's* founder. He explains that Rienzi is, among other things, in the liquor business. Then he refills her wine glass.

> **Mrs. Garrison:** Is that Rienzi's wine?
> **Hutcheson:** Hunh-hunh.
> **Mrs. Garrison:** Very good.
> **Hutcheson:** The best.

The line between good and evil, never easy to establish or maintain, has been all but erased. And if the number of fighting, independent newspapers continues to dwindle—the lighted sign on the *Day* building blinks out at the end of the film—who will be left to care?

As a counterpoint to, and an escape from, the bleak journalistic present, *Park Row* turned for its subject to the journalistic past. Written, produced, and directed by Sam Fuller, this film took a nostalgic look back at the beginnings of the modern American press on New York's "Newspaper Row." It re-created or at least alluded to actual historical events: Steve Brodie's leap from the Brooklyn Bridge; Ottmar Mergenthaler's development of the linotype; the newspaper-orchestrated campaign to raise money to buy a pedestal for the Statute of Liberty. Of course, the film's hero, cigar-chewing editor Phineas Mitchell (Gene Evans) of the fictitious *New York Globe*, is instrumental in them all.

At a 1969 retrospective of his films, Fuller was asked what he would like to do most. "Own and edit my own newspaper," he said. He had been a copy boy on the *New York Journal* at age twelve and then worked on the *New York Graphic*. In 1928 he joined the *San Diego Sun*, becoming at seventeen one of the youngest crime reporters in the country. "I was involved in strikes, executions, and that kind of thing," he recalled. "I interviewed lots of people, murderers who had committed appalling crimes. . . . Did you know I discovered the body of Jeanne Eagles? I wrote a prize-winning article about it."[65] *Park Row* was Fuller's homage to his origins.

According to Fuller, he was offered studio backing on the condition that he make the film as a musical with Gregory Peck, Rita Hayworth, Mitzi Gaynor, and Dan Dailey. Instead, he made it with his own money—$200,000—most of which he lost when the film flopped at the box office.[66] The small budget was reflected not only in the cheap-looking sets, but also in what *Variety* called the "fulsome use" of long, continuous takes.[67] Fuller described the technique in a magazine interview in 1970:

> I open up in a saloon, 1886, and a fight starts. The men come out from the saloon into the street. They fight down the street. They upset different people. And the first man defeats the second man. He goes into an office and has a big scene with a woman in there, shakes her up a little bit, comes out, walks down a block, goes behind a big statue of Benjamin Franklin and goes into the *third* set. Now that scene is taken without a cut. I had to have a little mike planted on my actor. And I had to strap the operator to the camera. In the first trial, the camera whipped around and the men flew in all directions. It was like a roller coaster. A good shot.[68]

Despite its technical cunning, the opening of *Park Row* just repeats an old cultural cliche—that a newspaperman's second home is the saloon. And the film comes full circle when, near the end, Mitchell goes on a drinking spree because goons from the *Star* have firebombed his office (this kind of violence, incidentally, belonged to the circulation wars in Chicago in the 1920s, not those in New York in the 1890s). "The *Globe* is dead, long live the *Globe*," Mitchell says before passing out on the street.

Not only does the film represent newspapermen as hard-drinking, but it also represents newspaper work itself as dangerously addictive, a concept derived, you may remember, from temperance tales via turn-of-the-century newspaper novels by the likes of Jesse Lynch Williams and Edna Ferber. A boy who applies for the job of printer's devil on the *Globe* tells Mitchell, "I got printer's ink in me, too," confirming his identification with all those newspapermen in fiction and film who can no more survive without the next scoop than alcoholics can survive without the next drink. In addition, newspaper work has the same capacity as alcohol to destroy the family. Mitchell's partner, who owns the press on which the *Globe* is printed, admits that the machine came between him and his wife.[69]

"To make a real newspaper film," Fuller wrote in 1975, long after the critical and commercial failure of *Park Row*, "is as difficult as to make a real war film. The censor is not the only barrier. People who buy tickets and walk into a peacock temple to crack popcorn in soft chairs have been doped over the years. They have been doped over the years [by] what a newspaper is like on the screen."[70] Fuller was saying in effect that most newspaper films try not to violate audience expectations, including the expectation that all newspapermen drink, and quite heavily. In this regard, *While the City Sleeps* (1956), directed by Fritz Lang, seems very Hollywood, very mainstream. As Denise Herd and Robin Room noted in their analysis of the film, "Alcohol use is interwoven through the various layers of the film's structure. . . . The characters are always drinking, but seldom drunk—the glass and bottle are so pervasive that they are virtually invisible and entirely 'normal.' "[71]

But what is normal? Lang, a German emigré who is generally considered one of the greatest directors of the studio era, uses drinking here to comment on "the hollowness of accepted morality."[72] Based on a 1953 novel, *The Bloody Spur,* by Charles Einstein, *While the City Sleeps* follows the competition among three bureau chiefs to find the "Lipstick Killer" and win the job of executive director at a news syndicate.[73] Although on one level the film is a hard-boiled, *noir*-ish murder mystery, it isn't really concerned with "whodunit." As in his masterpiece, *M* (1931), Lang reveals the identity of the murderer from the start. The film is more concerned with the effect of the string of sex murders on the other characters.

One of Lang's biographers said *While the City Sleeps* exposes "the treachery and disloyalty that can divide friendly colleagues in the rat-race for position."[74] A French critic claimed that the object of the film was "to destroy the myth of the journalist as a defender of widows and orphans."[75] But Lang himself didn't sound nearly so condemnatory of the press when discussing the film in a 1965 interview with Peter Bogdanovich. Asked whether most of the newspeople weren't worse than the murderer, he replied:

> You are very romantic. They are human beings. Maybe it's like [Peter] Lorre in *M*—he murders because he must—but these people . . . do exactly the things you probably do yourself but which you detest: running after a job, greedy for money. How many people have you met in your life who are ethical? So what do you expect from these people in *While the City Sleeps?*[76]

The putative hero of the film is Ed Mobley (Dana Andrews), a Pulitzer Prize-winning reporter on the *New York Sentinel* and a commentator on its sister TV station. Mobley professes no interest in becoming director of Kyne Inc., despite being offered the job outright. "I'm content the way I am," he says, "just to be able to write a book now and then, keep my nose clean. I have no appetite for power." But it soon develops that he isn't quite the ethical paragon he seems. He is willing to use his fiancee, Nancy (Sally Forrest), as bait to catch the killer (John Barrymore Jr.). He also is willing to betray her with Mildred (Ida Lupino), the gossip-columnist girlfriend of Mark Loving (George Sanders), one of the competitors for the directorship. In fact, the film draws parallels between Mobley and the sexually twisted killer. When Lt. Kaufman (Howard Duff), the detective on the case, observes, "This guy's a real nut on dames," Nancy bitterly cuts in, "And this description begins to fit Mobley."

Mobley and the Lipstick Killer aren't the only men in the film to use women for their own base ends. The ironically named Loving more or less pushes Mildred at Mobley in an attempt to win the star reporter over to his side. In addition, picture editor Harry Kritzer (James Craig) fully expects his affair with Dorothy Kyne (Rhonda Fleming), wife of owner Walter Kyne (Vincent Price), to give him an edge in the competition.

Kritzer: I'll play it my own way as Walter's best friend.
Dorothy: With Walter's best wife.
Kritzer: I don't want to involve you, darling.
Dorothy (*cynically*): My hero!

So let's tally it up: Mobley betrays Nancy with Mildred; Dorothy betrays her husband with Harry; Mobley uses Nancy as bait for the killer; Loving uses Mildred as bait for Mobley. Of course, the characters drink through all this intrigue and in-fighting. They drink in the wee hours of the morning and during the middle of the day and at night. They drink whether they feel up or down, whether they are on the job or just socializing. They drink in penthouses, secret love nests, cocktail lounges, restaurants, and basement bars. And if they aren't drinking, they are making plans to meet for drinks.

Lt. Kaufman: Here's the full text of the confession. Would you like to have it exclusive?
Mobley: Thanks.

Kaufman: Will you buy me a drink sometime?
Mobley: Sure, sure.

Drinking is sanctioned within the social context, but the social context itself is thoroughly corrupt. The characters discuss their various schemes over drinks—how to get ahead, how to get even, how to get laid. It is no accident that Walter, who instigated the Darwinian struggle among the bureau chiefs, is often filmed with his face stuck in a brandy snifter or an oversized whiskey glass. He is childishly oral, the very embodiment of selfishness and greed.

One shot neatly sums up the film's dark view of society. It is of a liquor glass resting on the front page of the *Sentinel,* just below the banner headline on Mobley's exclusive story about the Lipstick Killer's confession. The headline, in boldfaced capitals, reads: I KILLED FOUR WOMEN. Then a hand reaches into the frame and lifts the glass. As the camera pulls back, we see that the hand belongs to Mobley, who takes a desperate drink. The film proceeds from there to a happy Hollywood ending: Nancy and Mobley get married, and the least objectionable candidate, *Sentinel* editor John Day Griffith (Thomas Mitchell), is named director. But it is the earlier shot that lingers in the mind, linking sexual violence, yellow journalism, and excessive drinking in an unholy trinity.

Sweet Smell of Success (1957) isn't any brighter a film. Shot on location in Manhattan's Bistro Belt, it captures, as one reviewer said, "the feel of Broadway and environs after dark"—the fast tempo, the sleazy characters, the garish nightspots.[77] Alexander Mackendrick, a British director making his American debut, and James Wong Howe, his cinematographer, managed to give the film a gritty, hard-edged look in keeping with its *noir*-ish themes of diseased love and corrupt power. Low-angle shots abound, suggesting an urban society that is out of kilter. The streets are wet as if it had recently rained—"a classic *film noir* touch," Ruth L. Hirayama noted — and the neon lights glare off them.[78]

The film stars Burt Lancaster and Tony Curtis, both of whom were cast against type. In a major departure from his usual heroic athleticism, Lancaster appears bespectacled and restrained in the role of J.J. Hunsecker, a syndicated columnist read by millions and sought out by celebrities and wannabes. J.J. wields his power to make or break careers with a cold, deliberate sadism. He has, in the words of a rival columnist, "the scruples of a guinea pig and the morals of a gangster."

Curtis, a teen idol at the time, plays Sidney Falco, a double-talking, two-faced, client-hungry press agent determined to scratch his way to the top, "where the weather is always balmy." At the start of the film, J.J. is refusing to print any of Sidney's items because he has failed to break up a romance between J.J.'s pretty younger sister and a jazz guitarist (J.J. has an incestuous attachment to the girl, but reviewers were reluctant to call it that.)[79] To win back J.J.'s patronage, Sidney first smears the musician as a drug user and a communist and then frames him on a marijuana charge. "This is life," he tells his disapproving secretary. "Get used to it."

As in *While the City Sleeps*, drinking permeates the story. J.J. gathers items for his column by making the rounds of 21, Toots Shor's, and El Morocco, all famous watering holes. Although he personally doesn't drink much—power is his favorite intoxicant—the hustling guys and dolls around him do. Drinking is a normal and natural part of the hectic club scene, an accepted accompaniment to the search for sex, fame, and a fast buck. Sidney, after planting dope on the musician, winds up slumped over the bar of one of the clubs. Our immediate moralistic reaction is that he must be getting drunk to quiet an uneasy conscience. Not so. He is actually celebrating his comeback. Surrounded by other members of his slimy trade, he proposes a toast: "To success, the sweetest perfume."

Despite positive reviews, strong performances, and a literate screenplay by Clifford Odets and Ernest Lehman, *Sweet Smell of Success* failed at the box office. Hirayama attributed this to its "completely cynical outlook."[80] The films of the fifties, as another critic said, "tended to be expansive, lavish, and uplifting."[81] *Sweet Smell of Success* was none of these things. Its mood was downbeat, and its characters were unpleasant. The mass audience that enjoyed the bland programming on the new medium of TV shunned it.

Nor were they likely to line up for *The Tarnished Angels* or *Lonelyhearts*, late fifties films with a gloominess about them and a cynical, hard-drinking journalist in them. Based on William Faulkner's novel *Pylon, The Tarnished Angels* (1957) was directed by Douglas Sirk, who once described the characters in his films as being on an "unmerry-go-round."[82] Sirk specialized in family melodramas—what used to be called "weepies"—a profitable, if critically despised, genre. Then, in the sixties, Andrew Sarris and other proponents of the *auteur* theory rediscovered him, placing his pictures as "actually among the most socially self-conscious and covertly 'anti-American' films ever produced by Hollywood."[83]

The Tarnished Angels was designed as a follow-up to *Written on the Wind,* a 1956 hit for Universal International that had the same stars (Robert Stack, Dorothy Malone, and Rock Hudson) and the same producer (Albert Zugsmith), screenwriter (George Zuckerman), and director (Sirk). Although now considered one of Sirk's best films, *The Tarnished Angels* was panned when released.[84] Bosley Crowther of the *New York Times* called it "badly written" and "abominably played," while *Variety* said, "Characters are mostly colorless, given static reading in drawn-out situations, and story line is lacking in punch."[85]

Set in the baroque atmosphere of New Orleans during Mardis Gras, 1932, the film traces the final disintegration of a "family" of aerial barnstormers, The Flying Shumanns—former World War I ace Roger Shumann (Stack), his trick parachutist-wife, LaVerne (Malone), their young son, Jack (Chris Olsen), and their mechanic, Jiggs (Jack Carson). The relationships among the family members are tangled and full of pain. Roger loves death-defying stunts, LaVerne loves Roger, and Jiggs loves LaVerne. In a flashback, we learn that Roger and Jiggs rolled dice to determine which of them would marry the pregnant LaVerne and be Jack's father. LaVerne is woman as object. The grease monkeys at the airport leer whenever she walks past. After Roger smashes up his plane, he barters her—or a few hours of her time—to get another.

Burke Devlin (Hudson), a hard-drinking reporter for the *New Orleans Times-Picayune,* becomes infatuated with these "gypsies of the air." As Devlin eventually confides to LaVerne, he went into journalism because he wanted to be a famous war correspondent like Richard Harding Davis, whom he saw in a newsreel when he was a kid. LaVerne herself ran away from home after seeing Roger's dashing figure on a Liberty bond poster. Both, that is, mistook image for reality and have been paying for it ever since. Sirk characterized Devlin in a 1977 interview as "just a shitty, drab reporter, who is really very pitiful."[86]

Drinking adds color to Devlin's drab existence. In the first of several newsroom scenes, Devlin, a cigarette in his mouth and a pencil behind his ear, is pounding out a yarn about the air show on his typewriter. "Keep it down," the city editor (Phil Harvey) says as he hurries through the newsroom. "We're tight for space." "I'll write it, you cut it," Devlin replies. This stops the editor in his tracks.

Editor: What do you you think that air show is? A cheap, crummy carnival of death. *(He picks up a container of coffee from Devlin's desk, sniffs it, and shoots him a dirty look.)*
Devlin: Did you expect me to spike it with cream?
Editor: No time for me to give you a temperance lecture now.
Devlin: I could tell you an idyll of winged knights jousting with death if I felt you could smell a story the way you smell whiskey.

Devlin then takes the container out of the editor's hand and drinks from it. Alcohol serves as a source of literary inspiration, fuel for his romantic vision of the fliers who zoom their little crates around the race course.

But the vision is unrealistic; the romance, inflated and false. The editor—who, shades of *Come Fill the Cup,* is a reformed drunk—is right to call the air show a "carnival of death." The men associated with it are all doomed or maimed in some way. The starter for the races, Colonel Fineman (Alan Reed), hobbles around on crutches because of injuries suffered in a crash. A pretty-boy flier (Troy Donahue) is killed trying to overtake Roger during a race. Toward the end of the film, Roger tells LaVerne that after this race he will give up flying. Then he takes off in a borrowed plane, and the engine begins to smoke and sputter. The crowd runs out onto the landing strip to get a better view. Roger dies when he crashes into a lake to avoid hitting them.

The Tarnished Angels, as noted German director Rainer Werner Fassbinder said, is "an incredibly pessimistic film," "nothing but an accumulation of defeats."[87] Its plot and imagery emphasize the tragic helplessness of humankind. Roger's final crash, for example, is intercut with shots of Jack watching it from a tiny plane on a carousel. "Let me out! Let me out!" the boy screams, but the carousel just goes round and round.

Mardi Gras furnishes Sirk with some of his starkest and most startling images. The camera frequently cuts away from the main action for glimpses of costumed celebrants—death's-head masks and devil masks and the distorted reflection of a couple kissing in a funhouse mirror. On the ground as in the air, the dance of death dominates.

The characters look for escape in all the usual places—work, sex, drink. After Devlin is fired from the paper for disobedience, he returns to his flat in a Southern Gothic mansion. LaVerne is there, and he breaks out two glasses and a bottle. The more they drink, the closer they draw to each other.

> **Devlin:** You better go easy on this wine,
> **LaVerne:** No, I, I got to talk. I want to. Tomorrow night the show moves on. Heaven knows when I'll be able to talk to anyone like I'm talking to you now.
> **Devlin:** A few more drinks, and I'd tell you how much I'm gonna miss you.
> **LaVerne:** Tell me. Please, tell me how much. I've forgotten how it feels to be missed.

Just as they are about to kiss, a man in a death's-head mask bursts in from a party next door, destroying the mood of tenderness and the chance for connection.

Lonelyhearts (1958) is another picture with a *film noir* sensibility. Producer Dore Schary, who adapted it from Nathanael West's impressively grim novel *Miss Lonelyhearts*, knew that films with sad endings often don't do well at the box office, and so tagged a happy ending onto his.[88] It convinced no one. Critics found the ending too pat under the circumstances, and audiences never bothered to find it at all.

Presented initially as a social tool, drinking plays an important symbolic role in the film. In the opening scene, aspiring writer Adam White (Montgomery Clift) joins Florence Shrike (Myrna Loy) at a table in Delahanty's, a "newshawk's pub." Adam is there to ask her husband, the feature editor of the *Chronicle*, for a job. As they settle down to wait for him to get off work, Adam orders a ginger ale—"on the rocks." Florence already has a drink in front of her.

> **Florence:** Did you ever try Cinzano? It isn't strong, but it's enough to relax you.
> **Adam:** It's embarrassing. I think I'm allergic to alcohol. Every so often I try to drink, but it makes me sick. . . . I don't know. God must have had a very careless worker on the assembly line when I came through.
> **Florence:** Perhaps the most careful one.

Adam's allergy to alcohol—a notion derived from AA ideology— marks him as innocent and pure. He is especially innocent and pure when compared to Bill Shrike (Robert Ryan), who, on arriving at Delahanty's, bellows, "Charlie, a double of the usual stomach-lining destroyer." A bitter cynic, Shrike hires Adam to write an advice-to-the-lovelorn column not because he likes him, but because he wants to corrupt him. "I know these good men," he tells his wife. "He's been good because there's no incentive to be bad. I'm intimate with the type."

At first, Adam laughs with his office mates at the letters that come to Miss Lonelyhearts from "Sick of It All" and "Concerned" and "So Unhappy," but then the pathetic pleas for advice begin to get to him. When his girlfriend, Justy Sargent (Dolores Hart), objects that he is taking the letters too seriously, he says: "What kind of crazy world is it where if you try to help somebody you're an oddball? Is it a sin to feel? Is do-gooder a dirty name?"

Shrike, of course, has the name of a predatory bird, certain species of which impale their prey on thorns to tear it. He continually tears at Adam's idealism, his belief in love and kindness. "The people who write these letters are fakers, like the rest of the human race," Shrike claims in one of his typical diatribes. "Cast your eye on our own daily bulletin of man's doings. Despair, deceit, duplicity, debasement recorded in headlines from Moscow to Minneapolis, from Cracow to Caracas. . . . People are animals, fakes, frauds, face it."

There is plenty in the film to support Shrike's brutal outlook. All the male-female relationships, for example, are flawed, characterized by dishonesty and disillusionment. Shrike tortures his wife over an adulterous affair she had ten years ago. Adam's father is in prison for shooting to death his wife and her boyfriend after catching them in bed. And Adam himself betrays Justy with Fay Doyle (Maureen Stapleton), a slattern who writes to Miss Lonelyhearts about her loveless marriage.

Consumed by guilt over this sexual lapse—a mini-version of the Biblical fall—Adam goes on a drinking spree. "You are right," he admits to Shrike at Delahanty's. "People are fakes and frauds, and, you know what, I lead the parade."

Shrike: You made a phone call.
Adam: I did. Also, I had a visitor.
Shrike: A lady who needed help?
Adam: So she said, but she didn't.
Shrike: And now your conscience grips you in an iron hand.

Adam: Hmm-hmm. And that's why I'm drinking, to release the iron grip.
Shrike (*sardonically*): The road to hell.
Adam (*to the bartender*): One more for the road.

Adam gets drunk, assaults a colleague, and then staggers out into the night. Shrike is triumphant. "The fortress is crumbled, the walls have been breached," he gloats. "Adultery, violence, and drunkeness have won the day."

The film doesn't end there, however. It continues for another half-hour during which everyone has his or her problems miraculously resolved. As critics attested, the happy ending lacks all credibility.[89] The hurts the characters have inflicted on each other seem far too deep to simply brush away. Which only goes to show, I suppose, that even if you don't believe in heaven, you can still believe in hell.

8

Happy Hour

He was the modern type of journalist . . . quick, efficient and direct. He was the type who did the job first and relaxed afterward.

—Maj Sjöwall and Per Walhöö, *The Man Who Went Up in Smoke*

In the late sixties and early seventies, researchers began speculating that men drink heavily in order to "hide self-perceptions of weakness, that their drinking represents a reaction against feelings of psychological dependency on others."[1] Films had proposed something of the same sort a whole decade earlier. *While the City Sleeps, Sweet Smell of Success, The Tarnished Angels,* and *Lonelyhearts*—all late fifties films—portrayed heavy drinking as a sign of modern man's alienation and pain. The characters in these downbeat stories drink to fortify their crumbling sense of self, to compensate for the human condition. They are fragile, neurotic creatures living on the edge of madness and death.

This existential portrayal of heavy drinking continued into the sixties with *The Luck of Ginger Coffey* (1964), a joint Hollywood-Canadian production shot in Montreal. Bleak images of the city in winter combined with the nightscapes and chiaroscuro of classic *film noir* to set a grim tone that critics equated with realism.[2] Adapted by Brian Moore from his novel, the film starred Robert Shaw as thirty-nine-year-old Ginger, who has struggled to make ends meet since immigrating from Ireland with his wife and teenage daughter. Ginger's oft-repeated motto, "Where there's life, there's hope," can't quite disguise his increasing desperation. Valuing himself more highly than anyone else does, he is too proud to take, or at least hold, the small jobs for which he is actually qualified.

One such job is as a proofreader for a newspaper. Although he believes the managing editor has promised to promote him to reporter soon, Ginger is a mere cog in the corporate machinery. "Tonight you become a proofreader," a drunken co-worker named Fox (Powry Thomas) says. "You're just a damn galley slave from now on." The bitterest of the proofreaders who gather at the Eagle Tavern every night, Fox walks with a limp, an outward symbol of the psychic wounds that a large, impersonal society inevitably inflicts on most of its members. Alcohol serves two contradictory functions for him—not only is it an anesthetic, but it is also a source of insight into the painful truths about life and work Ginger is so eager to deny.

The newspaper production process becomes a metaphor for the deadening, mechanical routine of modern existence. While the proofreaders bend over galley proof after galley proof, printers sharing the warehouse-like space with them bang on pages of type with mallets and rollers. The production process is rushed, noisy, dehumanizing. Yet Bosley Crowther of the *New York Times* enjoyed this part of the film. "As a newspaperman," he wrote in his review, "I like especially the atmosphere of the newspaper plant that is the scene of a lot of the action."[3] Crowther seemed not to realize how tormented the atmosphere was or what the torment might imply about the era. The proofreaders aren't at all like the carefree newspaper drunks of thirties films. They are paralyzed and impotent, caught in the vise of economic necessity. After work, they get drunk, but there is no release in their drunkenness, only further degradation.

Despite the occasional well-turned-out drama, such as *The Luck of Ginger Coffey*, the sixties weren't the most auspicious decade for newspaper films, perhaps because the real world supplied newspaper drama enough with the Vietnam War, political assassinations, and urban race riots. A somewhat representative example of the genre in this period was Samuel Fuller's *Shock Corridor* (1963) in which an undercover reporter investigating a murder in an insane asylum is attacked by nymphomaniacs. The following year brought another exploitation film, *Black Like Me,* in which a white reporter posing as a black to investigate race relations in the deep South hitches rides with people who quiz him about his sex life. There were also comedies on the order of *Critic's Choice* (1963) in which a critic debates the ethics of reviewing his wife's play; *Quick, Before It Melts* (1965) in which two New York newsmen study Antarctica; and *The Ghost and Mr. Chicken* (1966) in which a shy reporter played by Don Knotts—whose comic talent resides mainly in the fact that he looks like he suffers from a glandular disorder—solves a twenty-year-old crime to become a hero.

Alcoholism films underwent an even more drastic change in the sixties than newspaper films did. The decade marked the end of what many scholars consider the classic period of the genre, a span stretching from 1945–62, or from *The Lost Weekend* to *Days of Wine and Roses*, and defined by the presentation of Alcoholics Anonymous as an option for treatment.[4] Thereafter, the topic of problem drinking was steadily usurped by TV, supplying plots for soap operas, doctor shows, and network movies of the week. *Days of Wine and Roses* itself was adapted from a TV drama.[5]

None of this meant, however, that drinking or drunkenness disappeared from films, only that habitual drunkenness ceased to be portrayed there in medical terms. Films still pictured routine social drinking in bars and restaurants and still had a special affinity for theatrical drunk scenes. In fact, the sixties were bracketed by two films, *Inherit the Wind* (1960) and *Gaily, Gaily* (1969), that offered dynamic portrayals of the hard-drinking journalist.

Inherit the Wind, based on a play by Jerome Lawrence and Robert E. Lee, is a thinly disguised version of the Scopes "Monkey Trial" held in 1925 in the hill town of Dayton, Tennessee. John T. Scopes, a young high school teacher, volunteered to be the test case challenging a state statute that made it unlawful to "teach any theory that denies the story of the divine creation of man as taught by the Bible."[6] Featuring Clarence Darrow for the defense and the great Chautauqua orator and former presidential candidate William Jennings Bryan for the prosecution, the trial was ballyhooed in the press as a contest between Darwin and the Bible, scientific progress and ignorant superstition.

The real-life prototypes are given fictional names in the film: Scopes is called Bertram T. Cates (Dick York); Darrow, Henry Drummond (Spencer Tracy); and Bryan, Matthew Harrison Brady (Frederick March). H. L. Mencken, who reported the trial for the *Baltimore*

Sun, becomes E. K. Hornbeck (Gene Kelly). *Variety* remarked in its review that a "good measure of the film's surface bite" was contributed by Kelly in one of his few straight dramatic roles.[7]

An admirer once described Mencken as "omnibibulous," meaning he drank everything.[8] Although Hornbeck is shown drinking in only one brief scene—when he pours shots for Drummond and himself from a Prohibition-era hip flask—he gives the impression of drinking a lot more. That is because he displays throughout the film other characteristics that had come to be associated on the screen with the hard-drinking journalist: the hat worn at a decadent angle, the air of world-weary cynicism, the readiness with a wisecrack. For example, attending a camp meeting reverberating with shouts to the glory of God, he asks in his smart-alecky fashion, "Whatever happened to silent prayer?"

Like his cynical wit, his flask marks Hornbeck as a freethinker. The film seems initially to side with his progressive outlook, giving him many of the best lines. In the closing moments, however, its enthusiasm for his brand of urban sophistication cools, and Drummond denounces him in a surprisingly bitter speech:

> You have no meaning. You're like a ghost pointing an empty sleeve and smirking at everything people feel or want or struggle for. I pity you. . . . Isn't there anything? What touches you, what warms you? Every man has a dream. What do you dream about? What, what do you need? You don't need anything, do you—people, love, an idea just to cling to? You poor slob. You're all alone. When you go to your grave, there'll be nobody to pull the grass up over your head, nobody to mourn you, nobody to give a damn. You're all alone.

Critics hailed *Inherit the Wind* not only as "rousing" entertainment, but also as a film of ideas.[9] Stanley Kramer, its producer-director, was known in the fifties and sixties for social-problem films, including *The Men* (1950), *The Defiant Ones* (1958), *On the Beach* (1959), *Judgment at Nuremberg* (1961), and *Ship of Fools* (1965). *Inherit the Wind,* following close on the heels of the McCarthy era, was "very much an allegory of its time," an argument for the right of the individual to think and speak and choose for himself.[10] Yet the film ultimately betrays its own message. After putting Hornbeck in his place, Drummond weighs a volume of Darwin in one hand and the Bible in the other, and then walks out of the courtroom with both books tucked under his arm while an a capella voice sings "The Battle Hymn of the Republic." It is a perfect illustration of how mainstream films operate—how they often create narrative closure without actually resolving contradictions, how they visually reconcile what is ideologically irreconcilable.

Gaily, Gaily, coming at the end of the sixties, is a less cautious film than *Inherit the Wind,* reflecting the psychedelic atmosphere of experimentation and permissiveness the decade unleashed. This is most apparent in the film's bawdy humor. "Do you know what a sex maniac does?" a city editor asks at one point, and answers: "A good sex maniac sells newspapers." Such a joke might have been censored under the old Motion Picture Production Code, established in 1934 to set standards of proper decorum on the screen and just one of many traditional forms of authority swept away in the sixties.

Adapted from Ben Hecht's memoirs of his adventures as a cub reporter in the teens, *Gaily, Gaily* received mixed reviews. *Variety* called it "a lushly staged, handsomely produced, largely unfunny comedy."[11] On the other hand, Vincent Canby of the *New York Times* described it as "a movie of great and exuberant charm," though he added that it was based on "all sorts of questionable premises," including that "hard-drinking newspapermen are lovable."[12]

Francis Sullivan (Brian Keith with a brogue) has the unusual distinction of representing two hard-drinking stereotypes at once, the drunken Irishman and the newspaper drunk. Even *Variety* found him endearing. "He is the Irish soul of any good city room," it said, "a hustling deadline bard and philosopher, devious and cynical."[13] Young Ben Harvey (Beau Bridges), as Hecht is renamed for the film, becomes his protegé on the *Chicago Journal.* In addition to the tricks of yellow journalism, Sullivan introduces Ben to the seductive world of the saloon.

The extended scene in which Sullivan leads Ben on a drinking spree imparts several different meanings to drinking and drunkenness. After Ben drinks his first-ever schooner of beer in one gulp, Sullivan says, "Done like a man," as if drinking were a rite of manhood. He then pulls the cork from a whiskey bottle and tosses it over his shoulder, remarking, "Well, we won't be needing that any longer." It is a comic gesture, but one with anti-social overtones, suggestions of licentiousness and disorder. Later when Ben asks, "Mr. Sullivan, have I had enough yet?" Sullivan peers into his eyes for a moment. "Ah no," he responds, "there's still the soul of innocence lurking down there somewhere." Sullivan, though billed as a libertine, acts on the old, moralistic assumption that alcohol is corrupting. His cure for Ben's excessive naiveté is to drown it in booze.

By the time they leave the saloon, Sullivan and Ben are both rubber-legged, but still coherent. They stumble down a shadowy, deserted street—it might easily be one of the streets of existential dread found in *film noir*—discussing their reasons for getting plastered.

> **Ben:** What are we after?
> **Sullivan:** We ain't after anything. We're running away from something.
> **Ben:** What are we running away from?
> **Sullivan:** The truth, the entire truth. You see, none of it is the way they told it to us, lad, not one bloody word of it.

So drinking doesn't function only, or even mostly, as a measure of masculinity. It functions mostly as a means of escape. Men drink because they are scared and lonely and can't bear the truth, because they want to blot out consciousness of their actual circumstances. The bottle represents regression, a glass teat on which they hang for comfort.

Gaily, Gaily never shapes its various explanations of drinking into a unified theory or pattern, and director Norman Jewison never intended it to. The film simply absorbed some of the conflicting notions of drinking circulating through the culture and then squeezed them back out. In one scene, drinking disinhibits Ben sexually; in another, it renders Sullivan impotent. In one scene, drinking is treated as an answer to man's existential dilemmas; in another, it is treated as a joke. No matter. The journalist, as Hollywood entered the seventies, was still a drunk.

In 1974, the third version of the seminal newspaper film *The Front Page*, now directed by Billy Wilder and starring Walter Matthau as editor Walter Burns and Jack Lemmon as reporter Hildy Johnson, was introduced. The journalistic couple of the seventies, though, wasn't this unscrupulous pair, or even Clark Kent and Lois Lane, lifted out of comic books in 1978 into *Superman: The Movie*. No, it was

Bob Woodward and Carl Bernstein—sometimes known collectively as "Woodstein"—the young *Washington Post* reporters who took the lead in uncovering the Watergate scandal that eventually wrecked the Nixon White House. Their own account of how they got the story, *All the President's Men*, became a national best-seller and the basis for a critically acclaimed, commercially successful 1976 film.

But even before *All the President's Men* ever hit the bookstands or made it to the screen, the investigative reporter had achieved a certain celebrity because of highly publicized exposés of the Vietnam War, the nursing-home industry, prison conditions, and Wall Street.[14] "Armed only with his conscience and his wits," Robert Daley intoned in *New York* magazine in 1973, the investigative reporter "makes whole governments tremble, not to mention mere politicians and other millionaires. He is the glamour boy of journalism—in a country suddenly without glamour anywhere." Watergate just further confirmed his status as "the new American folk hero."[15] In 1978, four years after President Nixon resigned in disgrace, columnist Tom Wicker wrote that the investigative reporter had inherited "the role played at various times in the American psyche by so many robust earlier heroes—Paul Revere, the watchman of liberty; the Western sheriff singlehandedly guaranteeing law and order; Lindbergh challenging the Atlantic in the name of progress—the fearless, fighting individual standing up for the many, daring the gods, alert on the barricades."[16]

All the President's Men, both the book and the film, benefited from this sort of mythologization of the investigative reporter, as well as contributed considerably to it. Historian William E. Leuchtenburg called the film "a significant moment in the elevation of the American journalist to mythical status."[17] Michael Schudson, author of *Watergate in American Memory,* said it "ennobled investigative reporting and made of journalists modern heroes."[18]

Classic newspaper films, such as *The Front Page, Five Star Final,* and *Nothing Sacred,* are largely scornful of the press. *All the President's Men* is just the opposite—in Leuchtenburg's words, "a milestone in the process of exalting the press while demonizing government."[19] Woodward, played by Robert Redford, and Bernstein, played by Dustin Hoffman, diligently follow the established routines of responsible journalism in their pursuit of the Watergate story. They are professional, dogged, serious. In fact, as Seth Cagin and Philip Dray pointed out in their *Hollywood Films of the Seventies*, the film derives comic relief from "the repudiation of newspaper-hero characterstics, which usually involve misogyny and a gin-soaked universal view."[20] If Woodward and Bernstein bear any resemblance to their hard-drinking, cynical counterparts in thirties films, it is that they seem to come alive only when on the job.

But unlike their predecessors, Woodward and Bernstein aren't cynics, and they don't touch alcohol. Their total abstinence is remarkable in a genre where a surprisingly large number of films begin in barrooms, not newsrooms. What does it mean that *All the President's Men,* "the most popular and honored picture about journalism of modern times," leaves out some of the traditional basic ingredients of the newspaper-film genre—the newspaper bar, the newspaper drunk, the office bottle?[21] What does it mean that *All the President's Men* presents its reporter heroes and their editors and colleagues as stone-cold sober?

Clues to the answer may lie in sociologist Joseph R. Gusfield's essay "Passage to Play: Rituals of Drinking Time in American Society," summarized in a previous chapter.[22] Gusfield noted that ever since the emergence of industrial organization in the 1830s, work has been an area of sobriety, and play an area of permissible insobriety. To mix the two areas—permit drinking to occur during worktime—threatens bureaucratic order and factory discipline.[23] The fact that the journalists in *All the President's Men* don't drink on the job suggests that they accept the regimentation of modern life.

Instead of frequenting bars, as those roguish reporters in old newspaper films did, Woodward and Bernstein twice drop into a fast-food joint. On both occasions, they discuss their investigation between bites of mass-produced burgers and fries. The atmosphere is very different from that of a newspaper bar—less masculine and cozy, more anonymous. Woodward and Bernstein nonetheless appear quite at home sitting there in their little plastic booth.

And why not? The brightly lit but impersonal atmosphere of the fast-food place pervades the *Washington Post* as well. Film histories have described with awe the effort and expense—$200,000—to which director Alan J. Pakula went to construct an exact facsimile of the *Post* newsroom on two sound stages in Burbank, California.[24] He ordered nearly 200 desks from the same company that supplied the *Post* and even shipped in 270 tons of trash from the newspaper's waste baskets. The film would win an Academy Award for set decoration, but despite the great pains taken to achieve authenticity, the newsroom could be just any large office, with metal desks congregated in the middle of the floor and glass cubicles for the managers running along the walls. The newsroom doesn't reflect a romantic notion of reporting—the belief, implicit in classic newspaper films, that the best reporters are also the most drunk and insubordinate. Rather, it reflects the rigid, hierarchal organization of corporate America.

To associate the Watergate-era *Post* with corporate ideology may seem odd to anyone who remembers the Nixon administration's vitriolic attacks on the press for being too liberal, too effete, too negative.[25] *All the President's Men* itself contains news footage of White House press secretary Ronald Ziegler denouncing the *Post* for its Watergate coverage. But liberal and conservative are relative terms, and even at the height of Watergate, when the special prosecutor was subpoenaing White House tapes and the House Judiciary Committee was considering articles of impeachment, the core values of American corporate capitalism were never in danger of being abandoned by the press or Hollywood or the public both serve. If anything, all the controversy and struggle may have led to a kind of instinctive defense of those values.

All the President's Men defends the establishment by symbolically restoring parental authority, eroded by the intense generational conflict of the late sixties and early seventies, the famous "Generation Gap." The film identifies Woodward and Bernstein as belonging to the same side in the conflict as the twenty-something Republicans working for the Committee to Re-elect the President (CREEP). At one point Woodward even admits, to Bernstein's comic surprise, that he himself is a registered Republican.

Members of this generation all need careful mentoring. When Woodward and Bernstein go to interview CREEP treasurer Hugh Sloan (Stephen Collins), and later the bookkeeper (Jane Seymour) for CREEP finance chairman Maurice Stans, they find young people who have been abused by their symbolic fathers, whose love and trust have been betrayed. Sloan sits slumped in his living room with the lights out, while the bookkeeper is afraid to tell the dark family secrets she knows.

The reporters are more fortunate in their choice of fathers. Their editors—Ben Bradlee (Jason Robards in an Academy Award-winning performance), Howard Simons (Martin Balsam), and Harry Rosenfeld (Jack Warden)—are, as Thomas E. Leonard observed, "godly and wise."[26] Bradlee in particular warns the boys when they step out of line, motivates them when they feel discouraged, and stands up for them when they get criticized. He is the father they—and the country—need.

A scene near the end of the film illustrates how homey imagery is used to validate traditional authority. Woodward and Bernstein bang on Bradlee's door in the middle of the night. He answers it in his bathrobe and invites them inside. Fearing the house has been bugged, the reporters urge him to come out to the front yard, where they catch him up on their investigation. Bradlee then gives his own profane version of fatherly advice:

> You know the results of the latest Gallup poll? Half the country never even heard of the word "Watergate." Nobody gives a shit. *He pauses, looking thoughtfully at the reporters.* You guys are probably pretty tired. Well, you should be. Go on home. Get a nice hot bath. Rest up—15 minutes. Then get your asses back in gear. We're under a lot of pressure, you know, and you put us there. Nothing's riding on this except, uh, the First Amendment of the Constitution, freedom of the press, and maybe the future of the country. Not that any of that matters, but if you guys fuck up again, I'm going to get mad. Good night.

The scene is filled with **dark**ness and paranoia, but underlying it is a certain sense of normalcy—home, family, the gruff affection between fathers and sons. Bradlee's authority is defined in terms of these old-fashioned American values. Small wonder his power, though as absolute as Nixon's, seems less ominous.

Whatever its contribution to the heroic myths of journalism, *All the President's Men* is actually an ideologically conservative film. Woodward and Bernstein may topple a government, but they aren't revolutionaries. They believe in authority and rules and the corporate power structure. They respect and defer to their bosses. And, of course, they don't drink while working.

Looking back in 1985 on the success of *All the President's Men,* Bob Woodward, himself by then an editor at the *Post,* said the film was an anomaly. "People are not going to look at the press normally as their friend," he explained. "My feeling always is that we're outsiders. The period of the mid-70s may have been a little different, but it wasn't a natural situation."[27] Actually, not even that period was totally exempt from negative films about the press. The very same year *All the President's Men* was released, so was *Network*, a prophetic and venomous satire of TV news that went on to win four Academy Awards. Peter Finch received one for best actor posthumously, Faye Dunaway for best actress, Beatrice Straight for best supporting actress, and Paddy Chayefsky for best original screenplay.

At the time *Network* was released, the line between news shows and show business was fast disappearing. Since the early seventies, local stations had been hiring consultants, so-called "show doctors," to tell them how to goose up audience ratings for the news.[28] The result was yet another variation on the old theme of sensationalism— "a little hit 'em in the guts there, a little soft shoe here, a little sex, a little blood, a taste of something out of the ordinary."[29] *Network* parodies this trend, with Diana Christensen (Dunaway), chief of programming for the United Broadcasting System, turning the evening news into a kind of carnival. The main attraction is Howard Beale (Finch), a fifty-eight-year-old anchorman who is suffering a mental breakdown. Rather than get him help, Christensen markets him as "the Mad Prophet of the Airwaves," "a magnificent messianic figure inveighing against the hypocrisies of our time"—most of which, incidentally, involve TV and its narcoleptic effect on viewers. "Television is not the truth ," Beale shouts in a typical diatribe.

> Man, you'll never get the truth from us. . . . We'll tell you any shit you want to hear. We deal in illusions, man, none of it is true. But you people sit there night after night, day after day, all ages, colors, creeds. We're all you know. You're beginning to believe the illusions we're spinning here. You're beginning to think that the tube is reality, and your own lives are unreal. You do whatever the tube tells you. You dress like the tube, eat like the tube, raise your children like the tube. . . . This is mass madness, you maniacs.

When Beale's ratings eventually falter, threatening the profits of UBS, management orders him assassinated. "It'll make a helluva kickoff show for the new season," Christensen says.

Both Chayefsky and *Network*'s director, Sidney Lumet, had learned their respective crafts working in TV in the fifties. "Everybody keeps talking about the brilliant satiric nature of *Network*,"

Lumet pointed out. "To me and Paddy it wasn't satire at all, it was sheer reportage. Everything you saw in *Network* had happened to either Paddy or myself—except for the actual shooting of Howard Beale on the air, and let's just give that a couple of more years. That is not out of the realm of possibility."[30] Executives along Manhattan's "Network Row" disagreed. "It's a piece of crap," a vice president at NBC fumed after seeing the film. "It had nothing to do with our business."[31] At least one reviewer objected to it almost as strongly. Richard Schickel of *Time* magazine found the plot "so crazily preposterous that even in post-Watergate America—where we know that bats can get loose in the corridors of power—it is just impossible to accept."[32]

As in earlier films that take a humorously cynical view of the press, including *Nothing Sacred* and *Roxie Hart*, *Network* begins with a drunk scene. Even before the opening credits, we see Beale and Max Schumacher (William Holden), head of the news division at UBS, weaving down a Manhattan street at night. Because of low ratings, Beale was fired that day as anchorman, the event that precipitates his breakdown. A voice-over narrator explains that after the firing, the two old friends "got properly pissed," or drunk. The implication is that drinking reaffirms male bonds, and that drunkenness is an appropriate response to career setbacks.

But if alcohol is portrayed as having the power to help one forget current misery, it is also portrayed as having the power to help one recall former glory. Right there on the street, Beale and Schumacher reminisce about their role in the early golden years of TV. "Anyway," Schumacher recounts, pausing often to let out a drunken laugh,

> they're building the lower level of the George Washington Bridge. We were doing a remote from there, and nobody told me. So after 7 in the morning, I get a call, "Where the hell are you? You're supposed to be on the George Washington Bridge." So I jump out of bed, throw a raincoat over my pajamas, run down the stairs, run out into the street, and hail a cab: "Take me to the middle of the George Washington Bridge." And the cabbie turns around and says, "Don't do it, buddy. You're a young man. You got your whole life ahead of you."

The world implied by this anecdote is very different from the world of the film. Social relationships hadn't yet become predominantly predatory. There was still a place for fellow feeling.

Howard Beale (Peter Finch), the "Mad Prophet of the Airwaves," rants against corporate capitalism in **NETWORK** *(1976), just one of many journalism films that opens with a drunk scene.*

We are dropped into another, darker world by a jump cut from the street to a dimly lit bar. The mood of the drunken journalists has deteriotated. Schumacher stares morosely into his glass, while Beale rests his head on the bar top. Then they begin to talk, and though their conversation is depressing, they exhibit an almost visionary insight into how the modern mass media operate. It is as if all the alcohol has heightened their consciousness, afforded them a degree of understanding unavailable to the sober.

Beale: I'm going to kill myself.
Schumacher: Oh shit, Howard.
Beale: I'm going to blow my brains out right on the air, right in the middle of the 7 o'clock news.
Schumacher: Get a helluva rating, I guarantee you that. Fifty share, easy.
Beale: You think so?
Schumacher: Sure. We can make a series out of it. Hell, why limit ourselves? "Execution of the Week."
Beale: Terrorists.
Schumacher: I love it. Suicides, assassinations, mad bombers, Mafia hit men, automobile smash-ups. "The Death Hour, great Sunday night show for the whole family." Wipe fucking Disney right off the air.

Here is proof of the ancient principle, *In vino veritas* (In wine there is truth). As they sit at the bar embellishing their concept of "The Death Hour," Beale and Schumacher describe many of the crazy things that eventually happen in the film: Beale announcing on the air his intention to kill himself; Christensen adding a soothsayer to the broadcast; UBS contracting with a terrorist group, the Ecumenical Liberation Army, for exclusive footage of its bank robberies and assassinations. Unlike *All the President's Men*, which suggests that the truth is hard to find, *Network* suggests that it can found in a bottle. Beale and Schumacher may be blind drunk, but they are far-seeing.

9

Mixed Drinks

For art to exist, for any sort of aesthetic activity to exist, a certain physiological precondition is indispensable: intoxication.

—Friedrich Nietzsche

There have always been bad films, but as psychiatrist and film aficionado Harvey Roy Greenberg pointed out, the bad films of the 1980s seemed bad in a whole new way. He dubbed them "McMovies," explaining that they were the cinematic equivalent of fast food—brightly packaged, familiar tasting, and full of empty calories. He attributed the emergence of McMovies and semi-McMovies, which now constitute, in his opinion, the bulk of Hollywood's output, to a "relentless mercantilism," an "unslakeable obsession with profit over value."[1]

A sequel is the quintessential McMovie, having no greater goal usually than to reprise a big payday, and the eighties were the decade of the sequel. Among the many hit films that spawned sequels were *Superman, Star Wars, Rocky, Rambo, Raiders of the Lost Ark, Beverly Hills Cop, Halloween, Friday the 13th, Mad Max,* and *Lethal Weapon.* After a while, it even stopped seeming odd that films had numbers as well as names: *Missing in Action II, The Karate Kid Part III, Death Wish 4.*

If Hollywood was infected with greed, it was no worse infected than the rest of society.[2] The eighties were characterized by an overwhelming interest in doing business and making money. Oil prices plunged, the stock market soared, and yippies became yuppies, young urban professionals who adopted, as Laurence Shames put it, "the curatorial approach to their possessions."[3] There was the status pen (Mont Blanc) the status loafer (Gucci), the status panties (Hanro), the status tennis racket (Prince Custom), even the status water (Evian). The eighties fashion for owning and consuming resembled the giddy acquisitiveness of the fifties, a time when the United States contained 7 percent of the world's population, but owned 75 percent of its cars and appliances.[4] In fact, film scholar William J. Palmer only half-jokingly suggested that the eighties should be called *The Fifties II*.[5]

The resemblance between the fifties and the eighties went beyond rampant materialism to include anti-communist paranoia. Ronald Reagan, a former film star and old Cold War soldier, was re-elected president. Following his ideological lead, Hollywood released in the eighties an attack force of muscular military fantasies, from *Uncommon Valor* to *Red Dawn* to *Rambo: First Blood Part II* to *Top Gun*.[6] The latter, described by *Time* magazine as "a 110-minute commercial for the Navy," was the highest-grossing film of 1986, earning about $175 million.[7]

Not that there weren't some eighties films that eschewed patriotic gore and John Wayne heroics, that repudiated the Decaturish phi-

*The 1980s brought a spate of foreign-correspondent films, including **THE YEAR OF LIVING DANGEROUSLY** (1983) in which Mel Gibson plays an Australian correspondent who tries to make sense of Indonesia from a stool in the hotel bar.*

losophy of "my country right or wrong," that refused to regard war with fondness or nostalgia. Prominent examples were *The Year of Living Dangerously, The Killing Fields, Under Fire,* and *Salvador.* These films were part of a subgenre that critic Marek Haltof summed up as "the adventures of Western journalists in countries experiencing political and economic turmoil."[8] The journalists may think of themselves as world-weary and cynical, incapable of being surprised, but their brittle shell of cynicism proves small protection against the atrocities they witness—death squads and body dumps and grinding Third World poverty. Most retreat to the hotel bar. A few, however, cross the line between observer and participant, and become involved in the conflicts they were sent to cover.

One such is photojournalist Richard Boyle (James Woods), the protagonist of writer-director Oliver Stone's *Salvador* (1986). At an embassy cocktail party Boyle, a lowlife whose conscience has finally been pricked, denounces U.S. officials for incubating the plague of death squads afflicting Central America:

> You were the ones who trained Major Max in the Police Academy in Washington. You were the ones who trained Jose Madrano and Rene Chacon. You taught them how to torture and how to kill, and then you sent them here, And what did Chacon give us? He gave us the Mano Blanco. I mean what are the death squads but the brainchild of the CIA? But you'll run with them because they're anti-Moscow. You let them close down the universities. You let them wipe out the best minds in the country. You let them kill whoever they want. You let them wipe out the Catholic Church. You let them do it all because they aren't commies. . . . You have created Major Frankenstein.

Incidentally, *Salvador* was financed by Hemdale, a fledging British film company. Hollywood studios had rejected Stone's script as "anti-American."[9]

In the mid-1980s Dana Bullen, executive director of the World Press Freedom Committee and former foreign editor of the *Washington Star*, remarked that the typical foreign correspondent was no longer the "here-today gone-tomorrow, hard-drinking adventurer" often featured in popular novels and Hollywood films. "Many have graduate degrees in international subjects," Bullen said, "and have learned the languages of the areas they will cover. In more and more cases, they are well-trained, culturally aware, sensitive students of the people and situations they will write about."[10] But if fictional foreign correspondents aren't the equals in education or cultural sensitivity to their real-world counterparts, neither are they quite the thrill freaks or drunken xenophobic brutes Bullen implied. Even early examples of the subgenre—Rudyard Kipling's 1899 novel *The Light That Failed* and various short stories by Richard Harding Davis and Stephen Crane—allowed an occasional journalist-adventurer at least a modicum of ironic self-awareness. Over the next century, the bloodiest in history, fictional correspondents would acquire deeper doubts about the morality of war and the glamor of their profession.

The Light That Failed is the bombastic story of Dick Heldar, a young painter who, after ten lean years of struggle for the sake of his art, goes as a freelance illustrator to the Sudan, where a British army is fighting its way across the desert to relieve Gordon at Khartoum. "There was a row," Dick simply says, "so I came." In an age that believed "the test and privilege of manhood was not complete . . . until a man had been shot at," no more explanation was needed.[11]

While accompanying the relief column, Dick meets Torpenhow, a seasoned correspondent for the Central Southern Syndicate. "The syndicate did not concern itself greatly with criticisms of attack and the like," Kipling writes in the half-smirky, half-preachy tone he uses whenever discussing the press. "It supplied the masses, and all it demanded was picturesqueness and abundance of detail; for there is more joy in England over a soldier who insubordinately steps out of the square to rescue a comrade than over twenty generals slaving even to baldness at the gross details of transport and commissariat."[12] On Torpenhow's recommendation, Dick is hired to draw for the syndicate. He is now a full-fledged member of the "New and Honorable Fraternity of war correspondents, who all possess the inalienable right of doing as much work as they can and getting as much for it as Providence and their owners please. To these things are added in time, if the brother be worthy, the power of glib speech that neither man nor woman can resist when a meal or bed is in question, the eye of a horse-coper, the skill of a cook, the constitution of an ostrich, and an infinite adaptability to all circumstances."[13]

Dick and Torpenhow grow extremely close, "for they ate from the same dish, they shared the same water-bottle, and, most binding of all, their mails went off together."[14] They also endure together the hazards of battle, shedding their non-combatant status with blood-thirsty alacrity when the Mahdi's dervishes break the British square:

> Dick was conscious that somebody had cut him violently across his helmet, that he had fired his revolver into a black, foam-flecked face which forthwith ceased to bear any resemblance to a face, and that Tor-penhow had gone down under an Arab whom he had tried to 'collar low,' and was turning over and over with his captive, feeling for the man's eyes. . . . It was to Torpenhow that Dick turned by instinct. The representative of the Central Syndicate had shaken himself clear of his enemy, and rose, wiping his thumb on his trousers. The Arab, both hands to his forehead, screamed aloud, then snatched up his spear and rushed at Torpenhow, who was panting under shelter of Dick's revolver. Dick fired twice, and the man dropped limply. His upturned face lacked one eye.[15]

After Dick and Torpenhow return to London from the desert, which occurs about forty pages into the novel, the story bogs down. It doesn't pick up again until the last chapter, when Dick goes on "the long trail" one last time.[16] In between, Kipling focuses on Dick's attempt to cope with his new-found success as a painter of military subjects and on his romantic pursuit of Maisie, a cold blonde beauty who causes him nothing but grief. Her presence seems mostly designed to prove the superiority of male friendship to heterosexual love. When Dick, at the height of his fame and artistic powers, goes blind as a result of the sword wound he received in the Sudan, it is Torpenhow, not Maisie, who is there to comfort him in a scene rife with homoerotic overtones: "Torpenhow thrust out a large and hairy paw from the long chair. Dick clutched it tightly, and in half an hour had fallen asleep. Torpenhow withdrew his hand, and, stooping over Dick, kissed him lightly on the forehead, as men do sometimes kiss a wounded comrade in the hour of death, to ease his departure."[17]

Kipling is divided in his opinion of war correspondents. On the one hand, he celebrates the excitement and romance of their job and implicitly praises their courage, perseverance, and esprit de corps. On the other hand, he satirizes them as rather ridiculous figures, mere puppets of the home office who suffer all kinds of deprivation and danger for the greater glory of their employers:

> With the soldiers sweated and toiled the correspondents for the news-papers, and they were almost as ignorant as their companions. But it

was above all things necessary that England at breakfast should be amused and thrilled and interested, whether Gordon lived or died, or half the British army went to pieces in the sands. The Soudan campaign was a picturesque one, and lent itself to vivid word-painting. Now and again a "Special" managed to get slain—which was not altogether a disadvantage to the paper that employed him—and more often the hand-to-hand nature of the fighting allowed of miraculous escapes which were worth telegraphing home at eighteenpence the word.[18]

One of the correspondents himself acknowledges the contradictions inherent in their work. "Our business—the business for which we draw our money—" he says, "is to do absurd and impossible things— generally with no reason whatever except to amuse the public."[19]

Stephen Crane, author of *The Red Badge of Courage*, added alcohol to this mix in short stories based on his experiences as a correspondent for the *New York World* during the Spanish-American War. In "The Lone Charge of William B. Perkins," the protagonist is a comically inept correspondent from the Midwest whose first battle in Cuba is with some whiskey, while "Virtue in War" features a post-battle debate among three hot, tired, dusty correspondents about mint juleps.[20] "Oh, no, Shackles!" one interrupts another. "Oh, no, you're wrong. The best mint juleps in the world are made right in New York, Philadelphia or Boston. That Kentucky idea is only a tradition."[21]

A friend and colleague of Crane's in Cuba, Richard Harding Davis, continued the identification of war correspondents with hard drinking in "A Derelict," a story from 1902 concerning two disparate reporters. One is Keating of the Consolidated Press Syndicate, a "mighty corporation" that daily fed, in a dry, objective writing style, the appetite of 700 papers for news. "We do not want descriptive writing," the manager of the syndicate was always reminding its correspondents. "We do not pay you to send us pen-pictures or prose-poems. We want facts, all the facts, and nothing but the facts." Keating had "worn the collar of the Consolidated Press" for so long that he had no enthusiasm or illusions left. "A board meeting—a mine disaster—an Indian uprising—it was all one to Keating. He collected facts and his salary." When assigned to cover the war in Cuba, he goes grudgingly, though it is "the chance of a lifetime."[22]

The other reporter is Charlie Channing, "a sort of derelict" who has worked for "pretty nearly every paper in the country." Unlike Keating, Channing is a "genius" at descriptive writing. "I'm a better news-gatherer than Charlie," a reporter who once worked with him on a New York paper says. "I can collect facts and I can put them together well enough, too, [but] I can't see the things that Charlie sees."[23] Channing is nonetheless stuck in Jamaica, broke and without a paper for which to report the war next door. Friends in the press—with the notable exception of Keating, who spitefully offers him a job as stoker on his syndicate's press-boat—try to get him a reporting spot on their papers. No paper will hire him, however, because of his reputation for drunkenness.

But it is Keating, not Channing, who has passed out from drink when the Spanish fleet attempts to run the American blockade of Santiago harbor and the climactic battle of the war is fought. Channing covers for the CP man, filing a sixty-eight-page story, though he himself is wracked by fever and chills. The story, credited to Keating, is celebrated in the States as "the only piece of literature the war has produced." On the strength of it, Keating becomes the star reporter of his syndicate, given choice assignments and honored by fellow reporters at a formal dinner. Channing never reveals his authorship of the great story, but merely has another newspaperman relay to Keating the message, "It's all right."[24]

The ending is, of course, unbelievable, animated by a Victorian gentleman's idea of honor and a sixth-grader's idea of irony. But though early novels and short stories about war correspondents tended to be fatuous, later works in the subgenre exhibited a certain moral complexity. Perhaps the biggest reason for this was the increasingly total, or horrific, nature of war.

George Orwell, in an essay on Kipling, noted that the small, imperialistic wars of the late nineteenth century were hardly wars at all by modern standards.[25] Due courtesy was extended to "the other fellow"; armistices were called to bury the dead; and battles ended at nightfall. To correspondents of the era, war resembled a splendid pageant, with brightly uniformed troops moving in serried ranks, their swords and helmets flashing in the sun.[26]

World War I marked a turning point in the history of warfare. The tank, the airplane, and the machine gun—particularly the machine gun, which "would keep a stream of bullets in the air so dense that no one could walk upright in front of the machine-gunner's position without being hit"—brought mass mechanized killing to the battlefield.[27] "What almost all the soldiers of the First World War . . . tes-

tify to," respected military historian John Keegan said, "is their sense
of littleness, almost of nothingness, of their abandonment in a physical wilderness, dominated by vast impersonal forces from which
even such normalities as the passage of time had been eliminated."[28]

As ugly and futile as World War I was—and soldiers dug enough
trenches during its four years to encircle the globe—it was but a pre-
view of horrors to come: Guernica, the London blitz, Hiroshima, My
Lai. The rising level of violence swept away the old-time glamor of war
correspondence. Just after World War II, Herbert L. Matthews of the
New York Times sighed nostalgically that "the joys of battle and cam-
paigning are, in ever-increasing measure, dissolving into suffering."[29]

Fictional correspondents also reacted with dismay to the mon-
strous new face of war.[30] "Big Belt" Boylan, a correspondent accompanying the Russian army in the World War I-era novel *Red Fleece*,
exclaims: "It's different from anything I knew. It's so damn busi-
nesslike. Something's come over the world. War was more like a pic-
nic before. I never saw it like this. I believe we've gone crazy."[31] In
Scoop by British novelist Evelyn Waugh, who had covered the Italian
invasion of Ethiopia in 1935, the press itself is an extension of the
craziness. As Corker of Universal News confides to Waugh's protagonist, the accidental war correspondent William Boot,

> You know, when I first started in journalism, I used to think that foreign
> correspondents spoke every language under the sun and spent their
> lives studying international conditions. Brother, look at us! On Monday
> afternoon I was in East Sheen breaking the news to a widow of her hus-
> band's death leap with a champion girl cyclist—the wrong widow it
> turned out. Next day the Chief has me in and says, "Corker, you're off
> to Ishmaelia." "Out of town job?" I asked. "East Africa," he said, just like
> that, "pack your traps." "What's the story?" I asked. "Well," he said, "a
> lot of niggers are having a war. I don't see anything in it myself, but the
> other agencies are sending feature men so we've got to do something. . ."
> "What are they having a war about?" I asked. "That's for you to find
> out," he said, but I haven't found out yet. Have you?[32]

While Waugh-like touches of black comedy appear in eighties
films about war correspondents, the novel that probably most fore-
shadows the films is Graham Greene's *The Quiet American*, set in Vietnam during the mid-fifties, when the French were fighting a losing
colonial war against the Vietminh. Its narrator, Fowler, is a middle-
aged correspondent for a London paper who came to the Far East

Photojournalist Russell Price (Nick Nolte) expected to enjoy cheap shrimp, good beer, and nice hotels when he arrived in Nicaragua in **UNDER FIRE** *(1983), but the Sandinista revolution soon destroys the Club Med aspects of his assignment.*

years ago to escape marital problems. He has since gone native, keeping a Vietnamese mistress and hitting the opium pipe. By his own admission, he no longer takes his job seriously. "Once I was interested myself in what for want of a better term they call news," he says. "But grenades had staled on me; they were something listed on the back page of the local paper—so many last night in Saigon, so many in Cholon; they never made the European Press."[33]

Yet Fowler isn't as cynical or broken down as he seems. "We all get involved in a moment of emotion," a French pilot warns him, "and then we can't get out." For Fowler, this moment comes when a terrorist bomb explodes in a noonday crowd in Saigon. He is undone by the carnage—a woman sitting on the ground with what is left of her baby in her lap, the legless torso of a rickshaw driver twitching "like a chicken which has lost its head."[34] Haunted by the image of the mangled baby, Fowler determines to try to prevent future bombings.

In eighties films Western journalists working in underdeveloped countries are confronted with the choice of maintaining their coveted professional cool or getting involved in the political and social struggles going on around them. The dilemma is neatly posed in a scene from *Under Fire* in which Nick Nolte, playing photojournalist Russell Price, shares a jail cell with a Nicaraguan priest who supports the Sandinista rebels.

> **Priest:** Whose side are you on?
> **Price:** I don't take sides. I take pictures.
> **Priest:** No side?
> (*Price shakes his head.*)
> **Priest:** Go home.

Journalists who won't take sides, who remain disengaged, are portrayed in the films as morally corrupt. Their corruption is underlined by their eager appetite for liquor and sex. Here again, Greene's 1955 novel led the way. In the book, when someone in the hotel bar praises an American correspondent's story of Road 66—"What did you call it? Highway to Hell"—the correspondent replies: "Do you think I'd really go near their stinking highway? Stephen Crane could describe a war without seeing one. Why shouldn't I? It is only a damned colonial war anyway. Get me another drink. And then let's go find a girl."[35] The implication is clear and reflects the demonology of the old temperance movement: war may be hell, but drinking only makes it worse.

The first Australian film to be financed and distributed by a Hollywood studio, *The Year of Living Dangerously* (1983) re-creates the ominous political atmosphere of Indonesia in 1965, when both the Communists and Muslims tried to overthrow the government of President Sukarno.[36] Bernard Kalb, who covered Indonesia in the sixties for the *New York Times*, slammed the film as "too superficial," claiming that it "turned out to be a couple of hours of living impatiently with a caricature of a coup attempt." But, of course, the film was never intended as a dissertation on Indonesian politics. Director Peter Weir concentrated primarily on the cultural clash between East and West, with the West represented by the British, American, and Australian correspondents who seem to live in the hotel bar. Even Kalb acknowledged that the film succeeded in capturing their world, "a fraternity spiked with sharp competition for exclusives, small talk, big talk, rivalry, camaraderie."[37]

The newest member of this fraternity is Guy Hamilton (Mel Gibson), a twenty-nine-year-old correspondent sent from Sydney on his first overseas assignment. Billy Kwan, a Eurasian cameraman played by Linda Hunt in a cross-dressing, Oscar-winning performance, takes the inexperienced Guy under his wing. "You supply the words, I'll supply the pictures," he proposes. "I'll be your eyes."[38] Though a dwarf, Billy is ironically the only character of any moral stature in the film. As he leads Guy on a tour of the foul slums of Jakarta, he murmurs, "What then must we do?" repeating a question asked by St. Luke and Tolstoy. Guy gives the typical journalist's answer: "We can't afford to get involved."

About all that really interests the correspondents are their own careers and sex lives. The film emphasizes their indifference to the suffering of the Asian poor through a series of bar scenes. In one such scene, American correspondent Pete Curtis (Michael Murphy) drunkenly teases Guy, who has just scored, with Billy's help, a front-page scoop.

> **Curtis:** Let me ask you something, Hamilton. I've been worried about this ever since you got here. What do you do for sex?
> **Guy:** You worry about that?
> **Curtis:** Yeah. Whenever I hit the front page, I get a hell of a hard-on.
> **Guy:** So what do you do?
> **Curtis:** I go up to the cemetery. Ever heard of the cemetery?
> **Guy:** What are you, a necrophiliac?
> **Billy:** No, it's where the prostitutes hang out.

Curtis: Fantastic girls, Hamilton. Best value for your money in Asia. I'm telling you you will love the action. Wanna spend the night, it'll cost you a dollar.
Billy: Starvation is a great aphrodisiac.

Later, Guy drives to the cemetery, and Curtis and Jack Daniels go along for the ride. The prostitutes mob the car. One presses a bare breast against the windshield; another runs her tongue over the driver-side window. Curtis laughs, enjoying the show, but Guy quickly sobers up. He leaves Curtis to his personal form of colonialism and drives away in shame and disgust.

Guy is better than his colleagues. That, however, is still not good enough. He never becomes "the man of light" Billy hoped he would, never becomes engagé. "You abuse your position as journalist," Billy says, "and grow addicted to risk. You attempt to rule neat lines around yourself, making a fetish of your career and making all relationships temporary, lest they disturb that career." Guy and the other correspondents are too busy scheming, drinking, and screwing to notice that out in the street people are scrounging for a few handfuls of rice to keep themselves alive for another day. In part because of their blindness, things end badly, with Billy dying in a suicidal gesture of protest against the government and Guy fleeing the country as soldiers shoot suspected Communists alongside the road to the airport.

Under Fire (1983) follows the rum-soaked adventures of yet another group of ambitious, globe-trotting correspondents. Starting out in Chad, they soon move their little cocktail party to Nicaragua, where the Sandinista rebels are fighting dictator Anastasio Somoza and his vicious National Guard. The $8-million film was actually shot in Mexico, though director Roger Spottiswoode and screenwriter Ron Shelton did visit Nicaragua to interview correspondents and gather anecdotes for the script.[39]

Reviews were mixed. "There's plenty of thought to be given," Vincent Canby wrote in the *New York Times*, "to journalists who get so caught up in the practice of their trade . . . that they forget that the events they're covering involve the lives and deaths of real people." But he felt *Under Fire* "just muddled the issue" by having Nick Nolte's Russell Price, a tough, laconic, Hemingwayesque photojournalist, fake a picture out of sudden sympathy for the rebel cause.[40] By contrast, *Variety* "highly commended" the film, saying it was "probably the first time that both the American media and p.r. agencies on the side of the Somoza regime . . . are openly taken to task in an American feature film production aimed for stateside commercial release. Hats off."[41]

Initially, war provides little more than an exotic backdrop for the tangled love lives of the three main characters. Claire Stryder (Joanna Cassidy)—a radio reporter who whispers into her hand-held tape recorder such scoops as "I see a woman running down a street carrying a pig"—is in the process of transferring her affections from *Time* magazine correspondent Alex Grazier (Gene Hackman) to the younger, less grizzled Russell.[42] Alex, perhaps Russell's best friend, has grown tired of living out of a suitcase; he is thinking of trading in his Banana Republic safari jacket for a $10,000-a-month job as a network anchorman. Russell himself still thrives on dangerous assignments in faraway places.

The film underscores the press' exploitative relationship to the miseries of war by drawing a parallel between the correspondents and an American mercenary named Oates (Ed Harris) who turns up in every war zone they cover. In fact, it is Oates who recommends Nicaragua to Russell as they ride in the back of a troop truck in Chad. "Nicaragua, that's the spot," he says. "Cheap shrimp, a lot of rays." A scene or two later, Alex echoes Oates's remark: "I hear it's a neat little war and a nice hotel." And when Russell finally gets to Nicaragua, Claire says, "You're gonna love this war, Russell. There are good guys, bad guys, and cheap shrimp."

There are also assassinations and grenade attacks and massacres, but it is the Club Med aspects of Nicaragua that occupy the correspondents' interest. "Give me the scoop on Nicaragua," Russell asks Claire shortly after he arrives. She begins to recount a half-century of American-supported tyranny. "No," Russell interrupts, "I don't mean the peasant stuff. I mean the real stuff. Come on." Claire smiles and says, "Well, there are two kinds of beer. . ." All the boozing the correspondents do in nightclubs and around the hotel symbolizes their callousness and self-absorption, puts them on moral par with Somoza, who is seen throughout the film indulging in carnal pleasures.

Russell eventually becomes the kind of journalistic activist Billy Kwan wanted Guy Hamilton to be in *The Year of Living Dangerously*, but the consequences are far more ambiguous than Billy ever foresaw. While Russell's doctored photo of the Sandinista leader Rafael contributes to the overthrow of the Somoza regime, some of his other photos fall into the hands of a double agent, played with sinister Gallic charm by Jean-Louis Trintignant, who uses them to identify rebels for extermination. Moreover, Alex abruptly returns to Nicaragua from his new TV job because of the Rafael picture, only to be gunned down in the street by the National Guard—a re-creation of the actual murder of ABC correspondent Bill Stewart.[43] It is part of the moral complexity of the film that even when Russell chooses loyalty to the revolution over loyalty to journalism or his old drinking buddy, dead, blood-spattered bodies continue to pile up.

The theme of the corrupt, hard-drinking, parasitic foreign correspondent who finds redemption amid the stains and stinks of some Third World shithole gets its most visceral—and, according to critic Pauline Kael, its "most politically simplistic"—treatment in *Salvador*.[44] In 1984 writer-director Oliver Stone, a Vietnam veteran, went to Central America to investigate reports that the situation there might be leading to another Vietnam. He was horrified by what he saw, especially in El Salvador. Working with freelance journalist and photographer Richard Boyle, who had served as his guide on the tour, Stone developed a script based on recent events in the country and Boyle's personal experiences. The script also drew on Raymond Bonner's book, *Weakness and Deceit*, a study of U.S. complicity in right-wing death squads. Shot in fifty days, mostly in Mexico, on a shoe-string budget, the film was rejected by major American distributors as too controversial and reached only a limited audience when released in 1986.[45] But it received some belated recognition, including Oscar nominations for best original screenplay and best actor (James Woods as Boyle), after Stone's Vietnam War film, *Platoon*, became a critical and commercial hit later the same year.[46]

As a character, Boyle is about as appetizing as blue mold. He is, in his own words, "a fucking weasel." Although a veteran of the news coverage of Vietnam, Cambodia, Lebanon, and other wars, he has earned a reputation for unreliability and drunkenness. At least a few critics found the film's suggestion that "you have to be half-juiced up to do war-zone journalism" intolerable. Gene Siskel of the *Chicago Tribune*, for example, complained rather primly, "That's an insult to the courageous men and women who regularly perform the media's most dangerous job—that of foreign correspondent."[47]

When we first meet Boyle in a scummy apartment in San Francisco, his wife has just walked out on him, taking their baby and leaving him broke. His motives for driving to El Salvador in his old red convertible (Jackson Browne's "Running on Empty" conveniently playing on the radio) are purely selfish. "If I can get some good combat shots for AP," he tells his sidekick, an out-of-work disc jockey named Dr. Rock (James Belushi), "I can make some money." Also, he can reunite with his girlfriend, Maria (Elpedia Carrillo), a peasant madonna.

Boyle has assured Dr. Rock that El Salvador is pig heaven. "You're gonna love it here," he says. "You can drive drunk and get anybody killed for fifty bucks." But what they encounter almost immediately on arrival are scenes out of hell—and other foreign-correspondent films: a dead body burning in the middle of the road, an officer shooting a kneeling man through the head, a roundup of the usual leftist suspects. With the help of cinematographer Robert Richardson, Stone renders it all with the apocalyptic gloom of Bruegel's "The Triumph of Death," the great sixteenth-century painting in which an army of skeletons slaughter men and women alike, and wild dogs feed on the corpses, and the sky is a smudge of black smoke.

Wandering this landscape of nightmare, Boyle is initially dazed by the sheer amount of horror he witnesses, but then increasingly radicalized. "You've got to think of the people first," he ends up lecturing U.S. embassy officials. "In the name of human decency, something Americans are supposed to believe in, you got to at least try to make something of a just society here." Yet he doesn't exactly become a model citizen—doesn't stop drinking or lying or borrowing money. "The emotional thrust of the movie," as Paul Attansio explained in the *Washington Post,* "comes in Boyle's odyssey from a sleazy operator to a sleazy operator with a conscience, and it's because he remains distasteful that the conversion carries such oomph."[48]

The film places Boyle in the middle of a kind of continuum of journalists. At one extreme is Cassady, a photojournalist played by John Savage and based on John Hoagland of *Newsweek,* who was killed in El Salvador. Cassady idolizes war photographer Robert Capa. "You know what made guys like Capa great?" he says. "They weren't after money. They captured the nobility of human suffering." At the other extreme is a golden TV correspondent, a bubble-headed blonde who parrots the Reagan administration line and with whom Boyle frequently clashes. Watching her work, he mutters: "Fucking yuppies. Doing a standup on the roof of the Camino Real. Think they got the whole story." Boyle may be a drunk, but now there are worse things than being a drunk—like being a yuppie.

The eighties were the height—or, if you prefer, depths—of yuppiedom. The yuppie lifestyle insinuated itself as the style of the decade. And the essence, the basis, of that style was making and spending money—lots of it. Ambition, Laurence Shames observed in his well-written *The Hunger for More: Searching for Values in an Age of Greed,* "was whittled down to mean getting on a career track." In pursuing eighties-style success, people gave up sleep, gave up friends, gave up freedom, gave up "all the many grounds for self-affection and self-esteem that lie beyond the paycheck."[49]

Some of the responsibility for turning the eighties into the yuppie decade rests with Hollywood. According to one study, the characters in eighties films were "more likely to inhabit the milieu and the economic strata of the yuppie than any other segment of the American public."[50] These characters were obsessed with their jobs, often to the neglect of everything else—relationships, family, morality. Over the years, journalists had been portrayed on the screen as truly alive only when working on a story. Now the newsroom, with its frantic pace and high burnout rate, became in films like *Absence of Malice* (1981) and *Broadcast News* (1987) the epitome of the pressurized yuppie workplace.

Ironically, yuppieness was growing in visibility at a time when the national economy was in questionable health. Housing prices and interest rates were up; the employment rate and wages down. In fact, William J. Palmer claimed that yuppies saw their competitive work ethic and relentless consumption as a buffer against an increasingly unstable world. The material icons of the yuppie lifestyle—BMWs and three-piece Armani suits and glassed-in condos—were, he said, all that was left of the American dream.[51]

Absence of Malice presents a yuppie journalist, Megan Carter (Sally Field), who apparently fails because of her ethical choices, but actually fails because of her choice of lifestyle. She is the first of several women reporters and editors in eighties films who are made to suffer for being ambitious, for preferring a career to marriage and motherhood. Susan Faludi, author of *Backlash: The Undeclared War Against American Women,* argued that such films were part of a broad attempt to roll back the social and economic gains of the seventies women's movement. "All that free-floating anxiety over declining wages, insecure employment, and overpriced housing need[ed] a place to light," she wrote, "and in the '80s, much of it fixed itself on women."[52]

When originally released, *Absence of Malice* was greeted by journalists with indignant mutterings.[53] Pulitzer Prize-winning former reporter Lucinda Franks called the film a "grotesquely distorted" portrayal of the press, while Robert Hatch of the *Nation* took issue with its premise that "a successful newspaper can be run by irresponsible fools."[54] But *Absence of Malice* doesn't indict only journalistic ethics; it also indicts the female yuppie. Megan is "the kind of careerist who rises in the world because of her convenient dumb ruthlessness."[55] The film suggests that she and society would both be much better off if she stopped trying to compete with men and started trying to marry one—if she conformed to traditional gender norms. It is more than coincidence that as she debates the use of anonymous sources with Michael Gallagher (Paul Newman), the target of an FBI leak she printed, the dialog seamlessly shifts focus to her age, looks, and marital status.

> **Gallagher:** How old are you?
> **Megan:** 34.
> **Gallagher:** How come you're not married?
> **Megan:** Well, maybe I am.
> **Gallagher:** How come you don't wear a ring?
> **Megan:** Haven't you ever heard of liberation?
> **Gallagher:** Most of them are ugly.
> **Megan:** Is that supposed to be a compliment?

Drinking functions in the film as a gender marker. Gallagher's old man was the Al Capone of Miami, a bootlegger and worse, and he himself operates a liquor wholesale business. For relaxation, he cruises around in the boat his father once used for rum-running. This history, and the informal, straightforward way Gallagher talks and dresses, renders him a comfortingly nostalgic figure of male strength and toughness. And as if all that weren't enough to prove his masculinity, we sometimes see him go to the fridge for a beer, just a regular guy without postmodern angst or yuppie affectations.

Megan also drinks, but in her case, alcohol use has negative over-tones. To the degree that drinking is considered primarily a male activity or prerogative, a woman who drinks is a contradiction in terms, a kind of freak. So when the film shows Megan as being on a first-name basis with bartenders and barmaids or getting slightly crocked, it is signaling that she has squandered her femininity. Her lack of feminine sympathy leads directly to a series of journalistic disasters.

For example, Gallagher's lifelong friend Teresa Perrone (Melinda Dillion) begs Megan not to publish the fact that she had an abortion ten months ago, but Megan is impervious to her pleas. "I'm a reporter," she says, placing loyalty to her job over loyalty to her gender. "You're talking to a newspaper right now." Teresa, assistant to the principal of a Catholic school, kills herself when the story comes out.

Megan's demoralizing, manlike aggressiveness extends to sex. As noted in a previous chapter, film portrayals of hard-drinking women reflect "a persistent and deeply felt association between drunkenness and sexuality."[56] Megan, after having some wine during a dinner out with Gallagher, becomes sexually disinhibited. In a reversal of traditional sex roles, she invites him up to her apartment, and he coyly declines.

Megan (*disappointed*): You're not interested.
Gallagher: Maybe I'd like to think it was my idea.
Megan: I'd like that, too. (*A reflective pause.*) Gallagher, I'm thirty-four years old. I don't need courting.
Gallagher: I'm from the Stone Age. I guess I do.
Megan (*sardonically*): I'll send you a dozen roses.

Absence of Malice gives Megan an editor named Mac (Josef Sommers) who encourages her aggressiveness. Despite a benign, almost professorial appearance, Mac is a close relative of the scoop-crazed editors in newspaper films of the thirties and forties, films in which there was always an excuse to fetch the office bottle. Late one night, when the newsroom is deserted except for Megan and Mac, he brings out a bottle in a brown-paper bag.

Mac: Want some coffee?
Megan: Might keep me up.
Mac (*indicating the bottle*): It's decaffeinated. (*He unscrews the cap*

and pours each of them a shot.) I've been thinking it might be time
for you to come on the desk.
Megan: I'm not over the hill yet.
Mac: I think you'd make a damn fine editor.

Which just proves how addled his judgment is even without alcohol.

Where *Absence of Malice* generally antagonized reviewers, *Broadcast News* generally amused them, even though it also portrayed the emotional and moral shortcomings of yuppie journalists. Set in the Washington bureau of a network news department, the film was written, produced, and directed by James L. Brooks, who worked for CBS News before going on to create such popular TV series as *The Mary Tyler Moore Show* and *Taxi*. Hal Hinson of the *Washington Post*, while admitting that the film "never comes close to being a great, penetrating work about television news," called it "a spunky romantic comedy with some of the snappiest lines heard onscreen" in years.[57] His colleague Desson Howe agreed, saying it was "easily the best movie out" for Christmas 1987.[58]

The film's three major characters—hard-charging producer Jane Craig (Holly Hunter), talented but untelegenic reporter Aaron Altman (Albert Brooks), and none-too-bright anchor-in-the-making Tom Grunick (William Hurt)—form a love triangle that doesn't quite square up. That is because work is their first passion. After Jane makes Tom look good during a live newscast by feeding him questions through his earpiece, he kneels at her feet and says it was like sex, having her voice inside his head. But, as Roger Ebert of the *Chicago Sun-Times* pointed out, "He never gets that excited about sex. Neither does she."[59]

There is no stigma attached in the film to public drinking. Characters drink at house parties, embassy affairs, and professional gatherings without drawing any special attention or criticism. It is just part of the routine of contemporary social life. Tom, for example, is behaving appropriately when he invites Jane to celebrate his successful debut as anchor with the rest of the office gang at a bar down the street.

All the heavy drinking in the film is done in private by Aaron, whose status with the network falls as Tom's rises. Passed over as anchor for the live newscast, he stays home and binges on screwdrivers, mixing the vodka and orange juice in a big goblet with his fingers. Drinking becomes his means of coping with competitive pressures and professional disappointments, his sudden downward mobility.

It is also his means of disinhibiting himself. Only when drunk can Aaron find the words or courage to reveal to Jane his true feelings for her. "In the middle of all this," he confesses as his binge winds down, "I started to think about the one thing that makes me feel really good, and that's you." He looks at her longingly for a moment, then adds: "I'm going to stop right now, except I would give anything if you were two people, so I could call up the one that's my friend and tell her about the one that I like so much. I'm, I'm not gonna say any more, primarily because I'm about to pass out." Aaron uses alcohol to alternately anesthetize his feelings and help him vent them. Of course, he is no worse off than Jane, who suffers periodic fits of uncontrollable weeping despite her glamorous, high-powered job.

Broadcast News is intended to be an insider's affectionately mocking view of TV journalism, a kind of latter-day *Network* (1976). But do we still need Hollywood to tell us that TV represents the triumph of flash over substance, that even the news on TV is entertainment, that profits have become all-important? The film, though it grants its main characters a last-minute reprieve, is most effective as a critique of the yuppie worship of success. Jane, Aaron, and Tom are frantic overachievers, careerists with an aching void at the center of their lives. It is a void that, in the end, no amount of work or drink can fill.

10

Last Call

Started out on burgundy, but soon hit the harder stuff.

—Bob Dylan

Alcohol is the beverage most often shown on TV today. Research indicates that high school students who watch a lot of TV, especially music videos, are more likely to start drinking than other teenagers. A Stanford University study published in the journal *Pediatrics* in 1998 found that each increase of one hour per day of watching music videos brought a 31 percent greater risk of starting to drink over the next 18 months. Each hour of watching other kinds of TV brought a 9 percent greater risk. The study also reported that teenagers who rented movies were less likely to start drinking, while playing video and computer games had no effect either way.[1]

The study's lead author, Dr. Thomas Robinson, said the findings weren't too surprising given that the "great majority of drinking on television is by the most attractive and most influential people, and [that] it is often associated with sexually suggestive content." He called for "a balance in the way alcohol is portrayed so that people who did drink did suffer some consequences from it." Alyse Booth of the National Center on Addiction and Substance Abuse echoed him, saying, "There is a tremendous glamorization of the use of alcohol. Alcohol use is portrayed as normal and glamorous, never with consequences."[2]

Although alcohol use may be more prevalent on TV, it is still extensive in films. Journalists, for example, drink in nineties films as lustily as they ever did, and their drinking is, if not always glamorized, then at least naturalized, made to seem a normal and natural part of the journalistic identity. Apparently, old stereotypes never die; they just go in and out of rehab.

The Bonfire of the Vanities (1990), directed by Brian DePalma and based on Tom Wolfe's satirical novel of eighties greed and ambition, revives the stereotype of the sleazy, alcoholic reporter in the persona of Peter Farrell, who also narrates the film. Despite its best-seller name, all-star cast (Tom Hanks, Bruce Willis, Melanie Griffith, and Morgan Freeman), and $45-plus million budget, *Bonfire* bombed at the box office and with critics. It was declared "gross, unfunny" by the *New York Times;* a "calamity of miscasting and commercial concessions" by the *Washington Post;* "a real mess" by the *Deseret News.*[3] In fact, the film was so awful it inspired a book-length exposé, Julie Salamon's *The Devil's Candy,* which blamed the disaster on the whole money-driven, ego-mad, convoluted process of Hollywood filmmaking.

Played by Willis in Clark Kent glasses, Farrell is in danger of being fired for drunkenness when he gets tipped to a story involving multimillionaire stockbroker Sherman McCoy (Hanks), self-proclaimed "Master of the Universe." Sherman and his sultry mistress, Maria Ruskin (Griffith), took the wrong exit off the expressway, wound up in the wasteland of the South Bronx, and, terrified, ran over a black teenager who may or may not have been trying to rob them. Farrell saves his job by turning the hit-and-run accident into a tabloid extravaganza.

Most reviewers thought Willis was OK in the role, but found the role itself less than compelling. Rita Kempley of the *Washington Post* said Farrell, "a minor, not very interesting character in the book, becomes a principal, not very interesting character in the movie."[4] And Roger Ebert of the *Chicago Sun-Times* observed that although he is the narrator, Farrell "provides few insights and little verbal grace." He "just mopes about, sighing and shrugging and raising his eyebrows."[5]

The film begins with the reporter arriving drunk at a banquet honoring him. A five-minute-long virtuoso shot—one reviewer joked that cinematographer Vilmos Zsigmond "never met a dizzying angle he didn't like"—follows Farrell without a cut as he emerges from a limousine, rides up in an elevator, lurches down a hallway, and is helped into formal wear, all the while guzzling from a whiskey decanter and downing glasses of champagne.[6] As in the old temperance tales, his excessive drinking represents moral weakness, the sort of weakness that allowed him to twist the facts in order to make a better story.

But the film is ultimately inconsistent in how it characterizes Farrell's drinking or, for that matter, Farrell himself. In flashback we see him passed out on the floor of his apartment, surrounded by old newspapers, dirty clothes, the detritus of his drunken, disorganized life. "I'd had my chance," he says regretfully in voice-over, "and I'd blown it away in a bottle." Nonetheless, when he rehabilitates his career, it is by exploiting someone else's troubles, not by swearing off booze.

Farrell drinks throughout the film. It is the symbolic meaning of his drinking that changes. He may have broken the Sherman McCoy story, but he eventually becomes disgusted with the media frenzy that ensues, all those reporters shouting prosecutorial questions at Sherman and sticking cameras and microphones in his face. Sitting on the courthouse steps, the brim of his hat comically turned up in front, Farrell takes nips from a flask while, in voice-over, he compares his scoop-hungry colleagues to "jackals, dogs yipping at the heels of prey." Drinking, which once signified his own corruption, now signifies his disappointment with the sordid, press-infested modern age.

Although very much a nineties film in its star power and lavish production values, *The Bonfire of the Vanities* is more like a thirties film in its ambivalent view of the press. Farrell, in the shifting significance of his alcohol use, reflects two of the oldest film stereotypes of the drunken journalist—the reprobate and the romantic anti-hero. Other nineties films with a hard-drinking journalist, such as *The Paper, Cobb,* and *I Love Trouble,* exhibit the same retro style. It is as if contemporary Hollywood, having run out of ideas, went into a film vault to get some.

Unlike *Bonfire, The Paper* (1994) was well received by critics, perhaps not least because it flatters the profession to which they belong. Rita Kempley, usually a tough judge of films, said, " 'The Paper' perfectly captures the hubbub of the nation's newsrooms, where amid the clatter of keys, the babble of reporters and the clarion of phones, deadlines are met and the daily is born." She described its characters as "colorful, dead-on re-creations of newspaper types" who are linked by "the printer's ink in their veins," an analogy between journalism and alcohol addiction that, whether she realized it or not, dates back to the 1890s.[7]

Roger Ebert also liked the film, which covers twenty-four hectic hours in the life of a New York tabloid. It put him in touch all over again, he said, "with how good it feels to work at the top of your form, on a story you believe in, on deadline"—something that evidently doesn't happen very often on the film beat. But just as interesting as Ebert's reaction to *The Paper* was his reaction in his review to Conrad Black, the new owner of the *Sun-Times*. A week before the film was released, Black had been quoted as criticizing journalists: "They get too involved in the story, they all want to be stars, they're cynical, they're disillusioned, and a lot of them drink too much." Ebert shrugged off these remarks. "A lot of the people I've worked with would use them as boasts," he wrote, thereby demonstrating the persistence of *The Front Page* image of journalistic drinking as romantic, even heroic.

Ironically, *The Paper* itself is less worshipful of the stereotypical hard-drinking journalist than reviewers were. The film's hero, metro editor Henry Hackett (Michael Keaton), guzzles a Coke for breakfast and about ten more before the day is done—a tongue-in-cheek version of *The Front Page* stereotype. His desperate bumming of change for the newsroom Coke machines during moments of stress becomes a running gag in the script, directed by Ron Howard and written by brothers David and Stephen Koepp.

The one journalist who drinks seriously in the film, editor-in-chief Bernie White (Robert Duvall), is a physical and emotional wreck. He has just learned he has prostate cancer; regrets his adulteries and failed marriages; and is estranged from his grown daughter. A decayed patriarch, he abdicates responsibilty for the day's front page, leaving Henry and bitchy managing editor Alicia Clark (Glenn Close) to fight out which story will be featured. Meanwhile, he hunkers down on a barstool and shares his troubles with the bartender and a fellow drinker (Jason Alexander). "Ninety-nine percent of your time," he sighs, "is spent on three things: your house, your work, your family. . . . If you put them all together, the three of them want more than you have to give, so what do you do about that?"

Bernie may not be portrayed attractively, but the bar is, with its dim light and dark wood and floating blue islands of cigarette smoke, its atmosphere of intimacy and male bonding. Part of the reason Alicia acts like such a bitch is that she has been left out of the staff's nightly expeditions there. "You assholes think I don't know that you wait until I leave before you sneak off to the Bear's Head," she says. "Can't even invite me for a lousy drink." Incidentally, if viewers are literary-minded and look quickly enough, they can see novelist Richard Price (*Bloodbrothers, Freedomland*) and journalist Pete Hamill playing extras in the bar scene. Hamill, who did his best at one time to live *The Front Page* stereotype, ultimately gave up drinking, as recounted in his 1994 memoir, *A Drinking Life.*

Only death will get the title character to give up drinking in *Cobb* (1994), a depressing, alcohol-drenched biographical film about Baseball Hall of Famer Ty Cobb, who once held forty major-league hitting and base-running records and whose .367 lifetime batting average remains unsurpassed. From the early forties to the mid-fifties, Hollywood produced a series of baseball biopics—*The Pride of the Yankees, The Babe Ruth Story, The Stratton Story, The Jackie Robinson Story, The Winning Team, The Pride of St. Louis, Fear Strikes Out*—that presented their subjects as self-made men, inspirational figures, examples of the American dream come true.[8] *Cobb*, directed by former minor league player Ron Shelton, is quite different. It presents its subject not as a hero or role model, but as a wife-beater, an alcoholic, and a racist.

A few flashbacks aside, the film concentrates on the last ten turbulent months of Cobb's life, most of which he spent with freelance sportswriter Al Stump, hired by Doubleday to ghostwrite his autobiography. Cobb had the final say over the book's contents, and the result was a sanitized, self-serving version of his career called *My Life in Baseball*, which sold moderately well. An article Stump later wrote for *True* magazine about their collaboration won the Best American Sports Story Award of 1962 and became the basis for the film.[9]

There are barroom scenes at either end of *Cobb* that could have come right out of *The Front Page*. At the beginning of the film, Stump (affably played by Robert Wuhl) saunters into the Sportsman's Lounge, where some rumpled sportswriters are in noisy conversation at a table in the back, gesturing with their drinks and cigars for emphasis. Stump pulls up a chair, listens for a while, then says in exasperation, "Look at us, look at us, we call ourselves writers, and all we do is watch ball games, argue about everything, and just get drunk a lot." Toward the end of the film, the scene is basically repeated. Stump, who has been on the road with Cobb (Tommy Lee Jones in a ferocious performance) for almost a year, returns to the bar and finds his friends at the same table, perhaps even in the same argument. Yet their drinking is minimal compared to that of Cobb, who, in actual fact, drank a pint of whiskey a day. When doctors warned him in 1960 that liquor would kill him, he defiantly upped his consumption to a quart or more.[10] The film portrays Cobb as surviving on a high-octane blend of morphine, lithium, insulin, and alcohol. Stump is horrified the first time he sees Cobb wash down a fistful of pills with a slug of Southern Comfort, but he gradually loses his squeamishness, evolving over the course of the film from Cobb's biographer to his secretary, chauffeur, nurse, and drinking buddy. It should be added that the occasional shot of Stump working at his typewriter always shows a bottle of booze and a glass within easy reach—a reflection, of course, of the old belief that alcohol is a necessary ingredient of good writing. How old? In 14 B.C., Horace asserted, "No poems can please for long or live that are written by water-drinkers."

Where *Cobb* repudiated the optimism of the baseball biopics of the forties and fifties, *I Love Trouble* (1994) tried to recapture the snappiness of the "classic spar-until-they-fall-in-love movies" of the thirties and forties, such as *His Girl Friday* and *Woman of the Year*.[11] This film, starring Nick Nolte as legendary Chicago columnist Peter Brackett and Julia Roberts as his crosstown rival, Sabrina Peterson, has everything those earlier films did except wit, charm, and intelligence. "Damon Runyon had a character called 'Waldo Winchell, the half-smart scribe,'" Jack Kroll began his review in *Newsweek*. "*I Love Trouble* is a half-smart movie. Well, maybe one-third."[12]

Drinking isn't accentuated in the film; it is simply another feature of Brackett's traditional masculine aura, like his trenchcoat or his compulsive womanizing or his big, fat, phallic cigars. He drinks a wide variety of alcoholic beverages in a wide variety of settings—vodka at a black-tie affair, champagne on an airplane, beer in a hotel room. Yet he never drinks to excess or while at work. The film, despite using Chicago as a backdrop and invoking Ben Hecht's name, has no real thematic relation to *The Front Page*, throughout which Chicago police reporters subversively boozed it up. Bumping into Peterson in a newspaper saloon at lunchtime, Brackett tells her, "Yeah, Ben Hecht used to eat here back in the twenties. They have a little plaque with his name on it in a back booth, right next to mine." He then orders a Coke—a Coke!—with his club sandwich.

Brackett is supposed to be an urban columnist in the tradition of

At one point in **WOMAN OF THE YEAR** (1942), the battle of the sexes between sportswriter Sam Craig (Spencer Tracy) and foreign affairs columnist Tess Harding (Katharine Hepburn) takes the form of a drinking competition that leaves both of them disinhibited and ready for love.

Runyon and Hecht. Jimmy Breslin, one of the last of this breed, claimed recently that newspaper writing lacks punch because "cigar-smoking guys with flasks in their desk drawers" are gone, replaced in newsrooms by well-educated, fitness-crazy types.[13] "Today the reporters have two or three college degrees," he said. "They're much better about living. And they don't drink. And they don't smoke. And they're probably the most boring group of people I've ever heard of. The writing has as much personality as the carpet on the health club floor."[14] But though newspapers can now get along without alcoholic star reporters, Hollywood can't—not completely. The stereotype is too symbolically charged, too useful, even in its watered-down yuppie form, for filmmakers to relinquish it.

Hunter S. Thompson has dubbed the wild stuff he writes "gonzo journalism." Beginning in the late sixties with his first-person reporting for *Rolling Stone* and *Scanlan's*, Thompson, as one editor said, "gleefully defenestrated all the traditional rules of journalism: conciseness, sobriety, objectivity, even accuracy."[15] His *Fear and Loathing in Las Vegas*, a strange, audacious, darkly comic account of a drug-fueled road trip, was hailed as the "Best Book of the Dope Decade" when published in 1971.[16] The Modern Library edition, brought out in 1996, solidified its status as a contemporary classic. Two years later, it was turned into a major Hollywood production starring Johnny Depp, who prepared for the role by hanging out with Thompson for four months and studying his every quirk.[17]

This wasn't the first attempt to bring Thompson's hallucinatory prose to the screen. In 1980 *Where the Buffalo Roam*, allegedly based on various of his writings, had a short run in theaters. Although the film itself was largely ignored, film posters with the slogan "I hate to advocate weird chemicals, alcohol, violence or insanity to anyone . . . but they've always worked for me" became collector's items.[18]

Directed by Art Linson and starring Bill Murray as Thompson and Peter Boyle as his lawyer, Carlos Lazlo, *Where the Buffalo Roam* took a terrible pounding from critics. "The movie is about manic energy," Dave Kehr said in the *Chicago Reader*, "but you can feel everyone straining just to get the next shot on the screen."[19] When the film version of *Fear and Loathing in Las Vegas* opened to unanimous negative reviews in 1998, critics recalled that *Where the Buffalo Roam* was also unsuccessful, a "mess of a movie."[20]

The film is a series of loosely connected flashbacks. It begins with Thompson in his Colorado cabin, working against deadline on a story about the late sixties and early seventies, the demon-ridden Nixon era. To help the creative process, he slurps Wild Turkey while he writes. Later, during a flashback sequence, Thompson arrives at a college lecture hall carrying an ice bucket in one arm and a bottle of Wild Turkey in the other. A student in the audience stands up and says, "I was just wondering if you could tell me, umm, if you thought that drugs and alcohol would make me a better writer." Thompson responds by reaching into a pocket, whipping out a joint, and lighting up. He then restates the film's tagline: "I would hate to advocate drugs or liquor, violence, insanity to anyone, but in my case, it's worked."

In his writings, Thompson presents drugs and alcohol less as a pathway to creativity than as a symbol of death, doom, and the failure of the American dream. The film avoids this apocalyptic outlook. Mostly it exploits drugs and alcohol for laughs. Thompson and Lazlo wander through major cultural events like Super Bowl VI and the 1972 presidential campaign stoned out of their minds and acting with comic disinhibition, a ludicrous disregard for rules or rationality. They wave around guns and knives, trash rooms, and discombobulate straights, including the White House press corps, whom they spray with a fire extinguisher.

Yet, for all its supposed hipness, *Where the Buffalo Roam* contains echoes of early newspaper films. In one extended flashback, Thompson owes a cover story to Marty, a character based on *Rolling Stone* publisher Jann Wenner and played with grand pomposity by Bruno Kirby. Tired of waiting for Thompson to show up, Marty tells an aide-de-camp, "Check the bars." It is an order at least as old as *The Front Page*, where editor Walter Burns sets a similar search in motion for missing star reporter Hildy Johnson.

The reviews of *Where the Buffalo Roam* may have been bad, but those of *Fear and Loathing in Las Vegas* eighteen years later were many times worse. *Boxoffice Online Reviews* called it "a two-hour slog through revulsion and boredom," while the *Deseret News* said it was so "nauseatingly vivid" as to be "headache-inducing." Mark Clark of *USA Today* compared it to "an oldies concert pervaded by amplified flat notes and the stench of '70s burnout." "If the movie were more amusing," he added, "it could probably be accused of glorifying drugs, but the problem has been averted. The movie really isn't pro-drugs. It's simply unwatchable."[21]

Murray had adopted Thompson's trademarks, from his bizarre hats and big sunglasses to his cigarette holder, for *Where the Buffalo Roam*. Now Depp, playing Thompson's self-parodying alter ego, Raoul Duke (the name also of a Thompson caricature in the "Doonesbury" comic strip), pulled off an even better impersonation using the same sort of props. Some critics complained, however, that this just made it harder to tolerate spending two hours with his character.[22]

Like *Where the Buffalo Roam, Fear and Loathing in Las Vegas* was criticized for being plotless, or, as *Boxoffice Online Reviews* bluntly put it, an "amorphous blob of disjointed scenes and spaced-out episodes."[23] Actually, the film is quite faithful to its source book. Thompson and his lawyer, Dr. Gonzo (Benicio Del Toro), load up the trunk of their convertible with an amazing array of drugs and booze, and drive to Las Vegas, where Thompson is covering the Mint 400, a desert motorcycle race, for *Sports Illustrated*. He stays to report on a convention of district attorneys, which he does with his typical aplomb—by getting stoned and creating chaos wherever he goes.

In an attempt to capture the various altered states experienced by Duke and Gonzo, director Terry Gilliam and cinematographer Nicola Pecorini drew up a list detailing the cinematic qualities of each drug the characters consume. The list included adrenochrome ("everything gets narrow and claustrophobic, move closer with lens"); ether ("loose depth of field; everything becomes non-defined"); amyl nitrate ("perception of light gets very uneven, light levels increase and decrease during the shots"); mescaline ("colors melt into each other, flares with no sources, play with color temperatures"); and LSD ("expanded consciousness, everything extremely wide, hallucinations via morphs, shapes, colors and sounds").[24] The result is a film whose frenzied visual style approximates Thompson's writing style, though critics didn't necessarily like it more because of that.

One of the most visually stunning sequences in the film occurs in a cocktail lounge, where Duke, having ingested a bunch of mind-blowing drugs, hallucinates genuinely reptilian "lounge lizards." Based on Ralph Steadman's illustrations for the original book, the lizards were animatronic replicas built by Rob Bottin, who had created creatures for *The Thing* and *Deep Rising*. "We were supposed to get about twenty-five of them," Pecorini said, "but we wound up with just seven or eight. As a result, we had to use motion-control techniques to make it look as if we had a whole room full of them. That sequence took two full days to film. We had to do all of these different passes with different costumes on the various lizards to get it right."[25] The sequence is a kind of throwback to the nightmarish attack of delirium tremens that had been a staple of the alcoholism genre until the sixties.[26] Shots of creepy crawly things representing alcoholic hallucinations were spliced into temperance films as early as 1913's *Ten Nights in a Bar-room.*[27]

Roger Ebert, reviewing *Fear and Loathing in Las Vegas*, claimed that the film itself has "an alcoholic and addict mind-set," by which he meant that it never stands outside "the need to use," that it lacks perspective.[28] But this isn't really so. Duke provides frequent voice-over narration, some of it laced with cultural notes and criticisms and almost all of it lifted verbatim from Thompson's book. Here he is, for example, describing the hideous effects of ether while on screen he and Dr. Gonzo snort the drug, then stumble around Bazooka Circus, a casino with a big-top theme:

> It makes you behave like the village drunkard in some early Irish novel. Total loss of all basic motor skills. Blurred vision, no balance, numb tongue. The mind recoils in horror, unable to communciate with the spinal column. Which is interesting because you can actually watch yourself behaving in this terrible way, but you can't control it. Ether is the perfect drug for Las Vegas. In this town they love a drunk: fresh meat.

Duke combines many of the previous incarnations of the drunken journalist within himself. He is the comic drunk, unaware in his stoned state that his cigarette is bent; the literary drunk, hands poised over the typewriter keys, a bottle nearby for inspiration; the outlaw drunk, destroying public decorum, private property, and just about anything else that crosses his path.

At the same time, though, Duke adds a final dimension to the stereotype of the drunken journalist. He carries certain tendencies, loose in the larger culture, to their logical, if horrible, conclusion— the tendency to consume to excess, the tendency to reinvent oneself according to whim and circumstance, the tendency to want to escape from reality. As Las Vegas is the modern twisted version of the

American dream, so Duke is the modern twisted version of Everyman, a failed seeker on the verge of physical and mental collapse. He doesn't uncover the truth; it covers him. Smashed out of his skull, pouring sweat, subject to grim memories and bad waves of paranoia, he is the last of his line, the unforeseen end product of centuries of cultural evolution. He is what the drunken journalist becomes— drug-crazed, feverish, incoherent—when life finally grows too problematic for drink alone to resolve.

Epilogue

> For me, one of the tests of a good idea is its ability to last through a hangover.
>
> —Jimmy Breslin

Journalists haven't been the only ones in American culture to be stereotyped as drunks or as peculiarly susceptible to drink. So have Indians, blacks, and Irish immigrants. The first white settlers, while all right with alcohol for themselves, feared Indian use of it. The settlers became convinced that Indians were prone to develop an inordinate craving for alcohol and to lose control over their behavior when they drank. Some even blamed atrocities committed by drunken Indians for starting the early Indian wars. Concerned about Indian violence, all the colonies enacted laws regulating the sale of alcohol to Indians. This, however, didn't prevent white traders and land speculators from trying to get Indians drunk before making deals with them.[1]

Modern anthropologists have termed the supposed weakness of Indians for alcohol the "firewater myth." "In the absence of the anthropological concept of culture," R. C. Dailey explained, "the first Europeans [in the New World] naturally interpreted the Indians' response to alcohol as a constitutional or racial difference."[2] The stereotype of the drunken Indian persisted well into the 1800s, following the white frontier line all the way to the Pacific.[3] One possible reason for this was that the stereotype characterized Indians as savages and so provided a convenient rationale for their removal to reservations or even their slaughter.[4]

Like Indian drinking, drinking among blacks was carefully regulated by colonial governments, and not only in the South. A Connecticut law mandated the flogging of slaves, indentured servants, and apprentices caught in taverns without their masters' permission. Other Northern statutes imposed fines on whites for selling alcohol to blacks, slave or free. Such regulations reflected white fears that blacks, like Indians, were especially prone to violence when drunk.[5]

The drinking patterns of blacks have been eyed with suspicion throughout much of American history. In the antebellum period, Southern whites believed that blacks were too childish and irresponsible to be trusted with alcohol.[6] "The poor slave," a North Carolinian said, "imbibes until he becomes intoxicated when he is ready for a general fight or any species of rascality."[7] The belief that blacks were addicted to the excessive use of alcohol continued after the Civil War, with Robert E. Lee, for example, observing that blacks were "spendthrifts and gullible," and "had a great liking for tobacco and whiskey."[8] By the beginning of the twentieth century, even black leaders were expressing versions of this stereotype. "Drink has hurt us socially," a minister claimed in 1910. "If there is one thing to which we may attribute our present social status, it is to the drink habit."[9]

Because Indians and blacks were racially and culturally different from whites, their drinking lent itself to myth-making and stereotyping. The Irish, who formed the largest group of immigrants to the United States in the first half of the nineteenth century, also became stereotyped as excessively fond of alcohol. In their case, the already stark cultural differences between native-born Americans and immigrants were deepened by religious prejudice. The vast majority of Irish immigrants were Roman Catholic, but the United States was a predominantly Protestant country with a historical mistrust of anything related to the Catholic Church.[10]

The almost 2 million Irish who arrived between 1830 and 1860 suffered social, political, and economic discrimination on a scale perhaps unmatched by other immigrants.[11] Invited to the United States to help meet the industrializing North's need for cheap labor, the Irish still had difficulty finding work. An important factor in their exclusion from many jobs was their reputation for hard drinking.[12] One student of Irish immigration noted that Americans "marked down drunkenness as natural to the Irish as their brogue."[13]

Coming from a hard-drinking culture to a strange and hostile one, the Irish expressed their ethnic solidarity through alcohol. "That is," historians Mark Edward Lender and James Kirby Martin said, "they drank to assert their Irishness; the harder they drank, the more Irish they supposedly became."[14] All this drinking gave a certain credence to the nativist stereotype of the drunken Irishman. "We are known as a religion of saloonkeepers, of men who drink and men who provide the means of drinking," leaders of the Hibernian temperance movement lamented.[15]

The fact that Indians, blacks, and Irish immigrants were all once stereotyped by the majority culture as drunks suggests a correlation between the production of negative stereotypes and the projection of negative power. In the instances just cited, the stereotypes served to stigmatize out-groups and to justify discriminatory practices against them. Journalists, another group considered partial to drink and prone to drunkenness, would seem to fit the same pattern of marginalization.

While the stereotype of the drunken journalist has some positive aspects—for example, its sardonic, anti-authoritarian humor—it more often reflects negatively on the press. Particularly in the late twenties and early thirties, and then again in the fifties, the hard-drinking journalist of Hollywood films represented the underside of the American dream—greed and Darwinian competition and the gutter ethics of survival. His cynical disregard for white, middle-class norms may have accorded with the secret inclinations of the audience, but it collided with their overt values. Excessive drinking was a sign of something demonic or uncivilized in the journalist's character. It placed him, as it placed the drunken Indian, black, and Irishman, beyond the pale of social respectability.

By so identifying the journalist with alcohol, films discredited the power of the press in a society where that power wasn't only constitutionally protected, but also had been rapidly compounding ever since the emergence of the mass-circulation newspaper in the 1830s. The stereotype of the drunken journalist functioned, in the absence of close legal controls on the press, as an ideological or symbolic form of control, a means of resisting the assault of an increasingly sensational press on American life. Like the stereotypes of proscribed racial or ethnic groups, it rose in defense of home and family against incursions by the new, the strange, the other.

Circumstances would seem ideal today for the stereotype of the drunken journalist to undergo a resurgence. As editor Richard Lambert recently said, "By any measure, public trust in America's news organizations has been declining for years. People are progressively less inclined to believe what they see and read."[16] The preliminary findings of a survey by the American Society of Newspaper Editors provide ample evidence of this:

- Eighty percent of those surveyed say journalists chase stories because they sell newspapers, not because they are important.
- The same percentage say journalists enjoy reporting on the failures of public figures.
- Seventy percent say journalists are more cynical than other Americans.
- Sixty-five percent say journalists let advertisers influence news coverage.
- Only 25 percent say journalists would ever tone down a story to avoid hurting people.[17]

Oddly enough, despite such widespread public skepticism about the press, the stereotype of the drunken journalist has become less, not more, prominent over the past couple of decades. The one exception was the foreign-correspondent films of the eighties, a subgenre that included *The Year of Living Dangerously, Under Fire,* and *Salvador,* and in which heavy drinking still signaled moral weakness.[18] Otherwise, the stereotype has largely been relegated to the back pages.

The reason is that the use of alcohol has been demythologized. Journalists continue to drink on the screen—in 1994's *The Paper,* for example, they adjourn to a smoke-filled bar every night after work—but their drinking is pictured as normal, unremarkable, a routine feature of nineties social life. And even when a journalist binges, as TV correspondent Aaron Altman (Albert Brooks) does in *Broadcast News* (1987), there is no implication that journalists as a group are being indicted. The binge represents a personal crisis rather than a statement on the moral squalor of journalism.

Alcohol is the second most popular drug among contemporary Americans (the most popular is caffeine). Sixty-eight percent of American men and about 47 percent of American women admit that they drink alcohol at least occasionally. In addition, public opinion of alcoholism has softened in recent years. Once thought to be caused by a failure of will or a lack of moral fiber, alcoholism is now viewed as a medical problem. According to a 1987 poll, almost 90 percent of Americans believe that alcoholism is a disease and more than 60 percent think that it may be inherited.[19]

These numbers reflect the cultural influence of Alcoholics Anonymous, which has preached the disease concept since the mid-thirties, helping break down the moral stigma attached to alcoholism.[20] In fact, it was an AA-influenced film, *Come Fill the Cup* (1951), that foreshadowed the decline of the stereotype of the drunken journalist. As you may remember, James Cagney plays city editor Lew Marsh, a recovering alcoholic who has hired several reformed lushes for his staff. When the managing editor complains that "this place is beginning to look like a branch of Alcoholics Anonymous," Lew replies that ex-drunks make the best newspapermen. "Work takes the place of liquor," he says. In other words, the underlying pattern of addictive behavior doesn't actually change; it just finds a more suitable object. The alcoholic becomes the workaholic, a transformation that may have seemed hopeful in the fifties, but that would seem less so as time went on.

In his essay "Passage to Play: Rituals of Drinking Time in American Society," Joseph R. Gusfield compared the alcoholic with the workaholic, presenting them as kind of Jungian archetypes, reflections of the national unconscious. He called the alcoholic "one of the symbols of a fear of falling; of a threat in the personal drama of success and failure that is the key story of American careers." The workaholic symbolizes the opposite. "Here," Gusfield wrote, "the danger lies in the inability to let go; to enjoy release from role," and added: "That one is pathology and the other only troubling is the difference between cultural subordination and dominance."[21]

The workaholic, however, has become more than just troubling in journalism films. Over the history of the genre, he (and the workaholic is usually a "he") has gradually supplanted the alcoholic as a major ominous figure, someone to revile, suspect, fear. Many older films included protagonists who were at least incipient workaholics—star reporter Hildy Johnson in *The Front Page* (1931) and editor Ed Hutcheson in *Deadline, U.S.A* (1952) immediately come to mind. But if they worked hard, they also drank hard, finding escape from the pressures and preoccupations of their jobs in alcohol. They were never so involved with work that they couldn't stop for a quick nip. At a time when drinking still carried subversive overtones, this marked them as free men.

It would be misleading to suggest that the workaholic journalists in later films always mean bad news. In *All the President's Men* (1976), for example, workaholism is raised to the level of a social virtue. The round-the-clock devotion of reporters Bob Woodward and Carl Bernstein to their jobs allows them to uncover the Watergate scandal. They seem to have no family, no friends, no hobbies. Their life is their work, and their work is their passion. From the film's perspective, their singlemindedness is heroic, recalling faded, knightly notions of honor and duty. Robert Redford, who produced *All the President's Men* as well as co-starred in it, felt that the interest of the story lies in the way Woodward and Bernstein dig up the facts on Watergate.[22] The film celebrates their techniques and persistence, their absorption in the gritty little details of investigative reporting.

But, by the eighties, workaholic journalists were behaving quite despicably on the screen. Various reasons have been advanced for this sharp downturn in their image, from the mob approach to reporting and the explosion of tabloid TV to the profits-above-all philosophy of media companies.[23] At any event, the symbol of a corrupt press was no longer the drunken journalist who looks like he slept in his clothes. It was the respectable-looking yuppie who spouts all the right slogans while doing all the wrong things.

Beginning approximately with *Absence of Malice* (1981), in which an obtuse reporter destroys innocent people in the name of the First Amendment, journalism films have grown increasingly critical of the press. And the chief criticism has been that journalists are more interested in professional privilege and glitzy careers than in public service. Nineties films like *Hero, Natural Born Killers, To Die For,* and *Mad City* give us journalists who will do anything for a story or a shot at celebrity. They aren't slaves to alcohol, but to something worse— ambition. Of all the journalists we have met in film history, the drunk and the cynical and the lazy, the comic and the idealistic and the glib, the sober, hard-driving workaholic has become at the end of the century the most stereotypical and, ironically, the most dangerous.

Notes

CHAPTER 1

1. Craig MacAndrew and Robert B. Edgerton, *Drunken Comportment* (Chicago: Aldine, 1969), p. 36.

2. Joseph R. Gusfield has pointed out that the most widely recognized attributes of alcohol—its ability to reduce tension and increase fellow feeling—have produced its ritualistic uses. Thus, in the bureaucratic organization of daily life, alcohol is used to cue the shift from one time frame to another. The cocktail hour, for example, serves as a transition between day and night, work and play. Gusfield, "Passage to Play: Rituals of Drinking Time in American Society," in *Contested Meanings: The Construction of Alcohol Problems* (Madison: University of Wisconsin, 1996), pp. 67, 69.

3. Susan Sontag, *Illness As Metaphor* (New York: Farrar, Straus and Giroux, 1977), p. 58.

4. Herbert Fingarette, *Heavy Drinking: The Myth of Alcoholism As a Disease* (Berkeley: University of California, 1988), p. 51.

5. For more on AA's recovery program, see Joan Curlee-Salisbury, "Perspectives on Alcoholics Anonymous," in *Alcoholism: Development, Consequences, and Interventions*, 2d ed., eds. Nada J. Estes and M. Edith Heinemann (St. Louis: C. V. Mosby, 1982), pp. 312–13.

6. "Study Challenges Alcoholic, Therapy Match," *Middletown (N.Y.) Times Herald Record*, Dec. 20, 1996, p. 42.

7. Sontag, *Illness As Metaphor*, p. 35.

8. Ibid., pp. 32–33.

9. Donald W. Goodwin, *Alcohol and the Writer* (Kansas City: Andrews and McMeel, 1988), p. 172.

10. Quoted in ibid, p. 37.

155

11. Alex Barris, *Stop the Presses! The Newspaperman in American Films* (South Brunswick, N.J.: A. S. Barnes, 1976), p. 135.

12. Sontag, *Illness As Metaphor*, p. 25.

13. Denise Herd and Robin Room, "Alcohol Images in American Film," *Drinking and Drug Practices Surveyor* 18 (Aug. 1982): 25.

14. Robin Room, "Alcoholism and Alcoholics Anonymous in U.S. Films, 1945–1962: The Party Ends for the 'Wet Generation,' " *Journal of Studies on Alcohol* 50 (July 1989): 381.

15. Norman K. Denzin, *Hollywood Shot by Shot: Alcoholism in American Cinema* (New York: Aldine De Gruyter, 1991), p. xiv.

16. Richard Dyer, "The Role of Sterotypes," in *Images of Alcoholism*, eds. Jim Cook and Mike Lewington (London: BFI, 1979), p. 20.

17. Quoted in Brendan Gill, *Late Bloomers* (New York: Artisan, 1996), p. 106.

CHAPTER 2

1. D. B. Bromley, *Reputation, Image and Impression Management* (Chichester, England: John Wiley & Sons, 1993), p. 71.

2. Walter Lippmann, *Public Opinion* (New York: Free Press, 1922), p. 55.

3. Bromley, *Reputation*, p. 72.

4. Lippmann, *Public Opinion*, p. 59.

5. Ibid., p. 60.

6. Ibid., p. 74.

7. Bromley, *Reputation*, p. 72.

8. Lippmann., *Public Opinion*, p. 65.

9. Bromley, *Reputation*, p. 71.

10. Lippmann, *Public Opinion*, pp. 65–66.

11. Michael H. Bruno, "Stereotype," *Grolier Multimedia Encyclopedia* (N.p.: Grolier Electronic Publishing, 1995), n. pag.; Edwin Emery and Michael Emery, *The Press and America*, 5th ed. (Englewood Cliffs, N.J.: Prentice-Hall, 1984), p. 141.

12. H. L. Mencken, *Newspaper Days*, in *The Days of H. L. Mencken* (New York: Alfred A. Knopf, 1947; reprint ed., New York: Dorset Press, 1989), p. 181. Although he no longer drinks, Pulitzer Prize-winning columnist Jimmy Breslin also pays homage to the culture of drinking in his memoir, *I Want to Thank My Brain for Remembering Me.* Breslin recalls standing at the bar of Gallagher's restaurant late one afternoon with M. L. Rosenthal, managing editor of the *New York Times,* and Dick Doughtery, deputy police commissioner. They were talking about newspapers when suddenly Breslin, who had a big cold beer in his hand, blurted out, "I don't have to keep chasing fires for a living. I'm going to do a book called *The Gang That Couldn't Shoot Straight.*"

According to Breslin, the title would become "one of the three or four most repeated titles of my time." It fell from him so perfectly, he says, because of the beer and the lights and the bright polished wood—the special vibes of a good bar on a workday. Breslin, *I Want to Thank My Brain for Remembering Me* (New York: Little, Brown, 1996), p. 33.

13. Lippmann, *Public Opinion*, p. 61.

14. Quoted in ibid., p. 56.

15. The reference to the desk bottle is a paraphrase of a line from Alex Barris, *Stop the Presses! The Newspaperman in American Films* (South Brunswick, N.J.: A. S. Barnes, 1976), p. 135.

16. This was the era when not only journalism, but many occupations underwent professionalization. Drinking among late nineteenth-century reporters may have represented a holdover of pre-professional behavior. Herbert Gutman discussed the survival into the modern era of traditional work habits among American craftsmen in *Work, Culture, and Society in Industrializing America* (New York: Alfred A. Knopf, 1976), pp. 36–38.

17. Frank Luther Mott, *American Journalism*, 3rd ed. (New York: Macmillan, 1962), p. 488.

18. The best study of working conditions in the late nineteenth-century newsroom is Ted Curtis Smythe, "The Reporter, 1880–1900," *Journalism History* 7 (spring 1980): 1–9.

19. Quoted in Alfred McClung Lee, *The Daily Newspaper in America* (New York: Macmillan, 1937), p. 625.

20. "Working on Space," *Journalist* 7 (March 31, 1888): 8.

21. Charles J. Rosebault, *When Dana Was the Sun* (New York: Robert M. McBride, 1931; reprint ed., Westport, Conn.: Greenwood Press, 1970), pp. 166–67.

22. "Our Seventeenth 'Special,'" *Journalist* 28 (Dec. 15, 1900): 276. The same editorial recalled that James Gordon Bennett, founder of the *New York Herald*, "once told one of his men that he had noticed that men of genius frequently got 'high'; that was then an accepted notion in newspaper circles. Many of the 'old timers' had little other claim to genius[;] happily, this particular variety of genius is dying out."

23. Julian Ralph, *The Making of a Journalist* (New York: Harper & Brothers, 1903), p. 27.

24. Samuel Blythe, *The Making of a Newspaper Man* (Philadelphia: Henry Altemus, 1912; reprint ed., Westport, Conn.: Greenwood Press, 1970), p. 238.

25. Lee, *Daily Newspaper*, p. 625.

26. "Those who imbibed," old newspaperman Jim Bishop recalled, "used what I presume is an incontrovertible defense: the daily tensions of newsgathering, of trying to get the whole story and get it in time for the aptly named 'deadline'; to wait to read competitive newspapers to learn if they had an integral part of the story which we missed; the frustration of researching a good yarn all the way into the ground and then have the City Editor hold up

two fingers pinched together, murmuring: 'Give me three graphs'. . . . Many left the office for the saloon next door, intending to have two before hopping the commuter train. However, the bar conversation was always so rich and revealing, the joy of jawing among one's confreres often led to one more, and one more, and one more." Quoted in Goodwin, *Alcohol and the Writer*, p. 204.

27. Ibid., p. 205.

28. Quoted in ibid.

29. Matthew C. Ehrlich, letter to author, Jan. 2, 1997.

30. Ezra Goodman, "Fourth Estate Gets Better Role in Film," *Editor & Publisher* 20 (May 10, 1947): 26.

31. Ibid.

32. Ibid.

33. Deac Rossell, "Hollywood and the Newsroom," *American Film* 1 (Oct. 1975): 18.

34. Goodwin, *Alcohol and the Writer*, p. 183.

35. See Robin Room, "A 'Reverence for Strong Drink': The Lost Generation and the Elevation of Alcohol in American Culture," *Journal of Studies of Alcohol* 45 (Nov. 1984): 540–46; Alfred Kazin, " 'The Giant Killer': Drink & the American Writer," *Commentary* 61 (March 1976): 44; and John W. Crowley, *The White Logic: Alcoholism and Gender in Modernist American Fiction* (Amherst: University of Massachusetts Press, 1994).

36. Goodwin, *Alcohol and the Writer*, p. 119.

37. Quoted in Elizabeth Benedict, "Alcohol and Writers: A Long Day's Journey into Destruction," *Changes* 4 (July-Aug. 1989): 27. More than any other group except bartenders, writers die of cirrhosis of the liver, a disease associated with alcoholism.

38. Tom Wolfe, "The New Journalism," in *The New Journalism*, eds. Tom Wolfe and E. W. Johnson (New York: Harper & Row, 1970), p. 3.

39. Goodwin, *Alcohol and the Writer*, p. 205.

CHAPTER 3

1. Alfred Kazin, " 'The Giant Killer': Drink & the American Writer," *Commentary* 61 (March 1976): 45.

2. "In most societies alcohol is a social drink taken in company for relaxation and conviviality." W. R. Rorabaugh, *The Alcoholic Republic: An American Tradition* (New York: Oxford University Press, 1979), p. 163.

3. "Study Challenges Alcoholic, Therapy Match," *Middletown (N.Y.) Times Herald Record*, Dec. 20, 1996, p. 42.

4. Associated Press, "Study: Drunken Drivers Abound," *Middletown (N.Y.) Times Herald Record*, Jan. 8, 1997, n. pag.

5. Kazin, " 'Giant Killer,' " 44.

6. Mark Edward Lender and James Kirby Martin, *Drinking in America: A History* (New York: Free Press, 1982), p. 9.

7. Rorabaugh, *Alcoholic Republic,* pp. 149–50; Lender and Martin, *Drinking in America,* p. 2.

8. Lender and Martin, *Drinking in America,* p. 14.

9. Ibid., pp. 14–15.

10. Rorabaugh, *Alcoholic Republic,* p. 6.

11. Ibid., p. 139.

12. Ibid., p. 19.

13. Quoted in ibid., p. 6. Like Washington, Jefferson and Benjamin Franklin also did a bit of brewing. Lender and Martin, *Drinking in America,* p. 6.

14. Rorabaugh, *Alcoholic Republic,* p. xii.

15. Lender and Martin, *Drinking in America,* p. 72.

16. Ibid.; Rorabaugh, *Alcoholic Republic,* p. 112.

17. Lender and Martin, *Drinking in America,* pp. 66, 92–93.

18. Ibid., p. 108.

19. Donald Newlove, *Those Drinking Days: Myself and Other Writers* (New York: McGraw-Hill, 1981), p. 23.

20. Lender and Martin, *Drinking in America,* pp. 151–52. For the effect of the rise of the consumer society on American sexual mores, see John D'Emilio and Estelle B. Freedman, *Intimate Matters: A History of Sexuality in America* (New York: Harper & Row, 1988), particularly pp. 189, 227, 234–35, 242.

21. Norman K. Denzin, *Hollywood Shot by Shot: Alcoholism in American Cinema* (New York: Aldine De Gruyter, 1991), p. 4; Lender and Martin, *Drinking in America,* p. 191.

22. Harry Gene Levine, "The Discovery of Addiction: Changing Conceptions of Habitual Drunkenness in America," *Journal of Studies on Alcohol* 39 (1978): 148–49.

23. Ibid., 149.

24. Lender and Martin, *Drinking in America,* pp. 36–37.

25. Quoted in Levine, "Discovery of Addiction," 152.

26. Lender and Martin, *Drinking in America,* p. 68.

27. Ibid., pp. 119–20.

28. Quoted in "Discovery of Addiction,"158.

29. Andrew Sinclair, *Prohibition: The Era of Excess* (Boston: Little, Brown, 1962), p.182.

30. Lender and Martin, *Drinking in America,* p. 185; Levine, "Discovery of Addiction," 162.

31. Denzin, *Hollywood Shot by Shot,* p. 4.

32. Lender and Martin, *Drinking in America,* p. 185; Levine, "Discovery of Addiction,"167; Rorabaugh, *Alcoholic Republic,* pp. 221–22.

33. Joseph R. Gusfield, "Passage to Play: Rituals of Drinking Time in

American Society," in *Contested Meanings: The Construction of Alcohol Problems* (Madison: University of Wisconsin, 1996), p. 69.

34. Newlove, *Those Drinking Days*, p. 111.

35. Mark Edward Lender and Karen R. Karnchanapee, "Temperance Tales," *Journal of Studies on Alcohol* 38 (1977): 1347–51.

36. Ibid., 1361.

37. Ibid., 1351–53.

38. Ibid., 1351.

39. Ibid., 1366. The most widely read primer was written by a militant advocate of Prohibition, Dr. McGuffey. Larry May, *Screening Out the Past: The Birth of Mass Culture and the Motion Picture Industry* (New York: Oxford University Press, 1980), p. 14.

40. Quoted in Lender and Karnchanapee, "Temperance Tales," p. 1366.

41. Harold W. Pfautz, "The Image of Alcohol in Popular Fiction: 1900–1904 and 1946–1950," *Quarterly Journal for Studies on Alcohol* 23 (1963): 131–46.

42. Jesse Lynch Williams, "The Old Reporter," in *The Stolen Story and Other Newspaper Stories* (New York: Scribner's, 1899; reprint ed., Freeport, N.Y.: Books for Libraries Press, 1969), pp. 217–91.

43. Douglas Gilbert. *American Vaudeville: Its Life and Times* (New York: Whittlesey, 1940), pp. 269–73.

44. Quoted in ibid., p. 273.

45. See Peter Finn, "Attitudes Toward Drinking Conveyed in Studio Greeting Cards," *American Journal of Public Health* 70 (Aug.1980): 826–29.

46. Denzin, *Hollywood Shot by Shot*, p. 20. Edgar Dale, author of one of the earliest quantitative studies of American film, found that if drunkenness was shown on the screen, chances were good that an element of humor would be attached to it. Dale, *The Content of Motion Pictures* (New York: Macmillan, 1935), pp. 168–69.

47. Finn, "Studio Greeting Cards," 829.

48. Newlove, *Those Drinking Days*, p. 22.

49. Ibid., p. 140.

50. Jack London, *John Barleycorn* (New York: Grosset & Dunlap, 1913), p. 276.

51. John W. Crowley, *The White Logic: Alcoholism and Gender in Modernist American Fiction* (Amherst: University of Massachusetts Press, 1994), p. 44.

52. Ibid., p. 169.

53. Kazin, " 'Giant Killer,' " 44.

54. Crowley, *White Logic*, p. 37.

55. Quoted in ibid.

56. H. L. Mencken, *The American Language*, 4th ed. (New York: Alfred A. Knopf, 1937), p. 568.

57. Edmund Wilson, "The Lexicon of Prohibition," in *The American Earthquake* (Garden City, N.Y.: Anchor Books, 1964), pp. 90–91.

58. Lender and Martin, *Drinking in America*, p. 139.

59. Quoted in Kazin, " 'Giant Killer,' " 45.

60. Quoted in Crowley, *White Logic*, p. 44. By the same token, Donald W. Goodwin observed of Fitzgerald: "His novels and stories are crowded with drunkards who bear a strong resemblance to the writer." *Alcohol and the Writer* (Kansas City: Andrews and McMeel, 1988), p. 40.

61. Ibid., p.155.

62. See Deac Rossell, "Hollywood and the Newsroom," *American Film* 5 (Oct. 1975): 14–18, and Nick Roddick, *A New Deal in Entertainment* (London: British Film Institute, 1983).

63. Quoted in Denzin, *Hollywood Shot by Shot*, p. 4.

64. Madeline Matz of the Motion Picture, Broadcasting and Recorded Sound Division of the Library of Congress, letter to author, Jan. 7, 1997.

65. Quoted in Goodwin, *Alcohol and the Writer*, p. 119.

66. Quoted in Newlove, *Those Drinking Days*, p. 129.

67. Denzin, *Hollywood Shot by Shot*, p. 4.

68. Craig MacAndrew and Robert B. Edgerton, *Drunken Comportment* (Chicago: Aldine, 1969), p. 53.

CHAPTER 4

1. Stanley Kunitz and Howard Haycraft, eds., *Twentieth Century Authors* (New York: W. W. Wilson, 1942), pp. 1522–23. The title of Williams's prize-winning play was *Why Marry?*

2. For a survey of early newspaper fiction, see Howard Good, *Acquainted With the Night: The Image of Journalists in American Fiction, 1890–1930* (Metuchen, N.J.: Scarecrow Press, 1986).

3. "Newspaper Stories," *New York Times*, May 6, 1899, sec. 2, p. 293.

4. H. L. Mencken, *A Choice of Days*, selected and with an introduction by Edward L. Galligan (New York: Vintage, 1981), p. 142.

5. See Mark Edward Lender and Karen R. Karnchanapee, "Temperance Tales," *Journal of Studies on Alcohol* 38 (1977): 1347–70.

6. Jesse Lynch Williams, "The Old Reporter," in *The Stolen Story and Other Newspaper Stories* (New York: Scribner's, 1899; reprint ed., Freeport, N.Y.: Books for Libraries Press, 1969), p. 218.

7. See Harry Gene Levine, "The Discovery of Addiction: Changing Conceptions of Habitual Drunkenness in America," *Journal of Studies on Alcohol* 39 (1978): 143–74.

8. Williams, "Old Reporter," p. 255.

9. Ibid., pp. 248–50.

10. Ibid., p. 250.

11. Levine, "Discovery of Addiction," 144.

12. Berton Roueché, *The Neutral Spirit: A Portrait of Alcohol* (Boston: Little, Brown, 1960), pp. 110–11.

13. Williams, "Old Reporter," p. 258.

14. Lender and Karnchanapee, "Temperance Tales," 1364.

15. Williams, "Old Reporter," p. 258.

16. Ibid., pp. 269–70.

17. Ibid., p. 291.

18. David Graham Phillips, *The Great God Success* (New York: Grosset & Dunlap, 1901; reprint ed., Ridgewood, N.J.: Gregg Press, 1967), p. 11.

19. Henry Justin Smith, *Deadlines* (Chicago: Covici-McGee, 1923), p. 193.

20. Ben Ames Williams, *Splendor* (New York: Dutton, 1927), p. 205.

21. Gene Fowler, *Trumpet in the Dust* (New York: Liveright, 1930), p. 294.

22. Edna Ferber, *Dawn O'Hara* (New York: Grosset & Dunlap, 1911), p. 47.

23. John C. Mellett, *Ink* (Indianapolis: Bobbs-Merrill, 1930), p. 32.

24. Mark Edward Lender and James Kirby Martin, *Drinking in America: A History* (New York: Free Press, 1982), pp. 186–87.

25. Levine, "Discovery of Addiction," 165.

26. Louis M. Starr, *Bohemian Brigade: Civil War Newsmen in Action* (New York: Alfred A. Knopf, 1954), pp. 5–7.

27. Quoted in ibid., p. 7.

28. Ibid.

29. Elmer Ellis, *Mr. Dooley's America: A Life of Finley Peter Dunne* (New York: Alfred A. Knopf, 1941), pp. 47–48.

30. Larry Lorenz, "The Whitechapel Club: Defining Chicago's Newspapermen in the 1890s," *American Journalism* 15 (winter 1998): 86.

31. Quoted in ibid., p. 93.

CHAPTER 5

1. Norman K. Denzin, *Hollywood Shot by Shot: Alcoholism in American Cinema* (New York: Aldine De Gruyter, 1991), p. 4.

2. Quoted in Denise Herd and Robin Room, "Alcohol Images in American Film, 1909–1960," *Drinking and Drug Practices Surveyor* 18 (August 1982): 24–35.

3. Denzin, *Hollywood Shot by Shot*, p. 3.

4. Denise Herd, "Ideology, Melodrama, and the Changing Role of Alcohol Problems in American Film," *Contemporary Drug Problems* 13 (summer 1986): 215.

5. Dashiell Hammett, *The Dain Curse*, in *The Novels of Dashiell Hammett* (New York: Alfred A. Knopf, 1966), p. 193.

6. John D'Emilio and Estelle B. Freedman, *Intimate Matters: A History of Sexuality in America* (New York: Harper & Row, 1983), pp. 223–34.

7. Ibid., pp. 230, 265–66.

8. Virginia Wright Wexman, *Creating the Couple: Love, Marriage, and Hollywood Performance* (Princeton, N.J.: Princeton University Press, 1993), p. 13.

9. D'Emilio and Freedman, *Intimate Matters*, p.173.

10. Fred., "Rummy," *Variety,* Sept. 29, 1916, p. 24.

11. "The Fringe of Society," *American Film Institute Catalog for Feature Films, 1911–1920* (Berkeley: University of California Press, 1988), p. 306.

12. "Don't Neglect Your Wife," *American Film Institute Catalog for Feature Films, 1921–1930* (New York: R. R. Bowker, 1971), p. 197; Rush., "Don't Neglect Your Wife," *Variety,* July 29, 1921, n. pag.

13. "His Parisian Wife," *American Film Institute Catalog for Feature Films, 1911–1920* (Berkeley: University of California Press, 1988), p. 413.

14. Fred., "Night Workers," *Variety,* May 25, 1917, p. 20.

15. See Chapter 3, "The Ghosts of Printing House Square."

16. "Night Workers," *American Film Institute Catalog for Feature Films, 1911–1920* (Berkeley: University of California Press, 1988), p. 659.

17. Fred., "Night Workers," p. 20.

18. Step., "Deadline at Eleven," *Variety,* March 12, 1920, p. 53.

19. "Deadline at Eleven," *American Film Institute Catalog for Feature Films, 1911–1920* (Berkeley: University of California Press, 1988), p. 200.

20. "A Certain Rich Man," *American Film Institute Catalog for Feature Films, 1921–1930* (New York: R. R. Bowker, 1971), p.116.

21. See Chapter 2, "Drink, Drank, Drunk."

22. Rush., "Don't Neglect Your Wife," n. pag.

23. "The Foolish Matrons," *American Film Institute Catalog for Feature Films, 1921–1930* (New York: R. R. Bowker, 1971), pp. 259–60.

24. "A Case at Law," *American Film Institute Catalog for Feature Films, 1911–1920* (Berkeley: University of California Press, 1988), p. 127; Ibee., "A Case at Law," *Variety,* Nov. 23, 1917, p. 53.

25. Fred., "Rummy," p. 24. The "Keeley cure"—also called the "Gold cure"—enjoyed popularity as a remedy for alcoholism and drug addiction in the late nineteenth century. See Mark Edward Lender and James Kirby Martin, *Drinking in America: A History* (New York: Free Press, 1982), pp. 120–22

26. "The Fringe of Society," *American Film Institute Catalog,* p. 306.

27. Louis M. Starr, *Bohemian Brigade: Civil War Newsmen in Action* (New York: Alfred A. Knopf, 1954), p. 6.

28. Arnold S. Linsky, "Theories of Behavior and the Image of the Alcoholic in Popular Magazines 1900–1966," *Public Opinion Quarterly* 34 (winter 1970–71): 575–76, 580.

29. Mike Lewington, "Alcoholism in the Movies: An Overview," in *Images of Alcoholism,* eds. Jim Cook and Lewington (London: British Film Institute, 1979), pp. 22–24; Linsky, "Theories of Behavior," 579–80.

30. Linsky, "Theories of Behavior," 580.

31. D. A. B., "The Fringe of Society," *New York Dramatic Mirror,* Nov. 17, 1917, p. 19.

32. Ibee., "Case at Law," p. 53.

33. "Truthful Tulliver," *American Film Institute Catalog for Feature Films, 1911–1920* (Berkeley: University of California Press, 1988), p. 954.

34. "The Tomboy," *American Film Institute Catalog for Feature Films, 1921–1930* (New York: R. R. Bowker, 1971), pp. 818–19.

35. Herd and Room, "Alcohol Images," 29.

36. Andrew Tudor, "On Alcohol and the Mystique of Media Effects," in Cook and Lewington, pp. 11–12.

37. E. S., "Rummy," *New York Dramatic Mirror*, Sept. 30, 1916, p. 30.

38. "Rummy," *Wid's Film Daily*, Oct. 19, 1916, p. 1046.

39. Genevive Harris, "The Night Workers," *Motography*, June 2, 1917, p. 1171.

40. "Melodrama of Newspaper Life Makes Average Program Feature," *Wid's Film Daily*, March 14, 1920, p. 9.

41. Louis Reeves Harrison, "Deadline at Eleven," *Moving Picture World*, March 20, 1920, p. 2009.

42. Fred., "Rummy," p. 24.

43. Fred., "Night Workers," p. 20.

44. A. G. S., "The Night Workers," *New York Dramatic Mirror*, May 26, 1917, p. 29.

45. Chip Rowe, "Hacks on Film" *Washington Journalism Review* (November 1992): 28.

CHAPTER 6

1. "A newspaper picture," film critic Pauline Kael once said, "meant a contemporary picture in an American setting . . . a tough modern talkie, not a tearjerker with sound." Kael, *The Citizen Kane Book* (Boston: Little, Brown, 1971), p. 20.

2. Andrew Bergman noted that the very titles of the films—*Big News, Five Star Final, Scandal for Sale*—indicated "their wonderfully hysterical tone and subject matter. Bergman, *We're in the Money: Depression America and Its Films* (New York: Harper & Row, 1971), p. 21.

3. Ibid., p. 18.

4. See Howard Good, *The Journalist as Autobiographer* (Metuchen, N.J.: Scarecrow Press, 1993).

5. Ezra Goodman, "Fourth Estate Gets Better Role in Films," *Editor & Publisher* 20 (May 10, 1947): 26.

6. Nick Roddick, *A New Deal in Entertainment* (London: British Film Institute, 1983), p. 6.

7. Bergman, *We're in the Money*, pp. 21, 90.

8. Ian Hamilton, *Writers in Hollywood, 1915–1951* (New York: Carroll & Graf, 1990), p. 30.

9. Deac Rossell, "The Fourth Estate and the Seventh Art," in *Questioning Media Ethics*, ed. Bernard Rubin (New York: Praeger, 1978), pp. 238, 248.

10. Goodman, "Fourth Estate Gets Better Role," 26.

11. Rossell, "Fourth Estate and Seventh Art," p. 242.

12. See Simon Michael Bessie, *Jazz Journalism* (New York: E.P. Dutton, 1938; reprint ed., New York: Russel & Russel, 1969); and Silas Bent, *Ballyhoo* (New York: Boni and Liveright, 1927).

13. Quoted in Marion Tuttle Marzolf, *Civilizing Voices: American Press Criticism, 1880–1950* (New York: Longman, 1991), p. 85.

14. Rossell, " Fourth Estate and Seventh Art," p. 243.

15. Unable to locate a viewing copy of *Gentlemen of the Press*, I reconstructed the film from reviews as well as from a synopsis in the *American Film Institute Catalog for Feature Films, 1921–1930*.

16. Mordaunt Hall, "A Newspaper Play," *New York Times*, May 13, 1929, sec. 2, p. 27. See Richard Harding Davis, "A Derelict," in *Ransom's Folly* (New York: Scribner's, 1904) and Jesse Lynch Williams, "The Stolen Story," in *The Stolen Story and Other Newspaper Stories* (New York: Scribner's, 1899; reprint ed., Freeport, N..Y: Books for Libraries Press, 1969). Williams was so fond of the incident that he recycled it for a novel, *The Day-Dreamer* (New York: Scribner's, 1906).

17. Hall, "Newspaper Play," p. 27.

18. Mori., "Gentlemen of Press," *Variety*, May 15, 1929, n. pag.

19. Ibid.

20. Stephen L. Hanson, "La Cava, Gregory," *International Dictionary of Films and Filmmakers*, v. 2 (Chicago: St. James Press, 1984), pp. 310–11.

21. Waly., "Big News," *Variety*, Oct. 9, 1929, n. pag.

22. Roger McNiven, "Gregory La Cava," *American Directors*, v. 1, ed. Jean-Pierre Coursodon, with Pierre Sauvage (New York: McGraw-Hill, 1983), p. 198.

23. Ibid.

24. Waly., "Big News," n. pag.

25. Robin Room, "Alcoholism and Alcoholics Anonymous in U.S. Films, 1945–1962: The Party Ends for the 'Wet Generation,' " *Journal of Studies on Alcohol* 50 (July 1989): 377.

26. Quoted in Matthew C. Erhlich, "Thinking Critically About Journalism Through Popular Culture," *Journalism Educator* 50 (winter 1996): 39. See also Vivian Sobchack, "Genre Film: Myth, Ritual, and Sociodrama," in *Film/Culture*, ed. Sari Thomas (Metuchen, N.J.: Scarecrow Press, 1982), pp. 145–65.

27. For more on Brush's novel, see Howard Good, *Acquainted With the Night: The Image of Journalists in American Fiction, 1890–1930* (Metuchen, N.J.: Scarecrow Press, 1986), pp. 6, 10, 14, 35.

28. Rush., "Young Man of Manhattan," *Variety*, April 23, 1930, n. pag.

29. "Norman Foster in Talkie," *New York Times*, April 19, 1930, sec. 1, p. 15.

30. Chip Rowe, "Hacks on Film," *Washington Journalism Review,* Nov. 1992, pp. 27–29; Jane Gross, "Movies and the Press Are an Enduring Romance," *New York Times,* June 2, 1985, sec. 2, p. 1.

31. Jeffery Martin Brown, *Ben Hecht, Hollywood Screenwriter* (Ann Arbor, Mich.: UMI Research Press, 1985), p. 42.

32. "Front Page," *Judge,* April 11, 1931, p. 19.

33. Mordaunt Hall, "A Newspaper Melodrama," *New York Times,* March 20, 1931, p. 29.

34. B. B., "A Rowdy Film," *New Republic,* April 29, 1931, p. 303.

35. Hall, "Newspaper Melodrama," p. 29.

36. "Front Page," *Judge,* p. 28.

37. Richard Corliss, "The Front Page and His Girl Friday," in *Movie Comedy,* eds. Stuart Byron and Elisabeth Weis (New York: Grossman, 1977), p. 63.

38. Alexander Bakshy, "Too Much Halo," *Nation,* April 15, 1931, p. 429.

39. Peter Roffman and Jim Purdy, *The Hollywood Social Problem Film: Madness, Despair, and Politics from the Depression to the Fifties* (Bloomington: Indiana University Press, 1981), p. 38.

40. Ibid., p. 38.

41. Mark Edward Lender and James Martin Kirby, *Drinking in America: A History* (New York: Free Press, 1982), pp. 129–36.

42. Quoted in Kurt Vonnegut, *Timequake* (New York: G. P. Putnam's Sons, 1997), p. 150.

43. Sinclair, *Prohibition: Era of Excess* (Boston: Little, Brown, 1962), p. 214.

44. Ibid., pp. 223–24, 230.

45. Corliss, "Front Page," p. 60.

46. Ibid., p. 61.

47. Sinclair, *Prohibition,* pp. 230–231, 234.

48. Quoted in ibid., p. 234.

49. Ibid., p. 235.

50. John W. Crowley, *The White Logic: Alcoholism and Gender in American Modernist Fiction* (Amherst: University of Massachusetts Press, 1994), p. 28; Donald W. Goodwin, *Alcohol and the Writer* (Kansas City: Andrew and McMeel, 1988), p. 133; Robin Room, "Alcoholism and Alcoholics Anonymous in U.S. Films, 1945–1962: The Party Ends for the 'Wet Generation,' " *Journal of Studies on Alcohol* 50 (July 1989): 372; Denise Herd and Robin Room, "Alcohol Images in American Film, 1909–1960," *Drinking and Drug Practices Surveyor* 18 (Aug. 1982): 29.

51. See Chapter 4, "The Ghosts of Printing House Square."

52 Joseph R. Gusfield, "Passage to Play: Rituals of Drinking Time in American Society," in *Contested Meanings: The Construction of Alcohol Problems* (Madison: University of Wisconsin, 1996), p. 62.

53. Ibid., p. 59.

54. Ibid., p. 73.

55. I'm drawing here on the ideas of Herbert G. Gutman, *Work, Culture and*

Society in Industrializing America (New York: Alfred A. Knopf, 1976), pp. 36–38.

56. Gusfield, "Passage to Play," p. 68.

57. Jeffrey Richards, "Discovery: Five Star Final," *Focus on Film* 23 (1975): 57; Thomas Schatz, *The Genius of the System* (New York: Pantheon, 1988), p. 141; Elizabeth Dalton, "Women at Work: Warners in the Thirties," *Velvet Light Trap* 6 (n.d.): 15.

58. For more on "B," or budget, pictures, see Don Miller, *"B" Movies* (New York: Curtis, 1973); Robin Cross, *The Big Book of B Movies* (New York: St. Martin's, 1981); Wheeler W. Dixon, *The "B" Directors: A Biographical Directory* (Metuchen, N.J.: Scarecrow Press, 1985).

59. Stanley Walker, *City Editor* (New York: Frederick A. Stokes, 1934), pp. 202–04.

60. Rush., "Famous Ferguson Case," *Variety*, April 26, 1932, p. 13.

61. Ibid.

62. Judith Harwin and Shirley Otto, "Women, Alcohol and the Screen," in *Images of Alcoholism,* eds. Jim Cook and Michael Lewington (London: BFI, 1979), pp. 39, 48.

63. Room, "Alcoholism and Alcoholics Anonymous in U.S. Films," p. 376.

64. Rush., "Famous Ferguson Case," p. 13.

65. Mordaunt Hall, "Sensational Journalism," *New York Times,* April 8, 1932, p. 25.

66. Strong's single-mindedness about his job recalls Professor Herbert Fingarette's definition of heavy drinking as "a central activity" that "affects the style and nature of all aspects" of the drinker's life. In other words, a workaholic may bear some psychological or other resemblance to an alcoholic. This idea is developed in my "Epilogue." Fingarette, *Heavy Drinking: The Myth of Alcoholism As a Disease* (Berkeley: University of California, 1988), p. 101.

67. Sinclair, *Prohibition*, p. 177.

68. Ibid., pp. 310–11.

69. Quoted in Edgar Dale, *The Content of Motion Pictures* (New York: Macmillan, 1935), p. 170.

70. Ibid., pp. 168–69, 173–74.

71. Char., "Platinum Blonde," *Variety,* Nov. 3, 1931, p. 27.

72. A. D. S., "Out of His Element," *New York Times,* Oct. 31, 1931, p. 22.

73. Herd and Room, "Alcohol Images," 29.

74. See Chap. 6, "Frank Capra's Super-Shysters and Little People," in Roffman and Purdy, pp.179–89.

75. Timothy W. Johnson, "It Happened One Night," in *Magill's Survey of Cinema: English Language Films,* First Series, v. 2 (Englewood Cliffs, N.J.: Salem Press, 1980), pp. 852–53.

76. Leland A. Poague, *The Cinema of Frank Capra* (South Brunswick, N.J.: A. S. Barnes, 1975), p.154.

77. Quoted in Goodwin, *Alcohol and the Writer*, p. 172.

78. Brooks Robards, "Newshounds and Sob Sisters: The Journalist Goes to Hollywood," *Beyond the Stars: Stock Characters in American Popular Film*, v. 1, eds. Paul Loukides and Linda K. Fuller (Bowling Green, Ohio: Popular Press, 1990), p. 131.

79. Leland A. Poague called *It Happened One Night* "the first and most definitive of the 'screwball comedies,'" but Donald Willis argued that its "significance as a progenitor of screwball comedy is questionable," explaining that "it seems too mild, sane, and quiet to be considered screwball." Poague, *Cinema of Capra*, p. 153; Donald Willis, *The Films of Frank Capra* (Metuchen, N.J.: Scarecrow Press, 1974), p. 146.

80. Odec., "Libeled Lady," *Variety*, Nov. 4, 1936, n. pg.

81. Fingarette, *Heavy Drinking*, p. 18.

82. Ibid.; Joan Curlee-Salisbury, "Perspectives on Alcoholics Anonymous," in *Alcoholism: Development, Consequences, and Interventions*, 2d ed., eds. Nada J. Estes and M. Edith Heinemann (St. Louis: C. V. Mosby, 1982), pp. 311–14.

83. Frank S. Nugent, "Nothing Sacred," *New York Times*, Nov. 26, 1937, p. 26; Ed Hulse, "Nothing Sacred," in *Magill's Survey of Cinema*, First Series, v. 3 (Englewood Cliffs, N.J.: Salem Press, 1980), p. 1224.

84. Graham Greene, *Graham Greene on Film: Collected Film Criticism, 1935–1940*, ed. John Russell Taylor (New York: Simon and Schuster, 1972), p. 218.

CHAPTER 7

1. V. N. Volosinov, *Marxism and the Philosophy of Language*, trans. Laduslav Matejka and I. R. Titunik (New York: Seminar Press, 1973), pp. 10, 23–24.

2. Robin Room, "Alcoholism and Alcoholics Anonymous in U.S. Films, 1945–1962: The Party Ends for the 'Wet Generation,'" *Journal on Studies of Alcohol* 50 (July 1989): 370.

3. Joan Curlee-Salisbury, "Perspectives on Alcoholics Anonymous," in *Alcoholism: Development, Consequences, and Interventions*, 2d ed., eds. Nada J. Estes and M. Edith Heinemann (St. Louis: C. V. Mosby, 1982), p. 314.

4. Ibid., p. 311.

5. Herbert Fingarette, *Heavy Drinking: The Myth of Alcoholism As a Disease* (Berkeley: University of California Press, 1988), p. 19.

6. Mark Edward Lender and James Kirby Martin, *Drinking in America: A History* (New York: Free Press, 1982), p. 188.

7. Quoted in Donald W. Goodwin, *Alcohol and the Writer* (Kansas City: Andrews and McMeel, 1988), p. 5.

8. For other notable performances by actors portraying alcoholics on the

screen, see J. M. Howard, "Hard Drinkers Plum Roles for Many Actors," *San Francisco Chronicle*, June 19, 1988, Datebook sec., pp. 26–28.

9. Denise Herd and Robin Room, "Alcohol Images in American Film, 1909–1960," *Drinking and Drug Practices Surveyor* 18 (Aug. 1982): 25.

10. John W. Crowley, *The White Logic: Alcoholism and Gender in American Modernist Fiction* (Amherst: University of Massachusetts, 1994), pp. 145–46.

11. Herd and Room, "Alcohol Images," 25. The poll is cited in Stephen Braun, *Buzz: The Science and Lore of Alcohol and Caffeine* (New York: Oxford University Press, 1996), p. 91.

12. Andrew Tudor, "On Alcohol and the Mystique of Media Effects," in *Images of Alcoholism*, eds. Jim Cook and Mike Lewington (London: BFI, 1979), pp. 11–12.

13. Eric F. Goldman, *The Crucial Decade: America, 1945–1955* (New York: Alfred A. Knopf, 1956), p. 13.

14. Tudor, "On Alcohol," p. 11.

15. Harold W. Pfautz, "The Image of Alcohol in Popular Fiction: 1900–04 and 1946–50," *Quarterly Journal for Studies on Alcohol* 23 (1962): 145.

16. Herd and Room, "Alcohol Images," 31.

17. Robert Redding, *Starring Robert Benchley* (Albuquerque: University of New Mexico Press, 1973), p. 137.

18. Donald Spoto, *The Dark Side of Genius: The Life of Alfred Hitchcock* (New York: Ballantine Books, 1983), p. 240; Thomas A. Hanson, "Foreign Correspondent," in *Magill's Survey of Cinema: English Language Films*, First Series, v. 2, ed. Frank N. Magill (Englewood Cliffs, N.J.: Salem Press, 1980), p. 557.

19. Quoted in Redding, *Benchley*, p. 138.

20. Quoted in ibid.

21. Bosley Crowther, "Foreign Correspondent," *New York Times*, Aug. 28, 1940, p. 15.

22. Hanson, "Foreign Correspondent," p. 557.

23. The one exception was Bosley Crowther of the *New York Times* who said in his review that Benchley "tends too heavily toward travesty—just a shade too heavily." Crowther, "Foreign Correspondent," p. 15.

24. *Hollywood Reporter*, Aug. 28, 1940, p. 3; quoted in Redding, *Benchley*, p. 141.

25. Herb Sterne, "Foreign Correspondent," *Rob Wagner's Script*, Sept. 28, 1940, p. 16.

26. For a fairly comprehensive list of alcoholic writers of the "Lost Generation," see Crowley, *White Logic*, pp. 38–39.

27. Bosley Crowther, "The Philadelphia Story," *New York Times*, Dec. 27, 1940, p. 22.

28. One scholar described screwball comedy as "an inheritor of the preoccupations and discoveries of Shakespearean romantic comedy." Stanley Cavell, *Pursuits of Happiness: The Hollywood Comedy of Remarriage* (Cambridge, Mass.: Harvard University Press, 1981), p. 1.

29. Bosley Crowther, "Meet John Doe," *New York Times*, March 13, 1941, p. 25.

30. Edwin Schallert, " 'Meet John Doe' Hailed as Capra Victory," *Los Angeles Times*, March 31, 1941, p. 16; James Shelley Hamilton, "New Movies," in *Meet John Doe*, ed. Charles Wolfe (New Brunswick, N.J.: Rutgers University Press, 1989), p. 228.

31. Otis Ferguson, "Democracy at the Box Office," *New Republic*, March 24, 1941, pp. 405–06.

32. Ibid.

33. Ibid.

34. Frank Capra, "Five Endings in Search of an Audience," in Wolfe, p. 210.

35. Ibid., pp. 212–13.

36. Schallert, " 'Meet John Doe'," p. 16.

37. For a sampling of contemporary reviews and scholarly reappraisals of *Citizen Kane*, see Richard Gottesman, *Focus on Citizen Kane* (Englewood Cliffs, N.J.: Prentice Hall, 1971), pp. 45–120.

38. For more on the Hearst-Kane connection, see Laura Mulvey, *Citizen Kane* (London: BFI Publishing, 1992), pp. 28–39.

39. Virginia Wright Wexman, *Creating the Couple: Love, Marriage, and Hollywood Performance* (Princeton, N.J.: Princeton University Press, 1993), p. 18.

40. Bosley Crowther, " 'Roxie Hart,' 'Chicago' Remake, With Ginger Rogers, Adolphe Menjou, George Montgomery, Seen at Roxy Theatre," *New York Times*, Feb. 20, 1942, p. 21.

41. Frank T. Thompson, *William A. Wellman* (Metuchen, N.J.: Scarecrow Press, 1983), p. 205.

42. Walt., "Roxie Hart," *Variety*, Feb. 4, 1942, np; Crowther, "Roxie Hart," p. 21.

43. Thompson, *Wellman*, p. 204.

44. Jane Feur, *The Hollywood Musical* (Bloomington: Indiana University Press, 1982), p. 88. For more on the self-reflexive dimension of popular culture, see Dana Polan, "Brief Encounters: Mass Culture and the Evacuation of Sense," in *Studies in Entertainment*, ed. Tania Modelski (Bloomington: Indiana University Press, 1986), pp. 99–118.

45. Herd and Room, "Alcohol Images," 31.

46. Harry Gene Levine, "The Discovery of Addiction: Changing Conceptions of Habitual Drunkenness in America," *Journal of Studies on Alcohol* 39 (1978): 161–62.

47. Room, "Alcoholism and Alcoholics Anonymous in U.S. Films," 368; Norman K. Denzin, *Hollywood Shot by Shot: Alcoholism in American Cinema* (New York: Aldine De Gruyter, 1991), p. 7.

48. Goldman, *Crucial Decade*, p. 289.

49. Quoted in William Manchester, *The Glory and the Dream: A Narrative History of America, 1932–1972* (Boston: Little, Brown, 1974), p. 777.

50. Ibid., pp. 774–75.

51. Ibid., p. 778.

52. Thomas Schatz, *Hollywood Genres* (New York: Random House, 1981), p. 226.

53. Quoted in Goldman, *Crucial Decade*, pp. 135–36.

54. Richard M. Huber, *The American Idea of Success* (New York: McGraw-Hill, 1971), p. 309.

55. Brandon French, *On the Verge of Revolt: Women in American Films of the Fifties* (New York: Frederick Ungar, 1978), p. 68.

56. Denise Herd, "Ideology, Melodrama, and the Changing Role of Alcohol Problems in American Films," *Contemporary Drug Problems* (summer 1986): 229.

57. Bosley Crowther, " 'Come Fill the Cup,' in Which James Cagney Takes Role of Newspaper Man, at Warner," *New York Times*, Nov. 22, 1951, p. 47.

58. Room, "Alcoholism and Alcoholics Anonymous in U.S. Films," 374.

59. Ibid., 373.

60. Philip Wylie, *Generation of Vipers* (New York: Holt, Rinehart and Winston, 1942), p. 29.

61. Crowther, " 'Come Fill the Cup,' " p. 47.

62. Bernard A. Weisberger, *The American Newspaperman* (Chicago: University of Chicago Press, 1961), pp. 193–95.

63. Bosley Crowther, "Deadline, U.S.A.," *New York Times*, March 15, 1952, p. 8.

64. Estes Kefauver, an ambitious senator from Tennessee, chaired a committee in 1950 investigating crime nationwide. See Manchester, *Glory and Dream*, pp. 600–01.

65. Phil Hardy, *Sam Fuller* (New York: Praeger, 1970), pp. 35–36.

66. Ibid., pp. 39–40.

67. Gilb., "Park Row," *Variety*, Aug. 6, 1952, n. pag.

68. Quoted in Hardy, *Fuller*, pp. 45–56.

69. In somewhat the same vein, old Mrs. Garrison, widow of the *Day*'s founder, tells the maritally challenged Ed Hutcheson in *Deadline, U.S.A.*, "You wouldn't have had a wife if that newspaper had beautiful legs."

70. Sam Fuller, "News That's Fit to Film," *American Film* 1 (Oct. 1975): 23.

71. Herd and Room, "Alcohol Images," 34.

72. Ibid.

73. The working title of the film was *News Is Made at Night*.

74. Lotte H. Eisner, *Fritz Lang* (New York: Oxford University Press, 1977), p. 351.

75. Quoted in ibid.

76. Peter Bogdanovich, *Fritz Lang in America* (New York: Praeger, 1969), pp. 102–03.

77. Gene, "Sweet Smell of Success," *Variety*, June 19, 1957, np.

78. Ruth L. Hirayama, "Sweet Smell of Success," *Magill's Survey of Cinema:*

English Language Films, 2nd series, v. 5, ed. Frank N. Magill (Englewood Cliffs, N.J.: Salem Press, 1981), pp. 2393–94.

79. "What sort of love does the imperious Hunsecker have for his young sister?" the *New York Times* reviewer asked. "Is this exaggerated possessiveness psychological or something else?" A. H. Weiler, "Sweet Smell of Success," *New York Times*, June 28, 1957, p. 29.

80. Hirayama, "Sweet Smell," p. 2394.

81. William O'Neill, *American High: The Years of Confidence, 1945–1960* (New York: Free Press, 1986), p. 175.

82. Quoted in Schatz, *Hollywood Genres*, p. 254.

83. Ibid., pp. 224–25.

84. For a positive re-evaluation of the film, see Janey Place, "The Tarnished Angels," *Magill's Survey of Cinema: English Language Films*, 2d series, v. 5, ed. Frank N. Magill (Englewood Cliffs, N.J.: Salem Press, 1981), pp. 2412–12.

85. Bosley Crowther, "The Tarnished Angels," *New York Times*, Jan. 7, 1958, p. 31; Whit., "The Tarnished Angels," *Variety*, Nov. 27, 1957, n. pag.

86. Quoted in Michael Stern, *Douglas Sirk* (Boston: Twayne, 1979), p. 156.

87. Rainer Werner Fassbinder, "Six Films by Douglas Sirk," in *Douglas Sirk*, eds. Laura Mulvey and Jan Halliday (Edinburgh: Edinburgh Film Festival, 1972), pp. 102–03.

88. Franklin Jarlett, *Robert Ryan: A Biography and Critical Filmography* (Jefferson, N.C.: McFarland, 1990), p. 234.

89. For summaries of the major reviews of *Lonelyhearts*, see ibid., pp. 235–36.

90. There was at least one film released in the late fifties that treated the drunken journalist humorously. *Teacher's Pet* (1958), starring Clark Gable as a streetwise city editor who believes nothing good comes from colleges and Doris Day as the blonde, shapely journalism professor who helps change his mind, delighted critics and audiences alike. *The New York Times* said the makers of the film "managed to coalesce journalism and romance, those frayed ingredients of too many standard movies, into a sensible, funny, sometimes fresh and trenchant diversion."

Gable had played a newspaperman before, most memorably in the Oscar-winning *It Happened One Night*, but this was Day's first foray into romantic comedy after twenty-one films, usually in musical roles. The box-office receipts for *Teacher's Pet* were such that she went on to make a series of very successful romantic comedies with Rock Hudson.

Teacher's Pet was a bit of a throwback to films of the thirties and forties, and not just because it returned Gable to the city room or because it found drunkenness amusing. It was also a throwback because it contained a definite drunk scene, a set piece. Rather than engaging in the routinized drinking so common in fifties films, Gable and Gig Young, playing Dr. Hugo Pine, a psychology professor, have a drinking contest at a nightclub. This gave both actors ample opportunity to mug it up in the farcical manner of Robert Benchley at the London pub in *Foreign Correspondent* or James Gleason at Jim's Bar in *Meet John Doe*. Young's life sadly paralleled his screen roles. He eventually destroyed himself with alcohol, winding up a suicide. For more on *Teacher's Pet*, see A. H. Weiler, "Teacher's Pet," *New York Times*, March 20, 1958, p. 33; Powe., "Teacher's Pet," *Variety*, March 19, 1958, n. pag.; Timothy W. Johnson, "Teacher's Pet," *Magill's Survey of Cinema: English Language Films*, First Series, v. 4, ed. Frank N. Magill (Englewood Cliffs, N.J.: Salem Press, 1980), p. 1683.

CHAPTER 8

1. Herbert Fingarette, *Heavy Drinking: The Myth of Alcoholism As a Disease* (Berkeley: University of California Press, 1988), *p. 61*.

2. See, for example, Whit., "The Luck of Ginger Coffey," *Variety*, Sept. 23, 1964, n. pag.

3. Bosley Crowther, "The Luck of Ginger Coffey," *New York Times*, Sept. 22, 1964, p. 44.

4. Norman K. Denzin, *Hollywood Shot by Shot: Alcoholism in American Cinema* (New York: Aldine De Gruyter, 1991), p. 7; Robin Room, "Alcoholism and Alcoholics Anonymous in U.S. Films, 1945–1962: The Party Ends for the 'Wet Generation,'" *Journal of Studies on Alcohol* 50 (1989): 368.

5. Room, "Alcoholism and Alcoholics Anonymous," 368.

6. Quoted in Karl W. Weimer Jr., "Inherit the Wind," *Magill's Survey of Cinema: English Language Films*, 2d Series, v. 3, ed. Frank N. Magill (Englewood Cliffs, N.J.: Salem Press, 1981), p. 1148.

7. Pry., "Inherit the Wind," *Variety*, July 6, 1960, n. pag.

8. Mark Edward Lender and James Kirby Martin, *Drinking in America: A History* (New York: Free Press, 1982), p. 140.

9. Pry., "Inherit the Wind"; Philip T. Hartung, *Commonweal*, Nov. 4, 1960, p. 151. *Inherit the Wind* was nominated for four Academy Awards—best actor, best screenplay from another medium, best black and white cinematography, and best editing—but lost in every category.

10. Weimer, "Inherit the Wind," p. 1150.

11. Rick., "Gaily, Gaily," *Variety*, Dec. 3, 1969, n. pag.

12. Vincent Canby, "Gaily, Gaily," Dec. 17, 1969, *New York Times*, p. 62.

13. Rick., "Gaily, Gaily."

14. Leonard Downie Jr., *The New Muckrakers* (Washington: New Republic, 1974), p. 7.

15. Robert Daley, "Super-Reporter: The Missing American Hero Turns Out to Be . . . Clark Kent," *New York*, Nov. 12, 1973, p. 19.

16. Tom Wicker, *On Press* (New York: Viking Press, 1978), p. 15.

17. William E. Leuchtenburg, "All the President's Men," in *Past Imperfect: History According to the Movies,* ed. Mark C. Carnes (New York: Henry Holt, 1995), p. 291.

18. Michael Schudson, *Watergate in American Memory: How We Remember, Forget, and Reconstruct the Past* (New York: Basic Books, 1992), p. 104.

19. Leuchtenburg, "All the President's Men," p. 291.

20. Seth Cagin and Philip Dray, *Hollywood Films of the Seventies* (New York: Harper & Row, 1984), pp. 249–50.

21. Thomas E. Leonard, *News for All: America's Coming-of-Age with the Press* (New York: Oxford University Press, 1995), p. 214.

22. See Chapter 6, "Bottoms Up."

23. Joseph R. Gusfield, "Passage to Play: Rituals of Drinking Time in American Society," in *Constructed Meanings: The Construction of Alcohol Problems* (Madison: University of Wisconsin, 1996), pp. 57–74.

24. Leuchtenburg, "All the President's Men," p. 288; Cagin and Dray, *Hollywood Films,* p. 250; Howard Good, *Outcasts: The Image of Journalists in Contemporary Film* (Metuchen, N.J.: Scarecrow Press, 1989), p. 156; Ruth L. Hirayama, "All the President's Men," *Magill's Survey of Cinema: English Language Films,* First Series, v. 1, ed. Frank N. Magill (Englewood Cliffs, N.J.: Salem Press, 1980), p. 54.

25. See J. Anthony Lukas, *Nightmare: The Underside of the Nixon Years* (New York: Bantam, 1977), pp. 366–67, 373–74.

26. Leonard, *News for All,* p. 214.

27. Quoted in Jane Gross, "Movies and the Press Are an Enduring Romance," *New York Times,* June 2, 1985, sec. 2, p. 19.

28. Edwin Diamond, *The Tin Kazoo: Television, Politics, and the News* (Cambridge, Mass.: MIT Press, 1975), pp. 92–93.

29. Bob Teague, *Live and Off Color: News Biz* (New York: A & W Publishers, 1982), p. 99.

30. Quoted in Stephen E. Bowles, *Sidney Lumet: A Guide to References and Resources* (Boston: G. K. Hall, 1979), p. 31.

31. Quoted in "The Movie TV Loves to Hate," *Time,* Dec. 13, 1976, p. 78.

32. Richard Schickel, "The Upper Depths," *Time,* Nov. 29, 1976, p. 79.

CHAPTER 9

1. Harvey Roy Greenberg, *Screen Memories: Hollywood Cinema on the Psychoanalytic Couch* (New York: Columbia University Press, 1993), pp. 185–86, 205–06.

2. In 1984 a film critic for *USA Today* observed, "In Hollywood, truth is measured in box office receipts." Quoted in William J. Palmer, *The Films of*

the Eighties: A Social History (Carbondale: Southern Illinois University Press, 1993), p. xiii.

3. Laurence Shames, *The Hunger for More: Searching for Values in an Age of Greed* (New York: Times Books, 1989), p. 141.

4. Ibid., p. 31.

5. Palmer, *Films of Eighties*, p. ix.

6. Greenberg called this "the New Decaturism," after Admiral Stephen Decatur, who said, "My country, may she always be right, but my country right or wrong." See his *Screen Memories*, pp. 93–110.

7. Jacob V. Lamar, "The Pentagon Goes Hollywood," *Time*, Nov. 24, 1986, p. 30.

8. Marek Haltof, *Peter Weir: When Cultures Collide* (New York: Twayne, 1996), p. 70.

9. Frank Beaver, *Oliver Stone: Wakeup Cinema* (New York: Twayne, 1994), pp. 7–8.

10. Quoted in Marcia Ruth, "Covering Foreign News," *presstime*, April 1986, p. 29.

11. Frederick Palmer, *With My Own Eyes* (Indianapolis: Bobbs-Merrill, 1933), p. 25. Palmer was a war correspondent himself.

12. Rudyard Kipling, *The Light That Failed* (New York: H. M. Caldwell, 1899), pp. 29–30.

13. Ibid., pp. 32–33.

14. Ibid., p. 33.

15. Ibid., p. 39.

16. Ibid., p. 115.

17. Ibid., p. 225.

18. Ibid., pp. 28–29.

19. Ibid., pp. 236–37.

20. Stephen Crane, "The Lone Charge of William B. Perkins," in *Wounds in the Rain* (London: Methuen, 1900), pp. 33–41.

21. Crane, "Virtue in War," in ibid., p. 176.

22. Richard Harding Davis, "A Derelict," in *Ranson's Folly* (New York: Charles Scribner's Sons, 1904), pp. 162–65.

23. Ibid., pp. 168–170.

24. Ibid., pp. 211–12.

25. George Orwell, "Rudyard Kipling," in *The Orwell Reader* (New York: Harcourt, Brace & World, 1956), p. 277.

26. Rupert Furneaux. *The First War Correspondent: William Howard Russell of the Times* (London: Cassell, 1945), pp. 41, 45.

27. John Keegan, *The Face of War* (New York: Viking Press, 1976), p. 240.

28. Ibid., p. 322.

29. Herbert L. Matthews, *The Education of a Correspondent* (New York: Harcourt, Brace, 1946), p. 9. The length of World War I trenches is noted in Paul

Fussell, *The Great War and Modern Memory* (London: Oxford University Press, 1975), p. 21.

30. For a fuller discussion of the literary portrayal of war correspondents, see Howard Good, "The Image of War Correspondents in Anglo-American Fiction," *Journalism Monographs*, No. 97, July 1986.

31. Will Levington Comfort, *Red Fleece* (New York: George H. Doran, 1915), p. 97.

32. Evelyn Waugh, *Scoop* (Boston: Little, Brown, 1977), pp. 88–89.

33. Graham Greene, *The Quiet American* (London: William Heinemann, 1955; reprint ed., Penguin 1981), p. 18.

34. Ibid., pp. 152, 162.

35. Ibid., pp. 35–36.

36. Haltof, *Weir*, p. 67.

37. Bernard Kalb, "Cinematic Art vs. Reality in Indonesia," *New York Times*, Jan. 23, 1983, sec. 2, pp. 1, 17.

38. James Roy MacBean examines the film's use of "seeing" as a metaphor for moral commitment in "Watching the Third World Watchers," *Film Quarterly* 37 (1984): 3–13.

39. Richard Bernstein, "Issues Raised by 'Under Fire,' " *New York Times*, Oct. 30, 1983, sec. 2, pp. 9–10.

40. Vincent Canby. "Screen: 'Under Fire,' " *New York Times*, Oct. 21, 1983, sec. 3, p. 12.

41. Holl., "Under Fire," *Variety*, Sept. 7, 1983, np.

42. The sarcastic characterization of Claire is from Canby, "Screen: 'Under Fire,' " p. 12.

43. For a critical analysis of press coverage of the Nicaraguan revolution, see Shirley Christian, "Covering the Sandinistas," *Washington Journalism Review* (March 1982): 33–38.

44. Pauline Kael, "Pig Heaven," in *Hooked* (New York: E. P. Dutton, 1989), p. 183.

45. Beaver, *Oliver Stone*, pp. 7–8.

46. Howard Good, *Outcasts: The Image of Journalists in Contemporary Film* (Metuchen, N.J.: Scarecrow Press, 1989), p. 63.

47. Quoted in Beaver, *Stone*, p. 77.

48. Quoted in ibid., p. 78.

49. Shames, *Hunger for More*, pp. 13–14.

50. Palmer, *Films of the Eighties*, p. 282. See also Carol M. Ward, "The Hollywood Yuppie: 1980–88," in *Beyond the Stars*, v. 1, *Stock Characters in American Popular Film*, eds. Paul Loukides and Linda K. Fuller (Bowling Green, Ohio: Popular Press, 1990), pp. 97–108.

51. Ibid., p. 280.

52. Susan Faludi, *Backlash: The Undeclared War Against American Women* (New York: Doubleday, 1991), p. 68.

53. Jonathan Friendly, "A Movie on the Press Stirs a Debate," *New York Times*, Nov. 15, 1981, sec. 2, p. 1.

54. Lucinda Franks, "Hollywood Update," *Columbia Journalism Review* (Nov.-Dec. 1981): 63; Robert Hatch, "Absence of Malice," *Nation,* Jan. 29, 1982, p. 27.

55. Pauline Kael, "Absence of Malice," *New Yorker,* Jan. 4, 1982, p. 85.

56. Judith Harwin and Shirley Otto, "Women, Alcohol and the Screen," in *Images of Alcoholism,* eds. Jim Cook and Mike Lewington (London: BFI, 1979), p. 48.

57. "It's not a scathing satire like *Network,*" Hinson added, "nor is it to broadcast journalism what *All the President's Men* was to print." Hal Hinson, "Broadcast News," *Washington Post,* Dec. 25, 1987, online.

58. Desson Howe, *Washington Post,* Dec. 25, 1987, online.

59. Roger Ebert, *Chicago Sun-Times,* Dec. 12, 1987, online.

CHAPTER 10

1. "Study: Music Videos Lead Youngsters to Drink," *Middletown (N.Y.) Times Herald Record,* Nov. 3, 1998, p. 14.

2. Ibid.

3. Reviews from major newspapers are quoted in Julie Salamon, *The Devil's Candy: The Bonfire of the Vanities Goes to Hollywood,* (New York: Dell, 1991), p. 405. See also Rita Kempley, "The Bonfire of the Vanities," *Washington Post,* Dec. 21, 1990, online; Chris Hicks, "The Bonfire of the Vanities," *Deseret (Utah) News,* Dec. 21, 1990, online.

4. Kempley, "Bonfire."

5. Roger Ebert, "The Bonfire of the Vanities," *Chicago Sun-Times,* Dec. 21, 1990, online.

6. Desson Howe, "The Bonfire of the Vanities," *Washington Post,* Dec. 21, 1990, online.

7. Rita Kempley, "The Paper," *Washington Post,* March 25, 1994, online.

8. See Howard Good, *Diamonds in the Dark: America, Baseball, and the Movies* (Lanham, Md.: Scarecrow Press, 1997), particularly pp. 53–80.

9. The article, "The Fight to Live," is collected in *The Art of Fact: An Historical Anthology of Literary Journalism,* eds. Kevin Kerrane and Ben Yagoda (New York: Touchstone, 1998), pp. 271–89.

10. Al Stump, *Cobb: The Life and Times of the Meanest Man Who Ever Played Baseball* (Chapel Hill, N.C.: Algonquin Books, 1994), p. 7.

11. Caryn James, "I Love Trouble," *New York Times,* June 29, 1994, sec. C , p.15.

12. Jack Kroll, "Kiss, Bang, Boom," *Newsweek,* July 4, 1994, p. 71.

13. Felicity Barringer, "Media," *New York Times,* Nov. 2, 1998, sec. C, p. 7.

14. Quoted in ibid.; see also Jimmy Breslin, *I Want to Thank My Brain for Remembering Me* (Boston: Little, Brown, 1996), pp. 141–43.

15. Ben Yagoda, Prologue to "The Scum Also Rises," in Kerran and Yagoda, p. 302.

16. A. J. Kaul, "Hunter S. Thompson," in *Dictionary of Literary Biography*, v. 185: *American Literary Journalists, 1945–1995*, ed. Kaul (Detroit: Gale Research, 1997), p. 311.

17. Stephen Pizzello, "Gonzo Filmmaking," *American Cinematographer* (May 1998): 31.

18. Kaul, "Thompson," p. 321.

19. Dave Kehr, "Where the Buffalo Roam," *Chicago Reader*, online.

20. Chuck Dowling, "Where the Buffalo Roam," *Jackson Film Journal*, n.d., online; Roger Ebert, "Fear and Loathing in Las Vegas," *Chicago Sun-Times*, n.d., online.

21. Wade Major, "Fear and Loathing in Las Vegas," *Boxoffice Online Reviews*; Jeff Vice, "Fear and Loathing in Las Vegas," *Deseret (Utah) News*, n.d., online; Mark Clark, " 'Fear' Is a Bad Trip for the '90s," *USA Today*, n.d., online.

22. Vice, "Fear and Loathing"; Ebert, "Fear and Loathing."

23. Major, "Fear and Loathing."

24. Pizzello, "Gonzo Filmmaking," 40.

25. Ibid., 38.

26. Throughout Hollywood history, actors have made the most of drunk roles, from inebriation to attacks of DTs. A number have gotten Oscars or Oscar nominations for playing dipsos, including Ray Milland in *The Lost Weekend*, Bette Davis in *Dangerous*, Geraldine Page in *Sweet Bird of Youth*, Susan Hayward in *I'll Cry Tomorrow*, Bing Crosby in *The Country Girl*, Claire Trevor in *Key Largo*, and Gig Young in *Come Fill the Cup*. Some actors are remembered more for these parts than for any others in their careers. See J. M. Howard, "Hard Drinkers Plum Roles for Many Actors," *San Francisco Chronicle*, June 19, 1988, Datebook sec., pp. 26–28.

27. Denise Herd and Robin Room, "Alcohol Images in American Film, 1909–1960," *Drinking and Drug Practices Survey* 18 (Aug. 1982): 32.

28. Ebert, "Fear and Loathing."

EPILOGUE

1. Mark Edward Lender and James Kirby Martin, *Drinking in America: A History* (New York: Free Press, 1982), pp. 21–24, 49–50.

2. Quoted in Joy Leland, *Firewater Myths: North American Drinking and Alcohol Addiction* (New Brunswick, N.J.: Rutgers Center of Alcohol Studies, 1976), p. 1. See also Joseph Westermeyer, "The Drunken Indian: Myths and Realities," *Psychiatric Annals* 4 (Nov. 1974): 29–36.

3. Lender and Martin, *Drinking in America*, p. 23.

4. Leland, *Firewater Myths*, p. 3.

5. Lender and Martin, *Drinking in America*, pp. 27–28.

6. John R. Larkins, *Alcohol and the Negro* (Zebulon, N.C.: Record Publishing, 1965), pp. 236–39.

7. Quoted in ibid, p. 236.

8. Quoted in ibid.

9. Quoted in ibid.

10. Lender and Martin, *Drinking in America*, p. 58.

11. Ibid.

12. Richard Stivers, *A Hair of the Dog: Irish Drinking and American Stereotype* (University Park: Pennsylvania State University Press, 1976), p. 137.

13. Quoted in ibid.

14. Lender and Martin, *Drinking in America*, p. 60.

15. Quoted in Stivers, *Hair of the Dog*, p. 136.

16. Richard Lambert, "Rebuilding Trust," *Columbia Journalism Review* (Nov.-Dec. 1998): 39.

17. Jim Godbold, managing editor, *Eugene (Ore.) Register-Guard*, e-mail, Nov. 1998.

18. See Chapter 9, "Mixed Drinks."

19. Stephen Braun, *Buzz: The Science and Lore of Alcohol and Caffeine* (New York: Oxford University Press, 1996), pp.16, 91. The best current estimate is that roughly one in ten drinkers is an alcoholic.

20. Joan Curlee-Salisbury, "Perspectives on Alcoholics Anonymous," in *Alcoholism: Development, Consequences, and Interventions*, 2d ed., eds. Nada J. Estes and M. Edith Heinemann (St. Louis: C. V. Mosby, 1982), p. 311.

21. Joseph R. Gusfield, "Passage to Play: Rituals of Drinking Time in American Society," in *Contested Meanings: The Construction of Alcohol Problems* (Madison: University of Wisconsin Press, 1996), p. 74.

22. Ruth L. Hirayama, "All the President's Men," *Magill's Survey of Cinema: English Language Films*, First Series, v. 1, ed. Frank N. Magill (Englewood Cliffs, N.J.: Salem Press, 1980), p. 54.

23. Christopher Hanson, "Where Have All the Heroes Gone?" *Columbia Journalism Review* (March–April 1996): 46–47.

Select Bibliography

Barris, Alex. *Stop the Presses! The Newspaperman in American Films.* South Brunswick, N.J.: A. S. Barnes, 1976.

Beaver, Frank. *Oliver Stone: Wakeup Cinema.* New York: Twayne, 1994.

Benedict, Elizabeth. "Alcohol and Writers: A Long Day's Journey into Destruction." *Changes* 4 (July–Aug. 1989): 24–27, 81–82.

Bent, Silas. *Ballyhoo.* New York: Boni and Liveright, 1927.

Bergman, Andrew. *We're in the Money: Depression America and Its Films.* New York: Harper & Row, 1971.

Bessie, Simon Michael. *Jazz Journalism.* New York: E.P. Dutton, 1938; reprint ed., New York: Russel & Russel, 1969.

Blythe, Samuel. *The Making of a Newspaper Man.* Philadelphia: Henry Altemus, 1912; reprint ed., Westport, Conn.: Greenwood Press, 1970.

Bogdanovich, Peter. *Fritz Lang in America.* New York: Praeger, 1969.

Bowles, Stephen E. *Sidney Lumet: A Guide to References and Resource.* Boston: G. K. Hall, 1979.

Braun, Stephen. *Buzz: The Science and Lore of Alcohol and Caffeine.* New York: Oxford University Press, 1996.

Breslin, Jimmy. *I Want to Thank My Brain for Remembering Me.* New York: Little, Brown, 1996.

Bromley, D. B. *Reputation, Image and Impression Management.* Chichester, England: John Wiley & Sons, 1993.

Brown, Jeffery Martin. *Ben Hecht, Hollywood Screenwriter.* Ann Arbor, Mich.: UMI Research Press, 1985.

Cagin, Seth, and Philip Dray. *Hollywood Films of the Seventies.* New York: Harper & Row, 1984.

Carnes, Mark C., ed. *Past Imperfect: History According to the Movies.* New York: Henry Holt, 1995.

Christian, Shirley. "Covering the Sandinistas." *Washington Journalism Review* (March 1982): 33–38.

Cook, Jim, and Mike Lewington, eds. *Images of Alcoholism*. London: BFI, 1979.

Crowley, John W. *The White Logic: Alcoholism and Gender in Modernist American Fiction*. Amherst: University of Massachusetts Press, 1994.

Dale, Edgar. *The Content of Motion Pictures*. New York: Macmillan, 1935.

D'Emilio, John, and Estelle B. Freedman. *Intimate Matters: A History of Sexuality in America*. New York: Harper & Row, 1983.

Denzin, Norman K. *Hollywood Shot by Shot: Alcoholism in American Cinema*. New York: Aldine De Gruyter, 1991.

Diamond, Edwin. *The Tin Kazoo: Television, Politics, and the News*. Cambridge, Mass.: MIT Press, 1975.

Eisner, Lotte H. *Fritz Lang*. New York: Oxford University Press, 1977.

Ellis, Elmer. *Mr. Dooley's America: A Life of Finley Peter Dunne*. New York: Alfred A. Knopf, 1941.

Erhlich, Matthew C. "Thinking Critically About Journalism Through Popular Culture." *Journalism Educator* 50 (winter 1996): 35–41.

Estes, Nada J., and M. Edith Heinemann, eds. *Alcoholism: Development, Consequences, and Interventions*, 2d ed. St. Louis: C. V. Mosby, 1982.

Faludi, Susan. *Backlash: The Undeclared War Against American Women*. New York: Doubleday, 1991.

Feur, Jane. *The Hollywood Musical*. Bloomington: Indiana University Press, 1982.

Fingarette, Herbert. *Heavy Drinking: The Myth of Alcoholism As a Disease*. Berkeley: University of California, 1988.

Finn, Peter. "Attitudes toward Drinking Conveyed in Studio Greeting Cards." *American Journal of Public Health* 70 (Aug.1980): 826–29.

French, Brandon. *On the Verge of Revolt: Women in American Films of the Fifties*. New York: Frederick Ungar, 1978.

Fuller, Sam. "News That's Fit to Film." *American Film* 1 (Oct. 1975): 20–24.

Furneaux, Rupert. *The First War Correspondent: William Howard Russell of the Times*. London: Cassell, 1945.

Fussell, Paul. *The Great War and Modern Memory*. London: Oxford University Press, 1975.

Gilbert, Douglas. *American Vaudeville: Its Life and Times*. New York: Whittlesey, 1940.

Gill, Brendan. *Late Bloomers*. New York: Artisan, 1996.

Goldman, Eric F. *The Crucial Decade: America, 1945–1955*. New York: Alfred A. Knopf, 1956.

Good, Howard. *Acquainted With the Night: The Image of Journalists in American Fiction, 1890–1930*. Metuchen, N.J.: Scarecrow Press, 1986.

———. *Diamonds in the Dark: America, Baseball, and the Movies*. Lanham, Md.: Scarecrow Press, 1997.

———. *The Journalist as Autobiographer*. Metuchen, N.J.: Scarecrow Press, 1993.

———. *Outcasts: The Image of Journalists in Contemporary Film*. Metuchen, N.J.: Scarecrow Press, 1989.

————. "The Image of War Correspondents in Anglo-American Fiction." *Journalism Monographs,* No. 97, July 1986.

Goodman, Ezra. "Fourth Estate Gets Better Role in Film." *Editor & Publisher* 20 (May 10, 1947): 26ff.

Goodwin, Donald W. *Alcohol and the Writer.* Kansas City: Andrews and McMeel, 1988.

Gottesman, Richard, ed. *Focus on Citizen Kane.* Englewood Cliffs, N.J.: Prentice Hall, 1971.

Greenberg, Harvey Roy. *Screen Memories: Hollywood Cinema on the Psychoanalytic Couch.* New York: Columbia University Press, 1993.

Gusfield, Joseph R. *Contested Meanings: The Construction of Alcohol Problems.* Madison: University of Wisconsin, 1996.

Gutman, Herbert G. *Work, Culture and Society in Industrializing America.* New York: Alfred A. Knopf, 1976.

Haltof, Marek. *Peter Weir: When Cultures Collide.* New York: Twayne, 1996.

Hamilton, Ian. *Writers in Hollywood, 1915–1951.* New York: Carroll & Graf, 1990.

Hanson, Christopher. "Where Have All the Heroes Gone?" *Columbia Journalism Review* (March–April 1996): 45–48.

Hardy, Phil. *Sam Fuller.* New York: Praeger, 1970.

Herd, Denise. "Ideology, Melodrama, and the Changing Role of Alcohol Problems in American Film." *Contemporary Drug Problems* 13 (summer 1986): 213–47.

Herd, Denise, and Robin Room. "Alcohol Images in American Film." *Drinking and Drug Practices Surveyor* 18 (Aug. 1982): 25.

Howard, J. M. "Hard Drinkers Plum Roles for Many Actors." *San Francisco Chronicle,* June 19, 1988, Datebook sec., p. 26ff.

Huber, Richard M. *The American Idea of Success.* New York: McGraw-Hill, 1971.

Jarlett, Franklin. *Robert Ryan: A Biography and Critical Filmography.* Jefferson, N.C.: McFarland, 1990.

Kael, Pauline. *The Citizen Kane Book.* Boston: Little, Brown, 1971.

————. *Hooked.* New York: E. P. Dutton, 1989.

Kazin, Alfred. " 'Giant Killer': Drink & the American Writer."*Commentary* 61 (March 1976): 44–50.

Keegan, John. *The Face of War.* New York: Viking Press, 1976.

Lambert, Richard. "Rebuilding Trust." *Columbia Journalism Review* (Nov.–Dec. 1998): 39–42.

Larkins, John R. *Alcohol and the Negro.* Zebulon, N.C.: Record Publishing, 1965.

Lee, Alfred McClung. *The Daily Newspaper in America.* New York: Macmillan, 1937.

Leland, Joy. *Firewater Myths: North American Drinking and Alcohol Addiction.* New Brunswick, N.J.: Rutgers Center of Alcohol Studies, 1976.

Lender, Mark Edward, and Karen R. Karnchanapee. "Temperance Tales." *Journal of Studies on Alcohol* 38 (1977): 1347–70.

Lender, Mark Edward, and James Kirby Martin. *Drinking in America: A History.* New York: Free Press, 1982.

Leonard, Thomas E. *News for All: America's Coming-of-Age with the Press.* New York: Oxford University Press, 1995.

Levine, Harry Gene. "The Discovery of Addiction: Changing Conceptions of Habitual Drunkenness in America." *Journal of Studies on Alcohol* 39 (1978): 143–74.

Linsky, Arnold S. "Theories of Behavior and the Image of the Alcoholic in Popular Magazines 1900–1966." *Public Opinion Quarterly* 34 (winter 1970–71): 573–81.

Lippmann, Walter. *Public Opinion.* New York: Free Press, 1922.

London, Jack. *John Barleycorn.* New York: Grosset & Dunlap, 1913.

Lorenz, Larry. "The Whitechapel Club: Defining Chicago's Newspapermen in the 1890s." *American Journalism* 15 (winter 1998): 83–102.

Lukas, J. Anthony. *Nightmare: The Underside of the Nixon Years.* New York: Bantam, 1977.

MacAndrew, Craig, and Robert B. Edgerton. *Drunken Comportment.* Chicago: Aldine, 1969.

MacBean, James Roy. "Watching the Third World Watchers." *Film Quarterly* 37 (1984): 3–13.

Manchester, William. *The Glory and the Dream: A Narrative History of America, 1932–1972.* Boston: Little, Brown, 1974.

Marzolf, Marion Tuttle. *Civilizing Voices: American Press Criticism, 1880–1950.* New York: Longman, 1991.

Matthews, Herbert L. *The Education of a Correspondent.* New York: Harcourt, Brace, 1946.

May, Larry. *Screening Out the Past: The Birth of Mass Culture and the Motion Picture Industry.* New York: Oxford University Press, 1980.

Mencken, H. L. *The American Language,* 4th ed. New York: Alfred A. Knopf, 1937.

―――. *The Days of H. L. Mencken.* New York: Alfred A. Knopf, 1947; reprint ed., New York: Dorset Press, 1989.

Mott, Frank Luther. *American Journalism,* 3rd ed. New York: Macmillan, 1962.

Mulvey, Laura. *Citizen Kane.* London: BFI Publishing, 1992.

Mulvey, Laura, and Jan Halliday, eds. *Douglas Sirk.* Edinburgh: Edinburgh Film Festival,1972.

Newlove, Donald. *Those Drinking Days: Myself and Other Writers.* New York: McGraw-Hill, 1981.

O'Neill, William. *American High: The Years of Confidence, 1945–1960.* New York: Free Press, 1986.

"Our Seventeenth 'Special.'" *Journalist* 28 (Dec. 15, 1900): 276.

Palmer,William J. *The Films of the Eighties: A Social History.* Carbondale: Southern Illinois University Press, 1993.

Pfautz, Harold W. "The Image of Alcohol in Popular Fiction: 1900–1904 and 1946–1950." *Quarterly Journal for Studies on Alcohol* 23 (1963): 131–46.

Pizzello, Stephen. "Gonzo Filmmaking." *American Cinematographer* (May 1998): 30–41.

Poague, Leland A. *The Cinema of Frank Capra* (South Brunswick, N.J.: A. S. Barnes, 1975.

Polan, Dana. "Brief Encounters: Mass Culture and the Evacuation of Sense." In *Studies in Entertainment*, ed. Tania Modelski. Bloomington: Indiana University Press, 1986, pp. 99–118.

Ralph, Julian, *The Making of a Journalist.* New York: Harper & Brothers, 1903.

Redding, Robert. *Starring Robert Benchley.* Albuquerque: University of New Mexico Press, 1973.

Robards, Brooks. "Newshounds and Sob Sisters: The Journalist Goes to Hollywood." In *Beyond the Stars: Stock Characters in American Popular Film*, v. 1, eds. Paul Loukides and Linda K. Fuller. Bowling Green, Ohio: Popular Press, 1990, pp.131–145.

Roddick, Nick. *A New Deal in Entertainment.* London: British Film Institute, 1983.

Roffman, Peter, and Jim Purdy. *The Hollywood Social Problem Film: Madness, Despair, and Politics from the Depression to the Fifties.* Bloomington: Indiana University Press, 1981.

Room, Robin. "Alcoholism and Alcoholics Anonymous in U.S. Films, 1945–1962: The Party Ends for the 'Wet Generations,' " *Journal of Studies on Alcohol* 50 (July 1989): 368–383.

———. "A 'Reverence for Strong Drink': The Lost Generation and the Elevation of Alcohol in American Culture." *Journal of Studies of Alcohol* 45 (Nov. 1984): 540–46.

Rorabaugh, W. R. *The Alcoholic Republic: An American Tradition.* New York: Oxford University Press, 1979.

Rosebault, Charles J. *When Dana Was the Sun.* New York: Robert M. McBride, 1931; reprint ed., Westport, Conn.: Greenwood Press, 1970.

Rossell, Deac. "The Fourth Estate and the Seventh Art." In *Questioning Media Ethics*, ed. Bernard Rubin. New York: Praeger, 1978, pp. 232–82.

———. "Hollywood and the Newsroom." *American Film* 1 (Oct. 1975): 14–18.

Roueché, Berton. *The Neutral Spirit: A Portrait of Alcohol.* Boston: Little, Brown, 1960.

Rowe, Chip. "Hacks on Film." *Washington Journalism Review* (Nov. 1992): 27–29.

Salamon, Julie. *The Devil's Candy:* The Bonfire of the Vanities *Goes to Hollywood.* New York: Dell, 1991.

Schatz, Thomas. *The Genius of the System.* New York: Pantheon, 1988.

———. *Hollywood Genres.* New York: Random House, 1981.

Schudson, Michael. *Watergate in American Memory: How We Remember, Forget, and Reconstruct the Past.* New York: Basic Books, 1992.

Shames, Laurence. *The Hunger for More: Searching for Values in an Age of Greed* New York: Times Books, 1989.

Sinclair, Andrew. *Prohibition: The Era of Excess*. Boston: Little, Brown, 1962.

Smythe, Ted Curtis. "The Reporter, 1880–1900." *Journalism History* 7 (spring 1980): 1–9.

Sobchack, Vivian. "Genre Film: Myth, Ritual, and Sociodrama." In *Film/Culture*, ed. Sari Thomas. Metuchen, N.J.: Scarecrow Press, 1982, pp. 147–65.

Sontag, Susan. *Illness As Metaphor*. New York: Farrar, Straus and Giroux, 1977.

Spoto, Donald. *The Dark Side of Genius: The Life of Alfred Hitchcock*. New York: Ballantine Books, 1983.

Starr, Louis M. *Bohemian Brigade: Civil War Newsmen in Action*. New York: Alfred A. Knopf, 1954.

Stern, Michael. *Douglas Sirk*. Boston: Twayne, 1979.

Stivers, Richard. *A Hair of the Dog: Irish Drinking and American Stereotype*. University Park: Pennsylvania State University Press, 1976.

Stump, Al. *Cobb: The Life and Times of the Meanest Man Who Ever Played Baseball*. Chapel Hill, N.C.: Algonquin Books, 1994.

Teague, Bob. *Live and Off Color: News Biz*. New York: A & W Publishers, 1982.

Thompson, Frank T. *William A. Wellman*. Metuchen, N.J.: Scarecrow Press, 1983.

Volosinov, V. N. *Marxism and the Philosophy of Language*, trans. Laduslav Matejka and I. R. Titunik. New York: Seminar Press, 1973.

Walker, Stanley. *City Editor*. New York: Frederick A. Stokes, 1934.

Ward, Carol M. "The Hollywood Yuppie: 1980–88." In *Beyond the Stars*, v. 1, *Stock Characters in American Popular Film*, eds. Paul Loukides and Linda K. Fuller. Bowling Green, Ohio: Popular Press, 1990, pp. 97–108.

Weisberger, Bernard A. *The American Newspaperman*. Chicago: University of Chicago Press, 1961.

Westermeyer, Joseph. "The Drunken Indian: Myths and Realities." *Psychiatric Annals* 4 (Nov. 1974): 29–36.

Wexman, Virginia Wright. *Creating the Couple: Love, Marriage, and Hollywood Performance*. Princeton, N.J.: Princeton University Press, 1993.

Williams, Jesse Lynch. *The Stolen Story and Other Newspaper Stories*. New York: Scribner's, 1899; reprint ed., Freeport, N.Y.: Books for Libraries Press, 1969.

Willis, Donald. *The Films of Frank Capra*. Metuchen, N.J.: Scarecrow Press, 1974.

Wilson, Edmund. *The American Earthquake*. Garden City, N.Y.: Anchor Books, 1964.

Wolfe, Charles, ed. *Meet John Doe*. New Brunswick, N.J.: Rutgers University Press, 1989.

"Working on Space." *Journalist* 7 (March 31, 1888): 8.

Wylie, Philip. *Generation of Vipers*. New York: Holt, Rinehart and Winston, 1942.

Filmography

The Rummy (Triangle, 1916)

Director: Paul Powell

Screenplay: Wilfred Lucas

Photography: Not available

Cast: Wilfred Lucas, Pauline Starks, William H. Brown, James O'Shea, Harry Fisher, A. D. Sears, Clyde Hopkins

A Case at Law (Triangle, 1917)

Director: Arthur Rosson

Screenplay: William Dudley Pelly

Photography: Roy Overbaugh

Cast: Dick Rosson, Pauline Curley, Riley Hatch, Jack Dillon, Ed Sturgis

The Fringe of Society (George Backer, 1917)

Director: Robert Ellis

Screenplay: Pierre V. R. Key

Photography: George K. Hollister, Edward Wynard, and H. J. Butler

Cast: Ruth Roland, Milton Sills, Leah Baird, J. Herbert Frank, George Larkin, Tammany Young, Ollie Kirby, Jules Cowles

The Night Workers (Essanay, 1917)

Director: J. Charles Haydon

Screenplay: J. Bradley Smollen

Photography: Not available

Cast: Marguerite Clayton, Jack Gardner, Julien Barton, Mabel Bardine, Arthur W. Bates

Truthful Tulliver (New York Motion Picture; Kay-Bee, 1917)

Director: William S. Hart

Screenplay: J. G. Hawks

Photography: Joe August

Cast: William S. Hart, Nina Byron, Milton Ross, Alma Reubens, Norbert A. Myles, Walter Perry

His Parisian Wife (Famous Players-Lasky, 1919)

Director: Emile Chautard

Screenplay: Eve Unsell (adapted from a novel by Andrew Soutar)

Photography: Not available

Cast: Elsie Ferguson, David Powell, Courtney Foote, Frank Losee, Cora Williams, Captain Charles, Louis Grizel

Deadline at Eleven (Vitagraph, 1920)

Director: George Fawcett

Screenplay: Lucien Hubbard (adapted from a story by Ruth Byers)

Photography: Arthur Ross

Cast: Corrine Griffith, Frank Thomas, Webster Campbell, Alice Calhoun, Maurice Costello, Dodson Mitchell, James Bradbury, Emily Fitzroy, Ernest Lambert

A Certain Rich Man (Great Authors Pictures, 1921)

Director: Howard Hickman

Screenplay: Not available (adapted from a novel by William Allen White)

Photography: Joseph A. Dubray

Cast: Carl Gantvoort, Claire Adams, Robert McKim, Jean Hersholt, Joseph J.

Dowling, Lydia Knott, Frankie Lee, May Jane Irving, Harry Lorraine, J. Gunnis Davis, Charles Colby, Walter Perry, Fleming Pitts, Grace Pike, Eugenia Gilbert, Gordon Dumont, Edna Pennington

Don't Neglect Your Wife (Goldwyn, 1921)

Director: Wallace Worsley

Screenplay: Louis Sherwin (adapted from a story by Gertrude Franklin Atherton)

Photography: Don Short

Cast: Mabel Julienne Scott, Lewis S. Stone, Charles Clary, Kate Lester, Arthur Hoyt, Josephine Crowell, Darrel Foss, Norma Gordon, Richard Tucker, R. D. MacLean

The Foolish Matrons (Maurice-Tourneur Productions, 1921)

Director: Maurice Tourneur and Clarence L. Brown

Screenplay: Wyndham Gittens

Photography: Charles Van Enger and Kenneth Gordon MacLean

Cast: Hobart Bosworth, Doris May, Mildred Manning, Kathleen Kirkham, Betty Schade, Margaret McWade, Charles Meredith, Wallace MacDonald, Michael Dark

The Tomboy (Fox, 1921)

Director: Carl Harbaugh

Screenplay: Carl Harbaugh

Photography: Otto Brautigan

Cast: Eileen Percy, Hal Cooley, Richard Cummings, Paul Kamp, Byron Munson, Harry Dunkinson, James McElhern, Leo Sulky, Grace MacClean, Walter Wilkinson, Virginia Stern, Wilson Hummel, Ethel Teare

SOUND FILMS

Gentlemen of the Press (Paramount Famous Lasky, 1929)

Director: Millard Webb

Screenplay: Bartlett Cormack

Photography: George Folsey

Cast: Walter Huston, Katherine Francis, Charles Ruggles, Betty Lawford, Norman Foster, Duncan Penwarden, Lawrence Leslie, Harry Lee

Big News (Pathe, 1929)

Director: Gregory La Cava

Screenplay: Jack Jungmeyer (adapted from a story by George S. Brooks; dialogue by Frank Reicher)

Photography: Not available

Cast: Robert Armstrong, Carole Lombard, Sam Hardy, Tom Kennedy, Louis Payne, Wade Boetler, Charles Sellon

Young Man of Manhattan (Paramount-Publix, 1930)

Director: Monta Bell

Screenplay: Robert Presnell (adapted from a novel by Katherine Brush; dialogue by Daniel Reed)

Photography: Larry Williams

Cast: Claudette Colbert, Norman Foster, Ginger Rogers, Charles Ruggles, Leslie Austin, H. Dudley Hawley

The Front Page (Howard Hughes for United Artists, 1931)

Director: Lewis Milestone

Screenplay: Bartlett Cormack (adapted from a play by Ben Hecht and Charles MacArthur)

Photography: Glen MacWilliams

Cast: Adolphe Menjou, Pat O'Brien, Mary Brian, Edward Everett Horton, Walter Catlett, George E. Stone, May Clark, Slim Summerville, Matt Moore, Frank McHugh, Clarence H. Wilson, Fred Howard, Phil Tead, Eugene Strong, Spencer Charters, Maurice Black, Effie Ellsier, James Gordin, Dick Alexander

Five Star Final (First National, 1931)

Director: Mervyn LeRoy

Screenplay: Byron Morgan with Robert Lord (adapted from a play by Louis Weitzenkorn)

Photography: Sol Polito

Cast: Edward G. Robinson, H. D. Warner, Marian Marsh, Anthony Bushell,

George E. Stone, Frances Starr, Ona Munson, Boris Karloff, Robert Elliott, Aline MacMahon

Platinum Blonde (Columbia, 1931)

Director: Frank Capra

Screenplay: Jo Swerling (adapted from a story by Harry E. Chandless and Douglas W. Churchill; continuity by Dorothy Howell; dialogue by Robert Riskin)

Photography: Joseph Walker

Cast: Loretta Young, Robert Williams, Jean Harlow, Louise Closser Hale, Donald Dillaway, Reginald Owen, Walter Catlett

Famous Ferguson Case (First National, 1932)

Director: Lloyd Bacon

Screenplay: Harvey Thew (adapted from a story by Courtenay Terrett and Granville Moore)

Photography: Dev Jennings

Cast: Joan Blondell, Tom Brown, Adrienne Dore, Walter Miller, Leslie Fenton, Vivienne Osborne, J. Carroll Naish, Purnell Pratt, Kenneth Thomson, Grant Mitchell, Leon Ames, Clarence Wilson, Bert Hanlon, Mike Donlin

Scandal for Sale (Universal, 1932)

Director: Russell Mack

Screenplay: Ralph Graves (adapted from a novel by Emile Gauvreau; continuity by Robert Keith)

Photography: Karl Freund

Cast: Charles Bickford, Rose Hobart, Pat O'Brien, Claudia Dell, J. Farrell MacDonald, Harry Beresford, Berton Churchill, Glenda Farrell, Tully Marshall, Mitchell Harris, Hans von Twardowski, Lew Kelly, Mary Jane Graham, Buster Phelps, Paul Nicholson, James Farley, Jack Richardson, Angie Norton

It Happened One Night (Columbia, 1934)

Director: Frank Capra

Screenplay: Robert Riskin (adapted from a story by Samuel Hopkins Adams)

Photography: Joseph Walker

Cast: Clark Gable, Claudette Colbert, Walter Connolly, Roscoe Karns, Jameson Thomas, Alan Hale

Libeled Lady (Lawrence Weingarten for Metro, 1936)

Director: Jack Conway

Screenplay: Maurine Watkins, Howard Emmett Rogers, and George Oppenheimer (adapted from a story by Wallace Sullivan)

Photography: Norbett Nordine

Cast: Jean Harlow, William Powell, Myrna Loy, Spencer Tracy, Walter Connolly, Charley Grapewin, Cora Witherspoon, E. E. Clive, Lauri Beatty, Otto Yamaoka, Charles Trowbridge, Spencer Charters, George Chandler, Greta Meyer, William Benedict, Hal K. Dawson

Nothing Sacred (David O. Selznick for United Artists, 1937)

Director: Wlliam A. Wellman

Screenplay: Ben Hecht (adapted from a story by James H. Street)

Photography: W. Howard Greene

Cast: Carole Lombard, Frederic March, Charles Winninger, Walter Connolly, Sig Ruman, Frank Fay, Maxie Rosenblum, Margaret Hamilton, Troy Brown, Hattie MacDaniels, Olin Howland, George Chandler, Claire DuBrey, John Qualen, Charles Richman

The Sisters (Warner Brothers, 1938)

Director: Anatole Litvak

Screenplay: Milton Krims (adapted from a novel by Myron Brinig)

Photography: Tony Gaudio

Cast: Errol Flynn, Bette Davis, Anita Louise, Ian Hunter, Donald Crisp, Beulah Bondi, Jane Bryan, Alan Hale, Dick Foran, Henry Travers, Patric Knowles, Lee Patrick, Laura Hope Crews, Janet Shaw, Harry Davenport, Ruth Garland, John Warburton, Mayo Methot, Irving Bacon, Arthur Hoyt

Foreign Correspondent (Walter Wanger for United Artists, 1940)

Director: Alfred Hitchcock

Screenplay: Charles Bennett and Joan Harrison (adapted from the memoirs of Vincent Sheean; dialogue by James Hilton and Robert Benchley)

Photography: Rudolph Mate

Cast: Joel McCrea, Laraine Day, Herbert Marshall, George Sanders, Albert Basserman, Robert Benchley, Edmond Gwenn, Harry Davenport, Eduardo Ciannelli

His Girl Friday (Columbia, 1940)

Director: Howard Hawks

Screenplay: Charles Lederer (adapted from a play by Ben Hecht and Charles MacArthur)

Photography: Joseph Walker

Cast: Cary Grant, Rosalind Russell, Ralph Bellamy, Gene Lockhart, Porter Hall, Ernest Truex, Cliff Edwards, Clarence Kolb, Roscoe Karns, Frank Kenks, Regis Toomey, Abner Bierman, Billy Gilbert, Pat West, Edwin Maxwell, John Qualen, Helen Mack

The Philadelphia Story (Joseph L. Mankiewicz for Metro-Goldwyn-Mayer, 1940)

Director: George Cukor

Screenplay: Donald Ogden Stewart (adapted from a play by Philip Barry

Photography: Joseph Ruttenberg

Cast: Cary Grant, Katharine Hepburn, James Stewart, Ruth Hussey, John Howard, Roland Young, John Halliday, Mary Nash, Virginia Weidler, Henry Daniell, Lionel Pape, Rex Evans

Meet John Doe (Warner Brothers, 1941)

Director: Frank Capra

Screenplay: Robert Riskin (adapted from a story by Richard Connell and Robert Presnell)

Photography: George Barnes

Cast: Gary Cooper, Barbara Stanwyck, Edward Arnold, Walter Brennan, Spring Byington, James Gleason, Gene Lockhart, Rod La Roque, Irving Bacon, Regis Toomey, J. Farrell MacDonald, Warren Hymer, Harry Holman, Andrew Tombes, Pierre Watkin, Stanley Andrews, Mitchell Lewis, Charles Wilson, Vaugh Glaser, Sterling Holloway

Citizen Kane (RKO Radio, 1941)

Director: Orson Welles

Screenplay: Orson Welles and Herman J. Mankiewicz

Photography: Gregg Toland

Cast: Orson Welles, Joseph Cotten, Dorothy Comingore, Everett Sloane, Ray Collins, George Coulouris, Agnes Moorehead, Paul Stewart, Ruth Warrick, Eriskine Sanford, William Alland, Georgia Backus, Philip Van Zandt. Gus Schilling, Fortunio Bonanova

Woman of the Year (Joseph L. Mankiewicz for Metro-Goldwyn-Mayer, 1942)

Director: George Stevens

Screenplay: Ring Lardner Jr. and Michael Kanin

Photography: Joseph Ruttenberg

Cast: Spencer Tracy, Katharine Hepburn, Reginald Owen, Fay Bainter, William Bendix, Gladys Blake, George Kezas, Sara Haden, Minor Watson, Dan Tobin, Roscoe Karns, William Tannen

Roxie Hart (Twentieth Century-Fox, 1942)

Director: William A. Wellman

Screenplay: Nunnally Johnson (adapted from a play by Maurine Watkins)

Photography: Leon Shamroy

Cast: Ginger Rogers, Adolphe Menjou, George Montgomery, Lynne Overman, Nigel Bruce, Phil Silvers, Sara Allgood, William Frawley, Spring Byington, Ted North, Helene Reynolds, George Chandler, Charles D. Brown, Morris Ankrum, George Lessey, Iris Adrian, Milton Parsons

Welcome Stranger (Sol C. Siegel for Paramount, 1947)

Director: Elliott Nugent

Screenplay: Arthur Sheekman with N. Richard Nash (adapted from a story by Frank Butler)

Photography: Lionel Lindon

Cast: Bing Crosby, Joan Caufield, Barry Fitzgerald, Wanda Hendrix, Frank Faylen, Elizabeth Patterson, Robert Shayne, Larry Young, Percy Kilbride, Charles Dingle, Don Beddoe

Come Fill the Cup (Henry Blanke for Warner Brothers, 1951)

Director: Gordon Douglas

Screenplay: Ivan Goff and Ben Roberts (adapted from a novel by Harlan Ware)

Photography: Robert Burks

Cast: James Cagney, Phyllis Thaxter, Raymond Massey, James Gleason, Gig Young, Selena Royle, Larry Keating, Sheldon Leonard, Douglas Spencer, John Kellogg, William Bakewell, John Alvin

Park Row (Sam Fuller for United Artists, 1952)

Director: Sam Fuller

Screenplay: Sam Fuller

Photography: Jack Russell

Cast: Gene Evans, Mary Welch, Bela Kovacs, Herbert Heyes, Tina Rome, George O'Hanlon, J. M. Kerrigan, Forrest Taylor, Don Orlando, Neyle Morrow, Dick Elliott, Stuart Randall, Dee Pollock, Hal K. Dawson

Deadline, U.S.A. (Sol C. Siegel for Twentieth Century-Fox, 1952)

Director: Richard Brooks

Screenplay: Richard Brooks

Photography: Milton Krasner

Cast: Humphrey Bogart, Ethel Barrymore, Kim Hunter, Ed Begley, Warren Stevens, Paul Stewart, Martin Gabel, Joseph De Santis, Joyce MacKenzie, Audrey Christie, Fay Baker, Jim Backus, Carleton Young, Selmar Jackson, Kasla Orzazewski

While the City Sleeps (RKO Radio, 1956)

Director: Fritz Lang

Screenplay: Casey Robinson (adapted from a novel by Charles Einstein)

Photography: Ernest Laszlo

Cast: Dana Andrews, Rhonda Fleming, George Sanders, Howard Duff, Thomas Mitchell, Vincent Price, Sally Forrest, John Drew Barrymore, James Craig, Ida Lupino, Robert Warwick, Mae Marsh

Tarnished Angels (Albert Zugsmith for Universal, 1957)

Director: Douglas Sirk

Screenplay: George Zuckerman (adapted from a novel by William Faulkner)

Photography: Irving Glassberg

Cast: Rock Hudson, Robert Stack, Dorothy Malone, Jack Carson, Robert Middleton, Alan Reed, Alexander Lockwood, Chris Olsen, Robert J. Wilkie,

Troy Donahue, William Schallert, Betty Utey, Phil Harvey, Steve Drexel, Eugene Borden, Stephen Ellis

Lonelyhearts (MGM/UA, 1958)

Director: Vincent J. Donehue

Screenplay: Dore Schary (adapted from a novel by Nathanael West and a play by Howard Teichmann)

Photography: John Alton

Cast: Montgomery Clift, Robert Ryan, Myrna Loy, Jackie Coogan, Dolores Hart, Mike Kellin, Frank Maxwell, Maureen Stapleton, Onslow Stevens

Inherit the Wind (Stanley Kramer for United Artists, 1960)

Director: Stanley Kramer

Screenplay: Nathan E. Douglas and Harold Jacob Smith (adapted from a play by Jerome Lawrence and Robert E. Lee)

Photography: Ernest Laszlo

Cast: Spencer Tracy, Frederic March, Gene Kelly, Florence Eldridge, Dick York, Donna Anderson, Claude Akins, Harry Morgan

The Luck of Ginger Coffey (Crawley Films; Roth-Kershner Productions, 1964)

Director: Irvin Kershner

Screenplay: Brian Moore (adapted from his novel)

Photography: Manny Wynn

Cast: Robert Shaw, Mary Ure, Powys Thomas, Libby McClintock, Liam Redmond, Tom Harvey

Gaily, Gaily (Mirisch, 1969)

Director: Norman Jewison

Screenplay: Abram S. Ginnes (adapted from a book by Ben Hecht)

Photography: Richard H. Kline

Cast: Beau Bridges, Brian Keith, Melinda Mercouri, George Kennedy, Hume Cronyn, Margot Kidder, Roy Poole, Wilfred Hyde-White, Melodie Johnson

All the President's Men (Wildwood, 1976)

Director: Alan J. Pakula

Screenplay: William Goldman (adapted from a book by Carl Bernstein and Bob Woodward)

Photography: Gordon Willis

Cast: Robert Redford, Dustin Hoffman, Jason Robards, Jack Warden, Martin Balsam, Hal Holbrook, Stephen Collins, Jane Alexander

Network (Howard Gottfried for United Artists, 1976)

Director: Sidney Lumet

Screenplay: Paddy Chayefsky

Photography: Owen Roizman

Cast: Faye Dunaway, William Holden, Peter Finch, Robert Duvall, Wesley Addy, Ned Beatty, Beatrice Straight, Marlene Warfield

Where the Buffalo Roam (Universal, 1980)

Director: Art Linson

Screenplay: John Kaye (adapted from writings by Hunter S. Thompson)

Photography: Tak Fujimoto

Cast: Bill Murray, Peter Boyle, Bruno Kirby, Rene Auberjonois, R. G. Armstrong

Absence of Malice (Columbia, 1981)

Director: Sidney Pollack

Screenplay: Kurt Leudtke

Photography: Owen Roizman

Cast: Sally Field, Paul Newman, Melinda Dillon, Josef Sommer, Bob Balaban, Barry Primus, Wilford Brimley, Luther Adler, Don Hood.

The Year of Living Dangerously (MGM/UA, 1983)

Director: Peter Weir

Screenplay: David Williamson, Peter Weir, and C. J. Koch (adapted from a novel by C. J. Koch)

Photography: Russell Boyd

Cast: Mel Gibson, Sigourney Weaver, Linda Hunt, Michael Murphy, Noel Ferrier, Bill Kerr, Mike Emperio, Bemboi Rocco

Under Fire (Orion, 1983)

Director: Roger Spottiswoode

Screenplay: Ronald Shelton and Clayton Frohman

Photography: John Alcott

Cast: Nick Nolte, Gene Hackman, Joanna Cassidy, Ed Harris, Alma Martinez, Holly Palance, Jean-Louis Trintignant, Richard Masur, Rene Enriquez, Hamilton Camp, Jenny Gago, Eloy Casados, Jorge Zepeda

Salvador (Hemdale, 1987)

Director: Oliver Stone

Screenplay: Oliver Stone and Richard Boyle

Photography: Robert Richardson

Cast: James Woods, James Belushi, Michael Murphy, John Savage, Elpedia Carrillo, Tony Plana, Colby Chester, Cynthia Gibb, Will MacMillian, Valerie Wildman

Broadcast News (Twentieth Century-Fox, 1987)

Director: James L. Brooks

Screenplay: James L. Brooks

Photography: Michael Ballhaus

Cast: William Hurt, Albert Brooks, Holly Hunter, Lois Chiles, Joan Cusack, Robert Prosky, Jack Nicholson

Bonfire of the Vanities (Warner Brothers, 1990)

Director: Brian DePalma

Screenplay: Michael Cristofer (adapted from a novel by Tom Wolfe)

Photography: Vilmos Zsigmond

Cast: Tom Hanks, Bruce Willis, Melanie Griffith, Morgan Freeman, Kim Cattrall, Saul Rubinek, Alan King, John Hancock

The Paper (Universal, 1994)

Director: Ron Howard

Screenplay: David Koepp and Stephen Koepp

Photography: John Seale

Cast: Michael Keaton, Robert Duvall, Glenn Close, Marisa Tomei, Randy Quaid, Jason Robards, Jason Alexander, Spalding Gray, Catherine O'Hara, Lynne Thigpen

Cobb (Warner Brothers, 1994)

Director: Ron Shelton

Screenplay: Ron Shelton (adapted from an article by Al Stump)

Photography: Russell Boyd

Cast: Tommy Lee Jones, Robert Wuhl, Lolita Davidovich, Lou Myers

I Love Trouble (Touchstone, 1994)

Director: Charles Shyer

Screenplay: Nancy Meyers and Charles Shyer

Photography: John Lindley

Cast: Nick Nolte, Julia Roberts, Olympia Dukakis, Robert Loggia, Marsha Mason, Saul Rubinek

Fear and Loathing in Las Vegas (Universal, 1998)

Director: Terry Gilliam

Screenplay: Terry Gilliam, Tony Grisoni, Tod Davies, and Alex Cox (adapted from a book by Hunter S. Thompson)

Photography: Nicola Pecorini

Cast: Johnny Depp, Benicio Del Toro, Christina Ricci, Craig Bierko, Cameron Diaz

About the Author

Howard Good (B.A., Bard College; M.A., University of Iowa; Ph.D., University of Michigan) is coordinator of the Journalism Program at the State University of New York at New Paltz, where he has taught since 1985. He is the author of five previous books, including *Girl Reporter* (Scarecrow, 1998), *Diamonds in the Dark* (Scarecrow, 1997), and *The Journalist as Autobiographer* (Scarecrow, 1993). His articles have appeared in *Journalism Monographs, Journalism Quarterly, Journalism Educator, American Journalism, Quill,* the *Chronicle of Higher Education, Education Week, Teacher Magazine,* and the *American School Board Journal.* He has contributed scholarly essays to several collections, including *American Literary Journalists, 1945–1995* (Gale Research); *A Sourcebook on American Literary Journalists* (Greenwood Press); and volumes 3 and 5 of *Beyond the Stars: Studies in Popular American Film* (Popular Press). His poems have been published in *Midstream,* the *Dalhousie Review,* and other small magazines. He is vice president of the Board of Education in the Highland (N.Y.) Central School District.